SOLE SURVIVOR: ONE MAN'S JOURNEY

SOLE SURVIVOR:
ONE MAN'S JOURNEY

Biography of John Norman Walton,
the Sole Survivor of HMS *Neptune*

by his daughter

NORMA HUDSON

The Memoir Club

First published in 2008 by
The Memoir Club
Arya House
Langley Park
Durham
DH7 9XE

British Library Cataloguing in
Publication Data.
A catalogue record for this book
is available from the
British Library

ISBN: 978-1-84104-184-1

Typeset by TW Typesetting, Plymouth, Devon
Printed by Cromwell Press Ltd, Trowbridge, Wiltshire

Dedicated to my children Nicola and Michael,
grandchildren Thomas and Alice and future generations
that follow so that they may know something of their forefathers,
the lives they led, the sacrifices they made
and how they came to be.

This biography of the sole survivor of HMS Neptune
is also dedicated to the memory of the men
who lost their lives on 19 December 1941
and to their relatives,
many of whom became friends of my father.

Contents

List of Illustrations

Foreword

I consider myself privileged to be asked to write this forward to the remarkable story of the life of Norman Walton. I met Norman when he visited New Zealand in what was a most moving experience.

For New Zealand the tragic loss of the *Neptune* had multiple impacts which permeated all levels of the country at that time; from those related to defence policy at the highest level, to the grief of the families of the 150 New Zealanders lost.

The story starts in early 1941 when the New Zealand Government, anxious over the security of shipping in the South Pacific, sought an additional cruiser to strengthen naval forces in New Zealand waters. The Admiralty demurred but the New Zealand Government persisted, even though it was aware of the critical shortage of ships. In April 1941 the New Zealand High Commissioner in London was informed that *Neptune*, a sister ship to *Leander* and *Achilles* already in the New Zealand naval forces, could be made available. The plan was that *Neptune* would sail for New Zealand in late May or early June 1941. The ship would be manned by diluting the number of fully-trained personnel serving in *Achilles* and *Leander* and replacing them with newly-trained recruits. Once the decision regarding *Neptune* had been made, the New Zealand personnel serving in the Royal Navy, who could be made available, were posted to *Neptune*.

In New Zealand, the immediate consequence of the loss of the ship was the decision not to have any further New Zealand manned cruisers, as the casualty impact of a loss would be too great.

In the overall context of World War II, for the Royal Navy the loss of the *Neptune*, although tragic, had no strategic significance. For New Zealand however, the loss of the *Neptune*, which followed the losses in the Greek and Cretan campaigns, and Japan's entry to the war, assumed a very real significance.

This book, in telling of the events at a personal level, greatly adds to the understanding of both the loss of the ship, and its impacts on New Zealand.

Rear Admiral Ian Hunter, CB, RNZN (Rtd)

Preface

This memoir charting the life of my father has been written in response to a restless desire to record his diaries, notes and letters found after his death in April 2005 in his wooden 'ditty' box bearing a brass name-plate inscribed John Norman Walton. I have quoted my father and the men and women in his life verbatim in the hope that this will provide an insight into his character and his great will to survive – during his early life in the north-east of England, his service with the Royal Navy during World War II, his time as Prisoner of War and throughout his life. Mainly, of course, this record of his writings and the stories he told serve as a lasting memory to me, his daughter, and is written for the grandchildren and great-grandchildren he left behind and the future generations that may follow. It serves as a reminder of the good times we shared, the friends we made and the lessons he passed on.

He forever remains my last beloved guru.

John Norman Walton, as named in the records that document his naval career was called 'Geordie' by his shipmates. During his boxing career he took the professional name 'Patsy Dodds', 'Patsy' from the nickname given to his father and 'Dodds', the maiden name of his wife Irene. I knew him as Dad but everyone else knew him as Norman, the name he preferred. However, because he was my father, I shall refer to him as such throughout the remainder of this story.

Norma Hudson
2008

Acknowledgements

I am greatly indebted to all who have contributed to the contents of this book. I am eternally grateful to my friend John McGregor whose help in making his comprehensive research material into the circumstances of *Neptune*'s sinking available to me and the painstaking checking of factual material regarding my father's service record with the Royal Navy has been invaluable in providing a context for my father's diaries in this book. Also a thank you to Adrian St Clair for photographs, assistance and advice gained from his publication of *Mediterranean Minefield*. My thanks go to John Newton, whose dogged determination brought my father to New Zealand resulting in a much neglected grieving process over fifty years later, for himself and many of the relatives of the 150 New Zealanders who perished with *Neptune*, and his wife Barbara whose diligence in recording every aspect of the tour enabled the visit to occupy a deservedly prominent place within the book. I have received much support from Tyneside and District Ex Boxers Association and I would like to thank Malcolm Dinning in particular for providing photographs, programmes and news articles on my father's boxing career from the 1940s/50s.

My gratitude also goes to the following people for their support and professional help:

Rear Admiral Ian Hunter CB, RNZN (Rtd)

Nick Ray for the cover photograph

Mike Madine for the author photograph

Nixie Taverner, author

Robin and Diana Clayton.

Finally a special thank you to the Neptune Association and its members for providing their kind permission to use photographs, and to the War Veterans for allowing me to quote personal accounts of their experiences during World War II with a special mention to: Harry Bradbear, Harry Jones, Frank Brown, Norman Stewart, George Laidlaw and Jack Williams. Thanks to the Walton family, and a special thank-you to Isabelle and Leslie for their memories of my father. Thanks to my own family for their patience.

I have written verbatim from my father's diaries, letters and notes as he describes the various events in his life, but I have to thank many authors who have already written about the sinking of *Neptune* and boxing events from that era that have improved my narrative and I list some of them here:

Neptune's Legacy	Nixie Taverner
Almost HMNZS Neptune	Jack Harker
A Fair Fight	Vanessa Toulmin, World's Fair Ltd
Malta at War Series	John Mizzie
A Sailor's Odyssey	Admiral Sir Andrew B. Cunningham DSO
Mediterranean Minefield	Adrian St Clair (Second Edition due November 2008) Neptune Association. www.hmsneptune.com

Introduction

As Chairman of the Neptune Association, I have much pleasure in writing the Introduction to Norma Hudson's book about her father's remarkable life. What makes his story so unique is that he was the one survivor of the 765 members of HMS *Neptune*'s crew and thus the only eyewitness to what happened. He was the only person the hundreds of relatives could ask for details of the tragedy and to answer the many questions surrounding her fate. He bore this burden alone for sixty-five years. In all the other major naval disasters of World War II, there was always a handful of survivors to tell the tale. Norman was rescued on his sixth day on a Carley raft and the fact that he was still alive gave testimony to his supreme fitness and immense determination to live.

It was 22 December 1941 and the fourth day on the Carley Float. Able Seaman Norman Walton aged twenty was trying to keep alive his Captain – Rory O'Conor, aged forty-four – whose ship HMS *Neptune* with a crew of 765 men had been sunk in an Italian minefield about 12 miles north of Tripoli. That night Captain O'Conor died in the arms of Able Seaman Walton. By Christmas Eve on 24 December just two were still alive – Leading Seaman Albert Price and Norman himself. An Italian aircraft flew over them; Norman waved hard and not long afterwards the Italian Torpedo Boat *Calliope* came alongside and pulled them on board. They confirmed that both Captain O'Conor and Albert Price were dead, and buried them at sea.

On Christmas Day 1941, Norman Walton found himself in hospital in Tripoli, Libya, as a Prisoner of War of the Italian Navy. His diary notes: 'I was blind all day and all I had to eat was a bowl of hot milk. I couldn't stomach anything. Next day, Boxing Day, towards night my eyesight came back and I took a look through a mirror to see a face, which was unrecognisable to me. My tongue was swollen twice its size, my lips were swollen, and my nose spread across my face which was black with oil due to the sun burning it in – all due, I suppose, to exposure. I was treated very well by the Italian naval ratings and nurses in Tripoli hospital. I didn't know then that the food I was getting in that hospital was by far the best and most I would get as a POW.'

Norman had joined the Royal Navy as a Junior Seaman in 1938 aged 17. By the time he joined the cruiser HMS *Neptune* in November 1941 he had already been at war for 2½ years and seen almost continuous action. In the destroyer HMS *Janus*, he had fought in the Norwegian campaign, sailed to the Mediterranean for convoy duties between Malta and Tripoli, fought in the Battle of Calabria, spent 60 days in Detention Quarters for striking a Petty Officer, been part of the naval brigade in the evacuation from Crete (hitching a lift home in the severely damaged HMS *Orion*), and been sunk twice by German air attack and had 'to swim for it' before being rescued. All this was exciting enough, but by no means exceptional in the hectic early days of the war. The events of 19 December 1941 and his extraordinary survival were to propel him into the history books. Norman was the only survivor of the crew of 765 men and the only eyewitness to what happened after *Neptune* was mined. Why more didn't survive remains a haunting mystery.

After 15 months as a POW, Norman's adventurous life continued. One day he was asked if he wanted to be freed by the Camp Commandant. 'Yes Sir!' He was instructed to go south to Bari where allied POWs were being gathered for a POW exchange and walked out of the camp in the clothes he stood up in. At Bari he joined up with other POWs and got on board the Italian hospital ship *Gradisca* and taken to Turkey – a neutral country. From there, a British transport ship took them to Alexandria, and he eventually arrived back in England in June 1943. The first thing he did on leave was to get married to his childhood sweetheart Irene Dodds. After three weeks survivor's and POW leave he was drafted to the destroyer HMS *Mermaid* in time for a Russian convoy. After celebrating too hard on return and getting in a fight, he was discharged from *Mermaid* for another spell of 45 days in Detention Quarters. Determined not to get into more trouble, he was drafted to the minesweeper HMS *Rowena* where he spent the last 18 months of the war sweeping mines. He did very well in *Rowena* being promoted to Leading Seaman and then Petty Officer and becoming the ship's Bosun.

On being discharged from the Navy in June 1946, and needing the money, Norman started boxing professionally as a middleweight in fairgrounds and on the circuit. By the time he finally retired he had fought 146 times, winning 83 losing 58 and drawing 5 times. Recalled to the Navy in 1952 for another 5 years' service due to the Korean War, he was finally discharged in September 1957.

I would like to finish by paying my own tribute to Norman Walton. I spoke to him for the first time in October 2001 and went up to see him in Pudsey four times before he died aged 84, in April 2005. His personality was the inspiration behind the Neptune Association and I regarded him as a personal friend. Put simply he was one of the most remarkable men one could ever wish to meet, and we were delighted when he became our first President.

In April 2007, sixty members of the Neptune Association made a pilgrimage back to Tripoli and went by Libyan ship to the site where it is believed *Neptune*'s wreck lies. We held a service, lowered an ensign over the spot and scattered over 200 flowers in memory of individual sailors. Norman's daughter Norma then scattered his ashes so that he could join his mates, according to his wishes. It was a most emotional end to an amazing journey.

John McGregor, OBE, Commander, Royal Navy
(Son of Paymaster Commander Jack McGregor – *Neptune* Casualty)

CHAPTER 1

The Memorial

LONDON WAS IN CHAOS, bombs blasting the city, frightened people emerging from the smoke, injured, bleeding, confused. Dead bodies from the carnage not yet identified. A bleak reminder of how fragile peace can be. It was a time to celebrate the sixtieth anniversary of the end of World War II, an end which was supposed to be the last of the fear and the suffering, a time of peace and hope. It was a time to prepare for a weekend that would see the celebration of the end of that war – and yet we were seeing across our television screens acts of hatred and war once again.

Thursday 7 July 2005

It was just after 9 a.m. that the first reports of the disaster unfolding in central London began to come in: three terrorist bombs ripped through London Underground trains during rush hour on Thursday, 7 July and a fourth destroyed a double-decker bus, killing fifty-two people and wounding more than 700 others. The Tube was shut down and bus services in the centre of the city halted causing travel disruption. Mainline stations were also closed for much of the day.

A permanent memorial to the victims of the 7 July suicide bombings was unveiled in London in the Victoria Embankment Gardens where thousands of mourners laid wreaths in the aftermath of the attacks. There was no official ceremony to mark its launch. The London Memorial Garden, littered with flowers and notes of public sympathy, opened at the site of the bombings in the days following the terrorist atrocities, was closed permanently, and Westminster City Council commissioned a plaque to replace it. It reads, 'Under this tree people of all faiths and nationalities, united in grief, laid wreaths in memory of those killed on 7th July, 2005, following the attacks on London's public transport system.'

Similar sentiments and actions applied on that day and the following days as people all over the country prepared to commemorate all past wars and those who gave up their lives for the safety and future of their children and the future generations.

1

Saturday, 9 July 2005

A unique event took place on Saturday 9 July at the National Arboretum in Alrewas when over 400 assembled for a moving ceremony and service to accompany the unveiling of a Memorial in honour of two ships, the cruiser HMS *Neptune* and destroyer HMS *Kandahar* that were trapped in the clutches of an enemy minefield in the Mediterranean on 19 December 1941, with the loss of 837 lives including 150 New Zealanders and nineteen South Africans. It was the fifth worst British Naval disaster of World War II and the worst for New Zealand. While sixteen men survived *Neptune's* sinking and managed to reach a raft, they all died within the next few days except for one, Norman Walton, who became President of a flourishing Neptune Association over sixty years later. Almost unbelievably, a 'wall of silence' about the Force K disaster prevailed for over fifty years.

A strange set of coincidences led to the reported event and the inception of The Neptune Association.

John McGregor, whose father, Paymaster Commander Jack McGregor, was a *Neptune* casualty and who is now Chairman of the Neptune Association, was attending a family wedding in South Africa in October 1991. While there he visited the Naval Museum in Simonstown where his brother had told him he had seen a newspaper cutting from England about the sole survivor of the *Neptune*. On visiting the museum he was interested and intrigued to read the newspaper cutting about the sole survivor of the *Neptune*, Norman Walton, saying that he was alive and well and living in Pudsey, Leeds. As a result of his visit to the museum he contacted Nigel Fawcett who lives in Cape Town. Nigel's service in *Neptune* from May 1940 to March 1941, had been chronicled in the first of Nixie Taverner's Naval trilogy *A Torch Among Tapers*, a biography of her adoptive father, Captain Rory O'Conor, Captain of HMS *Neptune*. Nigel advised John to contact Nixie on his return to England.

At their meeting, she was delighted to hear that my father, Norman Walton, the sole survivor, was alive and living in Leeds and he and my mother had by then just returned from a tour of New Zealand. Consequently, Nixie and John contacted my father and they became very good friends. He became the much-valued President of the Neptune Association which they agreed they should form and which held its inaugural meeting at the Union Jack Club, Waterloo, London in December 2002.

And so it was that on the morning of Saturday, 9 July 2005, I, his daughter and my husband John prepared for the journey to the National Arboretum. The purpose of the gathering at the Arboretum was the dedication of a spectacular Memorial to *Neptune* and *Kandahar*, listing the names of all the casualties and the story of my father's survival. He had followed the progress of the building of the monument with passion and interest helped by informative visits from John McGregor.

The National Memorial Arboretum is a living tribute to the wartime generations of the twentieth century, being planted in 155 acres of reclaimed gravel workings beside the River Tame at Alrewas, between Lichfield and Burton-on-Trent. It lies within the boundary of the National Forest and has been planted in such a way that it is a gift for future generations to reflect and enjoy. A Millennium Commission Grant provided for a visitor centre, restaurant and the country's only Millennium Chapel. Here there is a short service of remembrance at 11 a.m. every day of the year.

The members of the Neptune Association had a desire to build a monument to honour, after so many years of silence, the lives of their husbands, fathers, brothers, uncles, cousins, grandfathers and friends who died in the service of their country on 19 December 1941. It was decided that the monument should be in the shape of a pyramid, 7 feet 6 inches tall, with a 4-foot square base, chosen partly because of the ships' connections with the Egyptian port of Alexandria.

Sixty-four years after the tragic Force K disaster a permanent memorial was built to commemorate the 837 men who died; it is the only one dedicated solely to those who died in the *Neptune* tragedy, with every name listed. Gerry Wright, wife of Nicholas Wright (son of Lieutenant Humphrey Wright, HMS *Neptune*) undertook to design the three-sided pyramid. It was also decided to appeal to members and relevant organisations to raise the necessary funds for the build, and Nick and Gerry volunteered to run the appeal. The 'Memorial Appeal' was launched to raise the £15,000 required in December 2004. Diana Clayton (daughter of Sgt. William Crocker Royal Marines, HMS *Neptune*) undertook the responsibility of finding the materials and oversaw the cutting and erection of the stones. The final pyramid was built from five stones cut from a single block of Derbyshire gritstone weighing five tons and turned into a four-sided pyramid weighing about three and a half tons.

By 9 March the first stones had been cut and a hole was later drilled in the second stone, ready to take a 25-foot Roll of Honour. The Commonwealth War Graves Commission had provided a comprehensive list of names for each casualty from *Neptune* and *Kandahar* but many small errors were found as more and more relatives made contact with the Association. Inside the shaft a sealed container recording the names of all the 837 casualties and a prayer used at a *Neptune* memorial service held in New Zealand in 2003 together with the Naval Prayer was inserted. On the top of the stone was a painting of the night sky, as it would have been seen from the water at the time HMS *Neptune* sank. The pyramid was finally erected at Alrewas with the orientation of the pyramid base towards the point north of Tripoli where *Neptune*'s wreck is believed to lie, on a bearing of 145 degrees from its position at the National Arboretum. At last on 6 April 2005 the Neptune Association had a monument. John McGregor had visited my father to relay the good news and show him the photographs of the final pyramid, which my father cherished and kept with him to his dying day on 20 April 2005.

My son, Michael, pulled into the driveway of our home. We three set off in silence, Michael driving, and John in the passenger seat; I sat in the back staring down at the black briefcase by my side that held so many memories of my father. A recent telephone call from Nick Hewitt, Interpretation Officer with HMS *Belfast* in London had requested any memorabilia remaining from the sole survivor of *Neptune* in order to include them in an exhibition entitled 'A Shared Tradition' which would run aboard HMS *Belfast* from July 2005 to May 2006. I had spent many hours clearing my parents' home during the spring of 2005 after my father passed away and had found many diaries, notes, letters and telegrams from the war years many of which had never been taken out of the 'ditty box' in the loft during my lifetime. They made fascinating reading and brought home to me, probably for the first time, that my father had led a life before my birth unknown and unquestioned by me. It made me realise how absorbed in our own lives we become and it is only at the passing of a loved one that we hang on to all the evidence of their existence. In the briefcase was the telegram sent by the Admiralty informing his parents that he was missing, and a postcard from Tripoli, Libya which declared him alive. These were to be used in the exhibition along with family photographs of my father.

The colours of an English summer splashed across the horizon as we sped south down the motorway and the bright sunshine flickered through the trees coming to rest on the papers in my hands. I stared at them, remembering my father who should have been with me today. The papers contained the timetable of events and order of service for the Memorial Day, where the exhortation read:

Norma Hudson, daughter of Petty Officer Norman Walton – only survivor of HMS *Neptune* and President of the Neptune Association shall read on behalf of her father –

They shall grow not old, as we that are left grow old.
Age shall not weary them, nor the years condemn.
At the going down of the sun, and in the morning
We shall remember them.

A tear fell on my cheek as I thought how much my father wanted to be there, to at last pay a special tribute to his fellow shipmates after all those years. Unfortunately it was not to be.

We arrived in good time and welcomed my father's youngest sister Ethel and her husband who represented the Walton family. It was a beautiful day worthy of such a unique event.

The ceremony commenced with a parade and march to the site, led by Bas Bowyer and the Sea Cadets and followed by words of welcome from the Neptune Association Chairman, John McGregor. A moving service was then introduced and conducted by the Chaplain Rev. Ron Paterson (who had served on both *Hood* and *Neptune* at the start of his Naval career and was well known for his inspiring, informal addresses). Most appropriately, the opening prayer, taken from The Neptune Memorial Service at St Christopher's, New Zealand, was read by Royden Thomson whose father, Paymaster Lieut. Bruce Thomson, was a *Neptune* casualty. Royden had attempted to meet my father once before in 1992 when he visited New Zealand but just missed him in Dunedin. He was to be foiled again as my father did not make the event as planned.

Following the dedication by the Chaplain of a memorial tree in memory of both ships, voices were raised in song with 'Lead Us Heavenly Father Lead Us'. This was followed by a reading from the historical plaque on the Monument by Gillian Wadden (daughter of

Surgeon Commander Thomas Larkworthy, HMS *Neptune*), Sheila Lloyd (daughter of Petty Officer Thomas Star, HMS *Kandahar*), Jean Horsham (daughter of Corporal James Auchinlech Royal Marines, HMS *Neptune*) and Duncan Black (son of Leading Stoker Thomas Black, HMS *Neptune*).

The first reading – 'Storm at Sea' – given by Col. Johan Du Plessis of the South African Embassy, was followed by the Naval hymn 'Eternal Father Strong to Save' and a series of prayers. The second reading from John 15, v.9–17, given by Captain Martin Atherton, Commanding Officer of Her Majesty's Naval Base Clyde at Faslane, was followed by the Chaplain's Special Memorial Dedication, 'Let this Memorial stand as a symbol of the life they led, the duty they undertook, the courage with which they fought and the memories they created and shared.'

The climax of this service was the unveiling of the Memorial itself. This was carried out by Nixie Taverner (Captain Rory O'Conor), Diana Clayton (Sgt. William Crocker, Royal Marines), Gillian Cross (Lieut. Frank Woodward) all of HMS *Neptune* and Valerie Pennifer (Edmund Lidbury) of HMS *Kandahar*.

I stepped forward, filled with a gush of emotion wishing my father was here to speak; the exhortation was given. A poignant moment for me and everyone in the Association that knew him.

After the Last Post, played by Adrian Harper a Royal Marine Bugler, the traditional one minute's silence was observed, followed by the Reveille. The service ended with Samantha White, great-granddaughter of *Neptune* casualty Lieut. Frank Woodward, reading the Kohima Epitaph, 'When you go home, tell them of us and say: For your tomorrow, we gave our today.'

Finally, seven doves of peace were released on behalf of *Neptune*, *Kandahar*, the Royal Navy, Royal Marines, Royal New Zealand Navy, South African Forces and all other nationalities aboard the stricken ships. Wreaths were then laid to the accompaniment of a lament, played by Piper Peter Vanse, by Richard Earp (*Neptune*); Bill Young (*Kandahar*); Captain Atherton, RN; Col Du Plessis, SADF; Lt. Burnham, RM; Harry Bradbear (George Cross Island Association); and Ken Oakley for the Neptune Association, followed by other descendants of those who perished.

The proceedings were brought to a close by the National Anthem, an impressive parade 'form-up' and march past the Memorial with a salute taken by the four commanders before a piped dismissal.

In the large marquee where lunch was provided guests mingled, new friendships were made and stories told of how for many years relatives of the deceased had no news of how their loved ones had died and no place where their lives could be commemorated. It was a special day where descendants gathered and were able to celebrate an everlasting memorial to their lives. My father would have been very proud to be there in person; in spirit he was with the group.

My husband, son and I walked through the exhibition that had been set up in the Conference Room at the Visitors Centre showing a variety of aspects of the Neptune Association's work including the building of the monument, the ship's crests and a map plaque subsequently fixed to the monument. There were examples of the books written including Nixie Taverner's book *Neptune's Legacy* published in 2003 and Adrian St Clair's book *Mediterranean Minefield* published later in 2005 that commemorated the lives of those lost in the Force K disaster; an exact replica of the Roll of Honour made by Diana Clayton was there to examine. I was taken aback when reading some moving accounts of the story of my father and his rescue on display. These had been written by children from schools in Derbyshire and Norfolk and were kindly given to me after the exhibition had closed.

Sunday, 10 July 2005

Thousands of people travelled into the City of London to support the marches and the parades of men and women, veterans of wars, who passed along the streets in front of them. The people of the United Kingdom stood proud across the country in celebration of peace, no suicide bomber, no terrorist, no warmonger, would influence their resolve to pay tribute to all who lost their lives in war.

CHAPTER 2

Growing Pains

WHEN JOHN NORMAN WALTON met the beautiful Maud Elliott in the early 1900s they would walk by the River Derwent in the village of Rowlands Gill, County Durham, planning their future. By 1920 they were married and living in a small terrace cottage in Townley Street, Rowlands Gill on the banks of the Derwent where they had spent so many happy hours together and where on 15 January 1921 they were delivered of their first born, a baby boy. As was the custom at that time they named him John Norman Walton after his father, and they would call him Norman. John Norman Senior, given the nickname of 'Patsy' Walton, began his working life down the pit mining coal, alongside his brothers, his father and his father before him but he was an active and talented sportsman and was soon able to use his skills as a footballer to escape a life down the pit. He became a professional footballer playing for Burnley at the age of twenty-three when my father was born. Patsy Walton was a charismatic figure, an all-round sportsman, mainly soccer but also a well-known sprinter and boxer. His quick wit, honed timing and ability to make people laugh led him into the entertainment business where his comedy act as well as his sporting prowess brought him local fame.

During the Great War 1914–18, every town, village and hamlet throughout the country suffered terrible losses to their populations. Many men were killed and of those who survived a great many were injured. The villages of Blaydon, Swalwell and Winlaton that clustered near where the Derwent meets the River Tyne, were no exception. Patsy Walton had experienced only the tail end of World War I, serving in the Royal Navy and was lucky to return home unscathed. Out of the carnage of the war groups of young men from the local area, who were survivors, were interested in establishing a social club, a place where ex-servicemen could meet in a pleasant social atmosphere, relax and converse with one another over a pint of beer. Such a social club was set up in Swalwell. Patsy was a member of the Miners Concert Party, who used to perform in the social clubs around the north-east of England during the 1920s and 1930s. He continued for many years with his comedy performances as the popularity of social clubs in the area grew. Throughout his life Patsy Walton was well known on the clubland circuit in the north-east of England, and he was in later years a respected member of the Swalwell Social Club Committee.

It was easy to see how Maud had fallen for Patsy Walton, he was quite a personality in the 1900s. Maud was an attractive woman, tall and elegant with a rosy complexion and jet black hair that she would sweep up into a bun on her head. She was intelligent, well educated and able to play a number of musical instruments well including the accordion, the piano and an instrument called the 'Jew's harp'. In later years Maud would accompany her children as they entertained friends and neighbours singing and performing the plays and concerts that she would help them to produce. The couple had nine children in all, five sons and four daughters. All the sons had a go at sporting activities trying to live up to the name of Patsy Walton. My father and his brothers all played soccer for Swalwell School and he and his brother Leslie played in the Gateshead District League. His younger brothers Tommy and Seppy were involved in schoolboy, youth and senior football for the district. His brother William, the third in line, was the only boy not interested in sport, preferring to go his own way, with his head in a book most times. My father went on to excel in most sports during his life, including boxing and water polo. Physical fitness was always his major drive; he inherited this from his father and often quoted the times during his life where his fitness, as well as his dogged determination, had given him the advantage against all the odds.

William Walton was my father's beloved granddad. He was born in 1866 in the Lanchester area and married Ellen Beadling. All families in the area were mining families at that time. Coal mining was the main source of employment in the three collieries around the Swalwell area. The Garesfield Collieries' Henry pit opened in Victorian times, closed in August 1940 and was originally a drift mine. Hannington's Drift, part of Axwell Park Colliery, opened in 1839 and closed in 1954, and was where coal from Whickhambank Colliery was taken out. There was also Axwell Colliery owned by R. Bagnall and Sons and located near Bagnall's Cottages south of where the coke works were later built. Garesfield Collieries Ltd. employed

281 people in 1914 while Axwell Park pit, known as 'The High' employed 803 people. Both mines used the local rail transport. After the last war an opencast disposal point was built off Millers Lane and coal was brought by road from the local opencast mines such as Cut Thorn near Fellside Road, Horsemouth near Ravensworth, Lumley Castle, Plawsworth near Chester-le-Street, Horsley in Northumberland and Maiden Law near Lanchester, among others. It was at Maiden Law where my father's grandparents and great-grandparents and their families gained employment. At Derwenthaugh there were extensive railway sidings where coal from the pits at Pontop, and later Garesfield, and coke from Winlaton Mill Cokeworks was transferred from the collieries' own railway onto the main rail network which ran parallel with the River Tyne from Gateshead to Hexham. Upstream of the many bridges that spanned the Derwent at Swalwell was the forge where iron and steel were manufactured using water power from the river at the Dam Head. On the site now stands Swalwell Visitors Centre associated with the Derwent Walk where my father and I, some fifty years later walked and recalled the happy times he spent around the area in his youth; it was full of activity and noise in his younger days. The cokeworks could be heard from his home releasing large volumes of smoke accompanied by a loud hissing noise; trains went to and fro between the cokeworks and Derwenthaugh passing under the Swalwell Bridge.

As a child my father had been used to running free on the green hills and in the woods that spread across Rowlands Gill, Whickham and Winlaton, where the seams of coal ran. The areas past Rowlands Gill were covered in huge pit heaps and the big steel wheels that would bring the miners up from the coalface. Streams of men, their faces black with coal dust would march through the streets in the area on a daily basis as the working shifts changed.

As my father was growing up in the 1920s his grandfather became the gamekeeper on Lockhaugh Estate in Rowlands Gill, a large wooded estate run by the pit owners of the time and where he spent most of his young life. William Walton or 'Old Bill', as he was called locally, went to live in Lockhaugh Lodge with his family. The 'Big House', as my father referred to Lockhaugh Lodge, was a large stone house in the wooded area of Rowlands Gill and stood alone above the open fields that ran from the Gill during the 1920s and 1930s. Low Thornley Burn Wood, known as Stampley Moss was an expansive wooded valley between Winlaton and Lockhaugh, where my father and his granddad would lay traps and hunt.

In the summer of 2002 as my father and I walked the new Derwent Walk heritage site we both remembered many of the old sites. Passing the cokeworks, which are now out of operation, we walked through the woods and up the valley to Rowlands Gill, where my father found the woodland much depleted since he was a boy. There were many new houses built on the fields and a large brick house was now standing on the site still called Lockhaugh Lodge. Some of the old stone walls and outbuildings remained and the surrounding wooded area by the River Derwent is now a popular tourist site. In fact the site where the cottages stood where my father was born, now serves as a caravan park, an idyllic spot alongside the river enjoyed by the children of today in much the same way as he and his brothers and friends enjoyed the area in the 1920s. His memories of Lockhaugh Lodge were vivid as he described his childhood, 'Granddad would sit outside in his deckchair of an evening, smoking his clay pipe while my Aunt Dorothy, Dad's sister, cooked at the wood-burning range in the huge kitchen, making the meals and caring for her father and brothers. She was a hard woman, she had to be living with all them men.' His grandmother Ellen passed away in December 1925, leaving her only daughter Dorothy to inherit the task of caring for all the men in the family who were still at home, a role accepted without question in those days. Happy memories for my father as he describes his time with his granddad:

> He would get me up before dawn when we would set off with the dogs into the woods. Granddad taught me all about the animals around and how to lay traps. When he first let me use his gun, I let off the shot and ended up on my backside. He dragged me up and set me up again. He was a hard but fair man and taught me how to look after myself and keep safe. Sometimes we'd 'knab' a rabbit to bring back for my Aunt Dorothy to hang then she'd clean it and pop it into a stew or a pie.

His granddad, as well as being gamekeeper at the Lockhaugh Estate, also used to run the local hunt. The Fox and Hounds public house in the village of Coalburns was one of the regular meeting places for the 'Braes of Derwent' fox hunt. He had many hunting dogs at the Lodge but his favourite dog was a German Shepherd called Boris. He guarded the front gates of Lockhaugh Lodge and would meet my father from the bus stop and escort him into the gates at his granddad's. My father described Boris as the safest guard he could have had as he followed him everywhere.

My father was always a good swimmer, which served him well in later life. He was taught to swim by his father and tells the story of diving for pennies, 'My dad taught me to swim in the river when I was very young. As I got older I used to dive off the bridges that crossed the River Derwent and dredge the bottom for pennies. I could make quite a tidy sum for my age.' When his granddad died in 1935 my father was fourteen-years-old. He described how the death of his granddad affected him, 'When my granddad died I took it hard. From an easy-going kid', he explained, 'I started to go off the rails. Hanging around Swalwell and Blaydon with a crowd from the wrong side of the tracks.'

By the late 1920s his father was offered the chance of a rented flat for his family in Whorlton Terrace in the village of Swalwell, as part of a 'package' to encourage him to play football for the local area. Football teams were originally associated with one or other of the various churches, the Church of England, the Presbyterians, and the Primitive Methodists each having their own teams. His dad started with the Presbyterians. Swalwell Association Football Club existed from 1949 until 1998. They played in the Northern Combination League. His father was a popular footballer already playing professionally for Burnley and later offered a higher sum to play for a Scottish football team called Alloa, a thriving club in those days. His wife Maud was not happy with his move and would not go with him, so he eventually rejected the offer with Alloa.

My father moved with his family from Rowlands Gill to the flat in Whorlton Terrace, near the River Tyne. Whorlton Terrace was a row of terrace houses that had been made into flats that sat in what they called Swalwell Bottom, below the mass of terrace streets that ran up the hill from the industrial foundries and shipyards located on the River Tyne. Most flats and houses in the area were owned by the families that ran the factories and the coalmines and were rented out to their workers. Maud and Patsy Walton lived in an upstairs flat that had a kitchen, living room, a bedroom next to the kitchen, where my father and his new brother Leslie slept and two smaller bedrooms off the hallway. When he and I visited the area of Whorlton Terrace in 2002 alas the houses were gone and a scrapyard now sits on the site.

In April 2005, a number of obituaries for my father were published in national and local newspapers including *The Times*, the *Daily Telegraph*, the *Yorkshire Post* and the *Newcastle Chronicle* and I included a request in the *Newcastle Chronicle* to hear from anyone who might remember my father, receiving a number of replies. Sally Craggs, who telephoned me after reading the newspaper article, was a neighbour in the 1920s, now living in South Shields and aged eighty-three. She described the times with my father and Leslie:

> I remember the picnics with the Walton family and swimming in the river with my sister and the two Walton brothers, wearing only our underwear, in what seemed like long hot summers in those days. They would put on great entertainment and we would watch them do concerts and sing. We were all very close in Whorlton Terrace and the children from the Walton family, the Morpeth family, who lived in the flat below and the Finlay family, would play together in the street. Our mothers would always be hanging the washing out on Mondays and they'd sit and talk while we played by the communal sink that stood in the middle of the street.

My father later recalled a story from the time when they moved to Swalwell from Rowlands Gill:

> I walked down from Rowlands Gill to my new home in Swalwell and remember I was wearing this smart suit and pair of shoes that my granddad bought me. Not many kids in Swalwell had shoes to wear. I ended up hiding in the doorways and under the windows of the houses I passed, so that none of the local kids would see me.

A lot of bullying took place in the streets during his early schooldays but he would always escape to his granddad's at weekends. He and his brother Leslie, who was born eighteen months after him, were always very close. Leslie, who now lives in Indiana, USA, describes his younger days with his brother:

> When there was just Norman and me at home we would always visit our Granddad in Rowlands Gill at the weekends and have picnics with our Mam by the river on school holidays. Norman was always getting into scraps as we got older. He would be fighting with two or even more lads at a time in the schoolyard at Swalwell School. I would always be told when Norman was in a fight and then run to pitch in and help my brother. All us kids would help each other and stick together. We were a force to be reckoned with in those days.

Leslie recalls when he and his dad saw my father being beaten up during a game of hide and seek in the alley, 'Dad started giving

Norman boxing lessons. Dad would teach us how to handle the big boys, kneeling down to us in the kitchen, and giving us regular boxing lessons. He was always giving us lectures on how to handle ourselves.'

My father began to toughen up and by the time he was fifteen, after his granddad had passed away, he was getting about in Blaydon Town and the Scotswood Road area of Gateshead, mixing with what he called the 'harder set'. He joined St Joseph's Boxing Gym, in Blaydon and really enjoyed the sport. Although not a Catholic himself most of his teenage pals were, and they came from Blaydon and Winlaton to form a gang. All the villages in the area had rival gangs at that time. He began to make a name for himself, 'I got a name in the area for all the wrong reasons' as he put it, 'street fighting and dance hall capers'. The locals called him the 'big kid', probably because he was the eldest of a large family, and he certainly tried to live up to the name. The Waltons were a really close family who always stood by and took care of each other.

Leslie describes their school days, 'Norman and I had very good attendance at Swalwell School with good school reports, which our Mam was very keen to see. Norman was a good scholar and he was pretty sharp. We would walk home to a cooked dinner every day and our Mam used to help us with our homework.'

My father always spoke about his Mam with great fondness, he recalled,

> Our Mam would be the one who would help with our homework. She was really intelligent and would help me with my maths. I loved mathematics. I would finish off the homework sat on the 'netty' (outside lavatory) roof in the yard. Jackie Finlay and I would do our homework up there regularly, so we wouldn't be bothered by some of the local lads.

It was hard times, where survival tactics were learned as part of everyday life. My father, his brothers and sisters all remembered the times as very happy, with lots of love and support in the household and from the aunties and uncles and friends who lived around them. The smells that came from the kitchen stove and the cast iron oven set in the fireplace filled the house and the cooking seemed to be constant. Even though money was scarce he and his brothers describe how they helped in the lean days:

> We waited outside the back entrance to the butcher's shop to collect 'scrag ends' from the cuts of meat that were often thrown out at the end of the day.

Then we would take them home to our Mam who was a wizard in the making of soups and stews. When it was a very cold winter our family would often run out of coal for the fires. We scratched and scraped for bits of coal on the pit heaps, and took home what we managed to find, but the quality of it wasn't up to much. Sometimes we had lucky pickings on the railway lines that ran parallel with the path of Blaydon Burn, a stream that ran through the valley near where we lived. Colliery engines would chug up and down the valley all day, carrying coal in trucks from the Mary and Bessie coal drifts which were about three quarters of a mile further upstream. The wagon-loads of coal ended up in hoppers next to Cowen's Brick Yard in Blaydon.

It was a dangerous activity, not to be recommended but one that often kept the house fires burning longer and an activity that the Walton brothers remember fondly, 'The engine drivers were friendly blokes who often gave us a wave as they passed.' All the family was united in working hard to keep the house warm and food on the table.

At weekends the children would entertain family and friends. The women in the street were always home alone on Friday and Saturday nights, while the men frequented the local clubs and pubs. The Walton family described the entertainment:

Concerts would be put on using the washing line across the front room where we would hang blankets to act as curtains to a theatre. Our Mam would play the 'squeeze box' when we sang songs. Men would also sometimes entertain in the street. It was usually three or four of them, one playing a mouth organ, the other spoons and others would join if they had a kettledrum and maybe a ukulele banjo. Sometimes the women would send for a jug of beer, which the boys would wait patiently for outside the club. Everyone in the club would know our Dad's name, Patsy Walton.

The streets in Swalwell teamed with playing children in the 1920s and 1930s, and among the many games they used to play was a popular game called 'bays'. My father's sisters describe the games they played:

The girls would mark out the bays with chalk from one to ten, sometimes marking the last one with OXO or LONDON. The 'hitchy dabber' as it was called was usually an empty shoe polish tin and would be shoved along to reach one of the bays. The girls would hop to the 'dabber' pick it up, turn still with one foot on the ground and hop back. The game was usually played by the girls in the summer months. The boys and girls would play a variety of street games together like Bon-bon the biscuit tin, Harilevers, Statues, Muntikitty and Queeny, depending on whether we could get hold of a ball or not.

My father explained why he left school in 1935:

> I had the chance to go to grammar school further along the road towards Blaydon but in those days, for most lads, it was more important to earn money to help your Mam, especially when you were the eldest. I started work in the same foundry as my Dad as a trainee steel-worker and making tea for the men on the side for 'coppers'. I used to help my Mam calculate the racing bets and often go to collect the bets for my Dad who was a 'bookie' at the time. The work was running short in the north-east and not many men in Swalwell were working by the late 1930s. They all had ways of making money on the side. Being a 'bookie's runner' was very popular. They would carry the 'clock' and take bets just in time for the race, then run down to 'Kimber's (a local shop in Swalwell which used to take the bet money). Then a 'posh' car would turn up and take the 'clock' and the money. Some of the younger kids, Isabelle and Tommy would ask to sit in the car and show off.

Much of the activity involved in being a 'bookie's runner' was unlawful and arrangements would be made to take turns amongst the 'runners' who would pay the fines.

His father eventually found work as a crane operator at the Delta Foundry, making steel 'chairs' for the railways. Before and during the war he continued to run a 'book' on the side, taking racing bets from the punters in the factories. It was with the coming of the railway that industry began to appear at nearby Derwenthaugh with the cokeworks, firebrick works, situated on the west bank of the Derwent, adjacent to the staithes and the Delta ironworks, later known as Raine and Company. In the Second World War they employed 800 men, but by the fifties and sixties traditional markets in the shipbuilding and mining industries waned, leading eventually to the end of Raines.

It was when he was sixteen-years-old that my father met Irene Dodds at the local dance in the Miners Hall, Winlaton. Irene lived in Winlaton and was a lively, popular and beautiful-looking fifteen-year-old when he met her. He describes their first meeting, 'She could have the pick of the bunch, she was lovely and a great dancer. I knew she was the one for me straightaway but she wasn't interested in this cocky lad from Swalwell. I chased her till she eventually caught me'. His way of living in his teenage years was not improving. He'd left school with the idea of making his mark in the area, not the life his mother had hoped for her eldest son and Maud believed he was taking the wrong path, as she worryingly told his father. He loved his father dearly and wanted to be like him, aspiring to his great name in the town, but always felt he could never live up to him. One night he came home after drinking and fighting again, but this time his father was up waiting when he came into the house. His father remarked that it must be true the things he had heard about his son. He replied, 'I'm big enough and old enough to look after myself.' 'Pop' (as he always called his Dad) said, 'I'll tell you when you are, son', and swung round out of his chair, whereupon my father jumped in and 'tried the nut'. It was the first and last time he ever attempted a strike at his dad. His father struck him only once, then carried him to bed. In the morning his mother told my father that 'Pop' had come out of the room with tears in his eyes saying he never thought he would ever have to raise his hand to a son of his, least of all Norman. However, my father disappeared to his Aunt Dorothy's, at Lockhaugh Lodge in Rowlands Gill. He knew he was always welcome there as it had ever been his escape. He stayed with his Aunt Dorothy for a long while until his father bumped into him in Swalwell one day and told him how much his mother was missing him. 'Crafty Pop', said my father, 'he knew how much I loved my mother, and so I returned home.'

Over the next few months the house seemed to be more and more crowded. My father was in his father's room regularly undergoing the lectures, until finally 'Pop' said, 'the best thing for you, son, is the Royal Navy, they have some good jockeys in there, they'll tame you.' My father thought on this and the next day he caught the bus into Newcastle and joined the Royal Navy. He was seventeen and a half-years-old and volunteered on 13 September 1938 for twelve years' special service. On entry to training he was described as 5 feet 8 inches tall, chest measurement 36 inches, with fair hair, blue eyes and a fresh complexion. He remembered, 'It didn't go down too well, this Naval discipline at first. After a few 'run ins' with the Navy I turned my energies to sport.' He began his amateur boxing career in the Navy and boxed in the novices competition for 'New Entries'. He had fifteen fights to get into the final where he was runner-up. He also made it into the football team and his sporting career with the Royal Navy soon blossomed. He was proud of his sporting achievements and soon became keen to do well with the Royal Navy.

My father's first posting was with HMS *Curacao* which lasted a whole two days. An old WWI light cruiser launched in 1917, it was fortunate he did not stay with her. She was 'escorting' the RMS *Queen Mary* – the ship now permanently moored at Long Beach, California, and which was used as a foot troopship in World War II – across the Atlantic on the night of 2 October 1942. She 'zigged' when she should have 'zagged' putting her square across the bows of the *Mary*, travelling in excess of thirty knots at the time and displacing more than 81,000 tons. She was cut in two and trampled straight under. The *Mary* was under strict orders to stop for nothing, and she was capable of ferrying up to 15,000 troops at a time, an entire army division and therefore vital to the war effort, so the loss of life in the *Curacao* was total, no survivors at all. The incident was shrouded in secrecy for much of the war and, in fact, doesn't get much of an airing even now. The *Mary* suffered a slightly bent bow.

He was with HMS *Esk* by the 28 April 1939 then on to HMS *Argos*, 6 May 1939 to 2 July 1939. He was serving in the Mediterranean out of Gibraltar to Malta and Alexandria.

My father had been assessed on 20 September 1938 for swimming, and excelling in the assessment had decided to learn the game of water polo. Always a keen swimmer from being a boy he really took to the game and it became one his favourite sports. He was chosen to play for the ship and the team was playing at every opportunity. He played football from joining and as a keen and skilled boxer he continued to box as a welterweight in the interservice boxing matches against the Army and Air Force. In his words, 'I became the undisputed champion in the Mediterranean by the end of '39.'

He was granted his first leave on 3 July 1939, and returned to see his family. His eldest sister Isabelle and younger brother Tommy had been waiting at the end of the street all day for his return. They walked with him back to the house, proud as punch, holding hands with their eldest brother in his new uniform. The flat had a shared yard downstairs and his brothers and sisters remember he would teach the younger ones his fancy skills in skipping and exercise as he continued his boxing training at home.

Beyond the yards, the foundries and shipyards on the River Tyne were now again bursting with activity, preparing for a possible war with Germany.

My father had been spoiled as the first-born, spending quality time with his dad and beloved granddad. Leslie had arrived soon after and his brother William three years later. Even though my father had spent a great deal of his growing years with his granddad in Rowlands Gill the three boys were close, and returning home meant boys' nights out at the clubs with Patsy Walton proudly showing off his eldest lad, home from the Navy. There was five years between William and Isabelle, the first daughter, and then the children came roughly every two years, regular as clockwork. As John Norman Walton, Senior, used to say, 'I just had to throw my trousers on the bed and Maud would end up pregnant again.' Isabelle was followed by another son, Thomas, born in 1932. Tommy was nearly eight years old when my father first came home on leave. He idolised his older brother, following him everywhere he could. Dorothy, Seppy and Lillian were still little tots, running around being pests to their brother home on leave. There was certainly a full house, but a happy and loving house ruled and run efficiently by his mother Maud, whom my father loved dearly.

My father could not wait to see Irene, and he did so nearly every minute of his leave. She lived in Pioneer Street, Winlaton with her Dad, also called Norman, her mother Priscilla whom everyone called 'Lily', her brother Ronnie and two sisters, Hilda and Betty. My father was a very good dancer and she enjoyed being twirled around the floor by her good-looking sailor when he was home. While he was away Irene would go to Swalwell to see his mother, Maud, and often help her to care for the younger children. His brothers and sisters have many memories of Irene being at the Walton house while they were growing up. She was known as 'our Irene', a loving prefix to a name that lets everyone else know you are part of the family.

My father always wanted to do what was expected of him and listened intently to the many instructions John Norman Senior would pass on as they both sat by the fire late at night after the rest of the family had gone to bed. My father would often relay these instructions to me, many years later. The sound advice his father had passed on had great longevity and as most fatherly advice still applies today. On his first leave from the Navy his father sat him down and told him how to cope if he ended up in the 'drink', 'Never go to sleep and keep moving whatever happens, sleep and you say good-bye to life.' It was advice that my father found very useful during the next few years.

At the end of his leave he joined HMS *Janus* in Jarrow-on-Tyne. The J Class destroyer was built by Swan Hunter and Wigham

Richardson Limited in Wallsend-on-Tyne, ordered on 25 March 1937 and commissioned on 5 August 1939. He described how proud he was to join her:

> We did the running up trials with her then off to *Pompey* barracks in Portsmouth. A trip around Britain followed, visiting various ports and showing the flag. This is a great ship with a real happy crew. Captain sends me out on the motorboat to pick up visitors from shore. I'm showing off the ship to visitors, bringing them back and forth from the shore-base in Cleethorpes. Feeling proud as punch and enjoying my life in the Royal Navy, hope I do well with her.

At 11 a.m. on Sunday 3 September 1939, war was declared with Germany. He described the day, 'HMS *Janus*, "up anchor and off", across the North Sea to pick up Sir Neville Henderson (Ambassador to Germany) at the Hook of Holland. We drop depth charges in anger on the way back to England. HMS *Janus* off on North Sea Patrol, this is the real thing, fighting for my country.'

My father was filled with a mixture of pride, anticipation and fear of what was to come.

CHAPTER 3

This is War

IN APRIL 1940 HMS *JANUS* was involved in convoy escort duties in
Norwegian waters. The Norwegian Campaign lasted all of six
weeks. Six weeks of hard gruelling battles, endurance and bravery,
during which three Victoria Crosses were earned by men of the
Royal Navy (the first VCs of the 1939/45 war). Most of the action
took place in the Norwegian fiords mainly, Narvik, Namsos,
Trondheim, Andalsnes, Bergen and Stavanger. On the dark night of
7 April 1940, ships of both sides steamed through wild seas to their
various destinations and rendezvous.

The first battle action was by a British minelaying destroyer, HMS
Glowworm, which had separated from the company of three other
destroyers in order to search for a man swept overboard in the high
seas west of Trondheim. Not an unusual occurrence in high seas as
my father described, 'One minute you could have a shipmate
following you on deck the next he could be gone. The Captains did
not always detour from their task to search for a man overboard,
following the orders was priority.' The destroyer engaged ships of the
German navy at dawn on the 8 April, when the German cruiser
Admiral Hipper with her eight-inch guns reduced the *Glowworm* to a
wreck. However, her Captain, Lt. Commander Roope, in a last
desperate effort attempted to ram the German cruiser. She crashed
against the cruiser's side and tore away 130 ft of her armoured belt
and broke off her starboard torpedo tubes. Shortly after, the
Glowworm blew up and sank with thirty-eight survivors who were
rescued by the *Hipper*, which although damaged had not been put out
of action. Alas the skipper of the *Glowworm* fell back into the sea
whilst being rescued and drowned.

On 8 April 1940 at the opening of the Namsos campaign it was
the destroyers of the Home Fleet which first felt the weight of the
Luftwaffe. Meagrely and unsuitably armed for defence against the
dive-bombers, yet they more than held their own.

Throughout 30 April the Stukas had kept up an almost ceaseless
attack for nearly eighteen hours a day. My father described the day,

'getting hammered by aircraft, German "Stukas" on us most of the time making our way up to Namsos, it's a bad do here'. At about five o'clock a formation of three Stukas split up. Two came hurtling down on the destroyer HMS *Bittern*'s port bow, the third dived from right astern of her. It was this plane that released a bomb that struck the quarter-deck at the base of a steel locker holding high explosive demolition charges. The resultant blast and flash streaked the full length of the ship. The Captain was thrown to the deck on the bridge and when he picked himself up he saw the stern of his ship had been blown off. Fire spread between decks and the small arms ammunition of the magazine began to explode. All fire pumps were out of action. Lt. Commander R.H. Mills gave orders for all hands except the forward gun crews to abandon ship.

Fortunately the destroyer HMS *Janus* had come into the fiord during the day and her captain now brought his bow alongside that of the *Bittern*, allowing the survivors to trans-ship. My father described his actions on that day:

> *Bittern* taking some bad hits and we pull alongside. I volunteer, along with others, to go on board to help bring off some of the injured. On going in the Coxwain's Office, on the upper deck, I find the Cox. in his chair. He looks OK but when I touch him, find he is dead as a doornail. 'Stukas' are attacking again so make our way to trans-ship, back on board at the double. Me and the lads are jiggered, having had no sleep for forty-eight hours, action stations all the time. Don't care too much for this war lark, all getting a bit too serious.

Soon afterwards HMS *Janus* was ordered to sink her with a torpedo. HMS *Bittern* was the only major warship to be put out of action at Namsos. Previous to this, HMS *Janus* was sailing into Namsos when she sent a medical officer and attendant to the aid of the wounded on board the anti-submarine trawler *Arab*, whose Captain, Lt. Commander R. B. Stannard was awarded the VC for gallantry and leadership.

The need to prevent German aid reaching General Diebl's isolated force by the road running up the coast from Namsos had been foreseen as early as April, when a party of a hundred *Chasseurs-Alpins* (French troops) were sent in the destroyer HMS *Janus* from Namsos to Mosjoen, a hundred miles further north and at the terminus of the railway. They were landed there on 2 May 1940. My father described the event:

Asked for volunteers to take the cutter ashore to pick up some crack French troops, under cover of darkness. I volunteered with the others and we pick them up pretty smooth, considering. Sailed out of Namsos into the North Sea and trans-shipped the French troops to a cruiser.

In May North Sea patrols were carried out against German minelayers. During the Norwegian campaign, Captain William Richmond Fell commanded a group of five trawlers known as the Gubbins Flotilla, which was despatched to support soldiers landed in Norway under the leadership of Colonel Gubbins. About 11 May 1940, my father recalled being sent with the destroyers HMS *Janus* and HMS *Javelin* to Colonel Gubbins' aid. He was Officer Commander of Scissors Force, a group of five independent companies each with twenty officers and 270 other ranks, sent to harass and delay the enemy advance up the solitary road north. They found him at Sandnessjoen where some 350 of his men were already embarking on a coastal steamer. He himself with the remaining 100 went aboard HMS *Janus* and they were taken to Bodo, a little port near the entrance of the Vestfiord which was to be held at all costs as an outpost of the operations round Narvik.

My father did not expand on this too much in his diary, except to write:

Done a couple more pick-ups and put-downs around the coast – pretty dangerous rendezvous. Proceeded to Narvik area where we are Asdic sweeping for submarines. Waiting in case any ships come out, doing a holding job, while the battleship HMS *Warspite* and destroyers, are doing such a wonderful job against the German ships and shore batteries.

The second battle at Narvik, conducted by the battleship HMS *Warspite* and escorting destroyers, did result in the destruction of a number of large German destroyers, supply and troop ships, and shore installations, but it was all too late. German forces were already in Norway in decisive numbers, and the British and French contingents had to be pulled out. My father's final comments in his diary for the spring of 1940, described his return to England, 'On our way back to Immingham Docks for repairs and boiler clean, we've had six weeks at sea and are pretty run down.' The Norwegian part of the war finished on 8 June 1940.

The diary notes he made at this time and letters to his mother provide some detail of his personal contributions and more importantly his feelings at that time, the excitement and the fear amongst his first major experiences of war. It was a period where he gained a number of commendations and took great pride in being made up to Able Seaman.

They endured some pretty rough times during the summer of 1940, operating from Alexandria under the leadership of Admiral Sir Andrew B. Cunningham, Commander-in-Chief of the Mediterranean Fleet. Initially it was their job to escort convoys, loaded with provisions, from Alexandria to Malta and on their return carrying equipment for maintaining the Mediterranean Fleet. By July HMS *Janus* was a member of the 14th DD Flotilla based on Alexandria and was involved in the bombardment of Bardia. She formed part of Force C under the command of Vice Admiral Pridham-Wippell. This force was involved in the Battle of Calabria that occured just to the east of the toe of Italy on 9 July 1940.

My father's sporting activities kept his spirit up and lightened his mood between actions as he described his escapades in the shore bases, 'I'm taking up all the sports I can get, playing water polo for the ship and flotilla, football schedule for the ship and the inter-service matches representing the Navy, pretty hectic, plus boxing pretty regularly at the Alexandria Fleet Club.' This kept his shore-time pretty full and more importantly, it kept him out of trouble. In March 1941 *Janus* was involved in the Battle of Cape Matapan. During March 1941 my father volunteered for submarines. He was sent to hospital to have his appendix removed and after ten days in hospital and the stitches removed he was sent up to Nathanya, near Tel-Aviv, Palestine for six weeks' convalescence. The convalescence period lasted one week. He had 'a very good night in Nathanya', as he mildly put it, fell foul of the military police and Palestine police whilst under the influence of alcohol and was accused of 'causing a disturbance'. He finished up in a cell for the night then was taken in front of the Commanding Officer the next morning. 'They said junior rates could not drink spirits, you had to be a Petty Officer or a Sergeant. Silly Fellows!' he wrote as an explanation for his actions in a letter to his mother. This episode saw him sent back, under escort, to HMS *Janus* leaving the ship in March 1941.

It is highly likely that a troublesome character such as he was at that time, would have been sent straight to the hottest place, which in 1941 was Crete.

CHAPTER 4

The Evacuation of Crete

CRETE WAS UNDER ATTACK from crack German paratroopers over a period of twelve days from Tuesday 20 May to 31 May 1941. On the second night after the Germans attacked Crete the Navy was warned that the British forces ashore would make an attempt that night to decoy the enemy convoy of invading caiques toward Suda at a convenient moment. A British destroyer came upon that convoy first in the darkness. At about 23.00 hours an Italian escorting destroyer failed to release its torpedoes in time to damage the British vessel and soon the Navy was on the spot in strength. The British ships found themselves in the midst of a fleet of caiques, each carrying about a hundred Germans, so closely packed they were standing shoulder to shoulder. The Italian destroyer was sunk outright and the Navy turned its pom-poms and four-inch guns upon the caiques – often at point blank range. In a few minutes the sea was in chaos. In the gun flashes the sailors could see thousands of Germans swimming about in the sea, calling hysterically for help. Caiques were rammed head on and smashed to pieces, or raked by the pom-poms or sunk by the four-inch guns. In some vessels the Germans attempted to hide below and hoisted the Greek flag. In others they jumped overboard in terror as the warships bore down on them. A few who got near shore were met with machine-gun fire or ran foul of booms and, overturning, drowned their crews among the rocks. Some nine thousand Germans were either drowned or killed. They were the whole of the ground staff of the Ninth German Flieger Korps and the Bavarian Mountain Division with their artillery.

My father must have been told of these events before he left Alexandria as there is a note in his diary that reads, 'that was a bloody night, they say the sea ran red with blood.'

On 1 June at 03.00 hours the final evacuation of troops was carried out by Vice Admiral King in the cruiser *Phoebe* in company with the fast minelayer *Abdiel* and the three destroyers *Kimberley, Hotspur* and *Jackal*. Previously 21,000 British and Imperial troops had been taken from Greece to Crete to reinforce the army there, most without equipment except their rifles. The total strength on Crete was 32,000 including 6,500 Australians, 7,000 New Zealanders and some young Greek troops plus the British garrisons on the island – mostly at Heraklion.

My father was on HMS *Woolwich* until 22 May 1941 and described his actions, 'I go on the Asdic course in HMS *Woolwich*, which I'm really looking forward to. I pass with flying colours and I'm now a fully qualified Anti-Submarine Detection Operator. Itching to get my first draft.'

As an adventurous lad aged just twenty there was an enormous element of excitement and no doubt the adrenalin would be pumping during his involvement in the sea battles that were raging in the Mediterranean during 1940/41. He was never happy to be ashore for long.

In Alexandria base, shore parties were being grabbed to make up Naval brigades to be sent to help the soldiers get onto the boats during the mass evacuation from Crete. My father was up there, happy to be involved, and understood the plan was to be that ships from Alexandria would come under cover of darkness and get as many soldiers as possible away from the embarkation points. He was part of the brigade landing on the beaches in Crete working for the

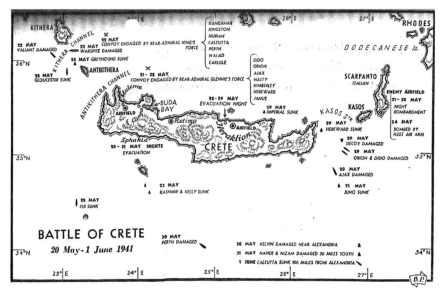

Map shows Maleme, Canea (Khania) and Heraklion where evacuation from Crete took place. My father was escorting the soldiers to the jetties as part of a naval shore party

beach master, Captain Morse, who had in fact been the previous Captain of *Neptune* from 1937 until he was relieved by Captain O'Conor in May 1940.

At 06.00 hours Wednesday 28 May, Rear Admiral Rawlings with Force B, the cruisers *Orion*, *Ajax* and *Dido*, six destroyers *Decoy*, *Jackal*, *Imperial*, *Hotspur*, *Kimberley* and *Hereward*, sailed from Alexandria with the objective to embark the Heraklion garrison of 4,000 that night. Enemy reinforcements were dropped in the Heraklion area that day. On their way Force B was under attack from German bombers, dive-bombers and torpedo bombers. Force B arrived at Heraklion at 23.00 hours. By 03.20 hours on 29 May, all 4,000 troops had been embarked in complete darkness, but not without trauma and casualties.

The context of my father's involvement on the beaches in the evacuation of Crete during late May 1941, is recorded in *A Sailor's Odyssey* written by Admiral of the Fleet, Viscount Cunningham:

By May 27th, after the decision to evacuate Crete, the troops from the Suda Bay area began wearily to fall back over the mountains to Spakia, a small fishing village on the south coast of the island. The village and the shingle beach, no more than 200 yards of which could be used by ships' boats, was hemmed in by a rugged escarpment of cliff 500 feet high. The road over the mountains from Suda Bay ended with a series of acute hair-pin bends and terminated abruptly at the cliff edge, from which a narrow zigzag track descended precipitously to the beach below. The ascent took at least two hours. At Heraklion, farther east, the Army had won its battle and the airfield was still in our hands. This was the only place where the jetties in the harbour were available for the embarkation of about four thousand men.

On the naval side the evacuation had to be undertaken with ships whose officers and men were on the verge of complete exhaustion, physically and mentally. As for the ships themselves, they had been driven hard for more than two months without the occasional two or three days' respite in harbour for boiler cleaning and running repairs. Their machinery had become unreliable, while many were struggling on as best they could after damage by enemy bombing. Moreover, their numbers were depleted. The navy had already lost two cruisers and four destroyers; while two battleships, aircraft-carriers, another cruiser and a destroyer were out of action for weeks or months. Another five cruisers and four destroyers had been damaged; but were still able to steam and to fight. The fleet was not really in favourable condition to evacuate some twenty-two thousand soldiers, most of them from an open beach, in the face of the Luftwaffe. But there was no alternative.

The general plan was as follows. Troops from the Maleme-Suda area were to embark from the beach at Spakia. Those from the Retimo area, if they could be contacted, were to come off from Plaka Bay. Troops from Heraklion would be taken off from Heraklion harbour, while a small number to the south of Heraklion were expected to make their way to Tymbaki, on the south coast. Evacuation was invariably to be carried out at night, usually between midnight and 3 a.m. This would allow ships to be as far as possible from the enemy air bases during daylight.

My father's part in the execution of this plan is described briefly in his notes for May 1941:

Crete was invaded by German Paratroops. I was sent ashore as part of a naval brigade to pick up troops. Standing on the road near the jetty watching them kicking their way down behind us I watched one 'Tommy' (the name given to British soldiers during the war), with his mounted Lewis gun shooting them down hard 'when they stop kicking they're dead', were his words to me. I said 'lets get going, there are hundred's of them'. I was explaining the way down to the jetty when the stukas came. I dived for cover in a crevice in the cliff side but he started running, he never had a chance. When I got onto the jetty it was crammed with Tommy's. We couldn't find the beach master, the beaches were crowded. The ships started coming in. Destroyers and smaller craft coming alongside while the cruisers stayed off shore.

Cunningham continued to describe the plan and wrote:

It had been decided that the main evacuation on the night of May 28th would be from Heraklion and it was planned to bring off the whole force in one lift. For this purpose a force under Rear Admiral Rawlings in the Orion with the cruisers Ajax and Dido, and the destroyers Decoy, Jackal, Imperial, Hotspur, Kimberley and Hereward, sailed from Alexandria at 6 a.m. on the 28th. They were to pass through the Kaso Straits at the eastern end of Crete.

My father noted at the time there was the realisation that there was no orderly escorting of troops to assigned embarkation in the smaller vessels and destroyers that lay around the harbour, not even in the expected organised transfer to cruisers outside the harbour:

We managed to get most of the soldiers aboard the small craft then a Lieutenant gave us the order 'every man for himself'. We all scrambled to board the few craft left. There was no order on how to return to our vessels so I climbed from one of the craft and boarded the Destroyer *Hereward*. HMS *Hereward* was packed so some of us transferred with the Tommies to the Cruiser *Orion*.

From 5 p.m., when about ninety miles south of the Straits at the eastern end of Crete the force was subjected to heavy air attacks – high-level and dive-bombing, as well as torpedo attacks. At 7.20 the

Imperial, Lieutenant-Commander C. A. de W. Kitcat, was narrowly missed by a bomb, though at the time she appeared to be undamaged. At 9 p.m. the *Ajax* had a close miss which started a fire, wounded twenty men, and caused some slight damage to the ship's side. It was unfortunate that exaggerated reports of the damage were given to the captain, and when he signalled them to the Rear Admiral the *Ajax* was ordered to return to Alexandria.

However, in spite of these mishaps the force arrived off Heraklion at 11.30 p.m., and the destroyers crept into the harbour, went alongside the jetties, ferried the correct quota of troops off to the cruisers, and embarked their own loads with steady efficiency.

In all 4,000 troops were embarked by 3 a.m. without alarming the enemy, a noteworthy performance, particularly without lights in pitch darkness.

My father described what he saw as he sailed with the force at 3.20 a.m. on 29 May, when twenty-five minutes later things started to go wrong, 'As daylight came so came the stukas. Four JU 88s appeared and dive bombing began, mainly on the *Orion* and *Dido*.' Out of the half-light of dawn, down they came, spitting gunfire and screaming bombs hurtling towards the ships, then off they went back to the airfields at Scarpanto for reloading and refuelling. 'About 06.30 hours I saw the *Hereward* was hit amidships, suffered a reduction in speed falling away astern of the squadron and apparently ran aground.'

The squadron had been delayed when Rawlings had ordered the *Hotspur*, Lieutenant-Commander C.P.F. Brown, to embark the troops and ship's company from the *Imperial*, and to sink her when her steering gear had failed. The delay had cost a precious ninety minutes and it was not until sunrise that the squadron turned south to pass through the Kaso Straits. Fierce air attacks started at 6 a.m. and continued at intervals until 3 p.m. Fighter cover promised by the RAF failed to appear. The *Hereward* was hit by a bomb and was seen to be making towards Crete, shrouded in smoke. Rear Admiral Rawlings took the difficult decision to push on. The *Hereward* was last sighted steaming slowly towards the shore with all her guns in action against the enemy aircraft. She was eventually sunk but Italian torpedo boats saved almost all the troops and the ship's company. My father was later to meet up with some of these fellows in the Italian prisoner of war camps and mentions the matelots in the diary notes of his time as POW.

Meanwhile the force was literally fighting its way south against wave after wave of attacking enemy aircraft. He continued to describe how the bombing was affecting himself and the crew of the *Orion*:

> Then it was *Orion*'s turn. 07.30 the *Orion* suffered a near miss. Many of the soldiers were firing their Bren Guns and Lewis Guns at the attackers. They machine gunned the ship, raking the bridge and wounded the Skipper and Rear Admiral Rawlings. The Commander T.C.T. Wynne, took over and we were bombed to hell, crippled for'd and aft.
>
> I got hold of a hose and we were trying to put out some of the fires, the screams were horrible – stayed in the memory for a long time. A Lt. Commander then ordered me to shut down a hatch as the water was coming up too fast. It was a communication hatch on the foc'sle and the crew was still down there, I felt sick. We gave up about 500 to the deep. Arms and spare body parts, we couldn't recognise most of them, it was pretty grim.

At 6.45 a.m. a close miss on the *Decoy*, Commander E. G. McGregor, fractured the turbine feet and reduced the speed of the squadron to twenty-five knots. A quarter of an hour later another very close miss on the *Orion* imposed a further reduction in speed to twenty-one knots. At 7.35, Captain G.R.B. Back was severely wounded by an explosive bullet from a dive-bomber, and he died two hours later. At 8.15 the *Dido*, Captain H.W.U. McCall, was hit by a bomb on 'B' turret, and at 9.00 the *Orion* was struck on 'A' turret. Both attacks were made by dive-bombers, and in each case the turrets were put completely out of action. At 10.45 the *Orion* was again attacked by eleven JU 87s. A bomb pierced her bridge, wrecked the lower conning tower, and burst on the stokers' mess deck. She had nearly 1,100 troops on board, and the casualties below were very heavy, a total of 260 being killed and 280 wounded. Among others three of the engineer officers were killed and all normal communications between bridge and engine-room were destroyed. The steering gear was put out of action and three boiler rooms were damaged, and the *Orion* was out of control until the emergency steering wheel could be connected and a chain of men organised to pass orders from the emergency conning position to the wheel. Because the fuel oil had been contaminated with seawater the *Orion's* speed fluctuated between twelve and twenty-five knots. To make matters worse the ship had also been badly on fire. At about 8 p.m. Rawlings brought his shattered squadron into Alexandria, the *Orion* herself with only ten tons of fuel and very few rounds of ammunition remaining. The ship was a terrible sight and the mess-deck a ghastly shambles.

My father described their return to harbour:

> We arrived into Alexandria harbour in the early hours of the morning. We were crippled, but the Commander done a magnificent job getting *Orion* into harbour. We were given cocoa and biscuits and bedded down in the warehouses, anywhere – jiggered and slept with exhaustion. I was transported back to Canopus shore station the next morning.

My husband and I took my parents on a package holiday to Crete, where we stayed in Heraklion over fifty years later. My father was very keen to see the island again and when he stood at the harbours and beaches it must have brought back striking memories from the events there in 1941. It was early spring when we visited and the weather was unusually cold but that did not deter my father's mission to tour the island. We hired a car and drove along the coast to Suda Bay where we all sat in silence in the very well-tended cemetery in Suda that looks out to sea. I watched as my parents slowly and silently walked amongst the rows of headstones marking the graves of the hundreds of young men who had perished in the hills and on the beaches in 1941. My father left us for a long while, walking down to the beach and looking out to sea.

Later that week we spent some time walking the beaches around the areas of Khania and Maleme. He recalled how there were legions of soldiers scrambling to the beaches and jetties. There now stands on that site a German monument in the shape of a diving eagle in memory of the 2nd Parachute Regiment.

I rarely heard him speak of the horrors he had witnessed during World War II, or of the memories that would plague him for years after. I witnessed only occasional moments when evidence of his emotions would rise to the surface. His nostrils would flare and tears would well in his eyes as the memories flooded back. The visit to Crete was one of those moments for my father as I watched the pain in his face.

CHAPTER 5

The Minefields

SEAMAN AND SHIPS ALIKE SPENT very little time in recovery between their actions in the Mediterranean during 1941. It was proving to be, as my father wrote, 'a very bad year for the Royal Navy'. There were few successes at sea for the Commander-in-Chief Mediterranean, Admiral Sir Andrew Cunningham, and as the year progressed the losses increased. My father had little respite in Alexandria after his traumatic experiences during the evacuation of the troops from Crete. He was immediately drafted to HMS *Abdiel*, which had also been involved in the evacuation of Crete. *Abdiel* was one of a class of six very fast minelayers. The others were *Manxman*, *Ariadne*, *Latona*, *Apollo* and *Welshman*. They displaced around 2,650 tons, about the size of a large fleet destroyer, but were given cruiser-size propulsion machinery: 72,000 shaft horsepower. They were known to be the fastest ships in the Navy and could top forty knots when required. Inevitably this meant they would get used in 'difficult' situations where speed was of the essence. This type of ship had a hard war, with *Abdiel*, *Latona* and *Welshman* all being lost.

My father recalled what transpired to be a short-lived duty on that ship in June 1941:

> I was next drafted to HMS *Abdiel*, a fast mine layer, I liked it aboard there. We had the job of taking grub and replacements up to Tobruk, what we called 'The Tobruk Run'. Had some lucky runs what with enemy submarines below us and Stukas above us. Then there was the torpedo carrying aircraft flying over us at night. We lost quite a few ships on those runs including our sister ship *Latona* later in the year. She went as opposite number to us. They went one night we went the next.

Latona was involved in what they called Operation Cultivate – the replacement of Australian troops in Tobruk with elements of the British 70th Division in October. The operation involved one fast minelayer of the *Abdiel* class running between Alexandria and Tobruk, escorted by three destroyers, on a nightly basis. At 21.05 hours on 25 October 1941, *Latona* was some thirty miles from Tobruk on the outward run when she was attacked by German aircraft. One bomb exploded in *Latona*'s after engine room. A considerable quantity of artillery and ammunition stowed for the Tobruk garrison lay on the upper deck and as fires started by the bomb spread the cargo exploded along with the ship's 4.7 in. magazine. There were thirty-seven casualties with the remainder being taken off the ship by the destroyers *Hero* and *Encounter*. Lieutenant Richard Coulton survived the sinking of *Latona* only to join *Neptune* two weeks before she sank. Another fateful twist in the tale.

My father's time with *Abdiel* ended sooner than expected as he described how he left his ship under escort:

> Coming off shore one night with three Petty Officers, I was an Able Seaman at the time, the duty Petty Officer kept me behind, for no reason I could fathom. He started dressing me down and digging me in the stomach with his torch, taunting me. I lost it, took the torch from him and put him in the Sick Bay. I got sixty days in Agami Detention Quarters. Had to do all sixty as I lost my remission through a boot-neck (naval term for detention guard). I had asked him for a smoke and he done my shins with the butt of his rifle. Proceeded to make a mess of him and got the rest of my sentence on punishment diet no. 1 (bread and water). Pleased to say the P.T.I. (Physical Training Instructor) looked after me while I was in there, he was a nice chap.

The Navy decided to loan him out to the small KOS whalers that were patrolling the coast around North Africa and my father described his first vessel, 'I'm loaned to a small coasting vessel carrying a 128-ASDIC set, which I'm operating. It's a tiny naval party of one officer and five men on board and we're supporting a Greek crew. The intention is to patrol off the North African coast, picking up any signs of enemy submarines.' KOS XXI was one of the small naval craft used in Crete and one of the few vessels that returned. She was a Norwegian whaler of 353 tons and used as an anti-submarine vessel. She was, unfortunately, sunk by bombs in October 1941 on his first trip. My father described the sinking, 'I'm overboard with six others. Luckily we're only in the water a few hours. We're picked up and taken to Alexandria barracks.'

It was his first dipping and he had survived without any ill effects.

His next loan was to another whaler the KOS XIX. The vessel was at the mercy of heavy air attacks as it patrolled the coast. The bombers came thick and fast and KOS XIX was sunk with only four survivors with my father being one of the lucky ones yet again. He was blissfully unaware at this time of just how many chances to survive he would be in for, as the sea battles in the Mediterranean heated up over the next few months. He just felt lucky to be still alive and as he put it when he recalled the events many years later, 'I didn't know then but the practice proved useful for my time "in the drink" to come'.

My father returned to depot for draft and joined HMS *Medway*, a depot ship for submarine duty. He was invited to the T Class submarine *Tetrarch* for a 'wet' before sailing, to celebrate a mate's birthday and after a bottle of rum or two he realised the submarine was leaving the harbour. He reacted quickly, jumped overboard and swam back to the breakwater. 'Another lucky dipping', he commented. She never returned from patrol. The *Tetrarch*, Commanding Officer Lt. Cdr. G. H. Greenway, RN, sailed from Alexandria on 17 October 1941, for the UK via Malta and Gibraltar. After leaving Malta on 26 October she was ordered to conduct a short patrol off Cavoli Island before proceeding to Gibraltar on 29 October. On crossing longitude seven degrees east she was to report her position. No signal was made by the submarine, nor did she respond to further requests to report her position. As there are no Axis claims for her sinking, it is most likely that she was the victim of a mine.

On 13 November 1941, the cruiser HMS *Neptune* was due to sail from Alexandria and was in need of an Anti-Submarine Detection Operator. My father was keen to get back to sea. He loved the seamanship, he hated being ashore for too long, and volunteered to join *Neptune*. HMS *Neptune* at that time was at sea in company with *Queen Elizabeth*, *Ajax* and *Hobart* and under constant air attack. The days at sea in November were the last recorded in her Navigation Log. This was a document submitted monthly by each ship, and the record of her movements in December had to be compiled from the logs of HMS *Aurora* and HMS *Ajax*. On 25 November, *Neptune* was at sea when the battleship HMS *Barham* exploded after being hit by four torpedoes fired by the submarine U–331. The following month the battleships HMS *Queen Elizabeth* and HMS *Valiant* were also disabled at Alexandria, but in this case it was Italian two-man submarines which delicately and courageously sneaked between the destroyers in the harbour to complete the task. Force B consisting of

Ajax, *Neptune*, *Kimberley* and *Kingston* sailed from Alexandria to Malta on 27 November to reinforce Force K, the cruiser-raiding squadron. The Italian bombing of Malta had reduced by this time and when *Neptune* returned from sea in early December the crew received some long-awaited respite from action stations.

My father described in his notes from the time, his role aboard *Neptune*:

> I was submarine detecting on a 124 set with the Asdic cabinet being below the Forward Mess Deck. We were 4 hours on and 4 hours off all the time at sea. There were two operators each watch, one on the asdic set and one on the range recorder. We finally berthed in Grand Harbour in Malta and get some light relief going ashore in the little dghajsas (small gondola) to the bars up 'the gut'. 'The gut,' as it was called by the sailors, was a long narrow street that ran up from the harbour, crowded with bars and cafés. The beer and wine in the bars was cheap and potent as were the girls who worked there. I had a tattoo showing a couple of bluebirds on my arm. One for my mother and one for Irene my sweetheart, so they would be close to me. Sometimes we had to pick through the rubble as the air raids on the island increased, but some bars remained as long as we sailors used them.
>
> There are a lot of New Zealanders on board *Neptune* and talk of handing the ship over to the New Zealand Navy. Nice-fellows these New Zealanders, they've even got me playing Rugby.

He described his enjoyment in sparring on the upper deck with one such Kiwi, 'Getting some sparring in with a fellow called Heeney, he's a good boxer and a great rugby player too. Also playing soccer for the ship, not as good a team as we had on *Janus*. Managed a couple of games of water-polo.'

My father boxed Leading Seaman Clarke in the Mediterranean Fleet Championships and recorded winning in two rounds. A photograph remains, which shows my father sporting a black eye, sitting drinking beer in a Valletta square in Malta with two of his mates. It was the last photograph his mother received from him during the war and she protected it well as it still remains, over sixty years later, in his 'ditty box' along with a note explaining how he received the black eye, this time in a legitimate fight.

The festive season was approaching and many of the crew on *Neptune* had managed to post Christmas cards home to their loved ones. A New Zealand Radio broadcast was made for the 'Forces Overseas' programme and all the Kiwis not on duty were gathered in the mess:

Calling New Zealand,

We are able to give you good tidings of 150 New Zealanders serving in the Royal Navy on HMS *Neptune*, most of whom have been away for 18 months. It is our good fortune today to have the opportunity of recording some personal messages from them. The High Commissioner of New Zealand, Mr W.J. Jordan has recently paid them an informal visit and saw and spoke with many of the New Zealand personnel, some of whom he had met some time ago in England.

By kind permission of Commander Berry, we have met the men in the Recreation Room and they are all extremely happy in this ship in the company of the Royal Navy.

With a diversity of nationalities aboard, *Neptune* is a very representative ship and it is most impressive to find all parts of the Empire gathered together, sharing in a common purpose. I'm sure you will be proud to know of the popularity of New Zealanders who were described to me as 'a splendid company of companionable fellows'. The best evidence of that was the wish most frequently expressed this morning to visit New Zealand someday. The men have spoken a good deal of *Leander* and *Achilles* and we exchange greetings on their behalf with this ship, should they be able to hear the broadcast.

Neptune's Captain, Captain Rory O'Conor, has kindly consented to speak to you now in New Zealand:

> I'm grateful for this opportunity of sending a warm greeting from HMS *Neptune* to you all in New Zealand and especially to the families of the large numbers of New Zealand officers and men now serving on board this ship. All goes well with *Neptune* and one of these days when we have beaten Hitler, I hope we shall have the privilege of welcoming many of you on board as visitors. Some of you will already know your way round as *Neptune* is a sister ship of *Achilles* and *Leander* – the finest class of ships in the Fleet. The thoughts of us all naturally turn homeward at this season and it is my earnest hope that this will be the last Christmas we have to spend away from our homes.
>
> On behalf of the *Neptune*, I wish you all as happy a Christmas as is possible in these grave days. We too shall be keeping it up this end.

Now with us is Lieutenant Woodward who has kindly prepared for us an account of the name of *Neptune* in the history of the Royal Navy and first-hand review of her important engagements in this war:

> Like other ships of the silent service, her deeds have so far, not been made public. This ship is HMS *Neptune* and she is manned by officers and men from all parts of the Empire among whom are 150 New Zealanders. The rest of the ship's company comes from Australia, Canada, South Africa, St Helena and Newfoundland, as well as the United Kingdom. There has been a *Neptune* in the Royal Navy for over 300 years continuously except

for a gap of about ten years. Her battle honours are many and include Quebec, Trafalgar and Jutland. At Trafalgar, it is interesting that three *Neptunes* took part; the British *Neptune*, a French one and the Spanish *Neptuno* . . . The present *Neptune* was the first ship to report 'Enemy fleet in sight', in action off Calabria, in February 1940, since 1805 when the French Fleet was reported to Nelson by the frigate *Zealous* . . . The last operation before *Neptune* left the Mediterranean in 1940 was in company with HMAS *Sydney* when a raid was made into the Aegean. On 28 July they intercepted and destroyed the tanker *Hermione* laden with petrol for the same enemy air forces who repeatedly bombed the ships in the Thermia channel during the operation.

The remainder of the year, *Neptune* was first employed protecting the trade routes in the Southern Indian Ocean, when on some occasions, the ship was at sea for nearly a month and experienced a climate varying from tropical heat to the cold temperature of the Antarctic, below latitude 50 degrees . . .

The deeds of cruisers only occasionally made headlines in the newspapers but this account of *Neptune*'s War efforts shows that her activities have been many and varied and in the first two years of the War, she steamed 158,900 miles, equivalent to seven and a half times round the world.

Her motto is *Regnare est servere* which means 'To rule is to serve' and we hope that her present service is helping Britannia rule the waves.

My father described his Captain favourably, 'O'Conor was a great Captain, spoke personally to everyone that joined the ship and made you all feel equal and just as important to the ship as the next man.' John Mizzie quotes from Rear Admiral Simpson's book *Periscope View* the following description of O'Conor's actions on 18 December:

> O'Conor was certainly a dashing leader. Cdr. G.W.G. Simpson, the captain of the submarine base at Lazaretto, and himself a New Zealander, saw O'Conor on the 18th December, in the operations room of the Naval Headquarters in Valletta at about 3 pm. *Neptune* was temporarily in command of Force K, Captain O'Conor being senior to Captain Agnew of *Aurora* (by date of seniority), who according to Simpson, 'had just conducted three convoy sinkings in as many weeks but was no longer in charge, despite his current experience.'

On his arrival at Naval headquarters Simpson found Vice Admiral Ford, the Admiral in Malta, and his Senior Staff Officer Operations, Cdr. Martin Evans, with their heads over a chart with Captain O'Conor. He had spent several minutes going through the contents of an envelope marked 'Secret' in silence. Simpson continued his description of what he saw that night:

Almost immediately O'Conor said, 'Right, I'll be off' and with his red hair, flashing blue eyes and cheerful smile he dashed from the room and down the 200 stone steps to the boat back to *Neptune*. As soon as Admiral Ford had left I said to Martin Evans, the Senior Staff Officer Operations, 'What's happening?' He explained that an important Axis convoy had been located well on its way to Tripoli, which it would be approaching from the east and entering that night. The question was a matter of time. Had the ships left early enough to intercept well east of Tripoli? How far east would the force have to be to evade all mines? What a horrible low featureless unlit coast to approach at night at really high speed! The project seemed highly dangerous to me and I said to Commander Evans: 'I fear the approaches to Tripoli, since I lost P32 (submarine) to the north and P33 (submarine) to the east in early August.'

Evans reassured me that O'Conor knew that minefields existed on the port's approaches, but that nobody could say what radius from the port they might be expected. He added that this opportunity could not be ignored. All sorts of things might happen, the convoy might have its speed reduced and so fall into our hands. Only the man in command could decide how and where to intercept the enemy. All this was straightforward sense: risks had to be taken and the man on the spot made the decisions. I fully agreed, but I still felt unhappy because of the ghastly temptation for an officer full of offensive enthusiasm to cut corners in order to fall upon the convoy.

Captain O'Conor returned to his ship just as urgently as he had left it and thereafter, a series of signals alerted cruisers *Aurora* and *Penelope*, together with destroyers *Kandahar*, *Lively*, *Lance* and *Havock* to raise steam and prepare for sea. He remarked when back on *Neptune* that there was no reference to enemy minefields, so a hand-written note was added to all copies inviting captains' and senior officers' attention to be drawn to the two known fields outlined in documents QB10 and QB11, after which O'Conor said that he and his navigator were up to date on all current Q messages.

What could not be revealed at the time was the planning by the Italians that had taken place very early in 1941, which was to lay a minefield between the seventy- to eighty-fathom line from about twelve miles north of Tripoli, minelaying at a depth the British could not have anticipated, since Italian mines could only be laid at a maximum depth of seventy fathoms. The Italians were concerned that British warships might bombard Tripoli, which was the only harbour they had in North Africa. They decided to plot an east-west path that such warships would be likely to take during the bombardment between the seventy- and eighty-fathom depth, and

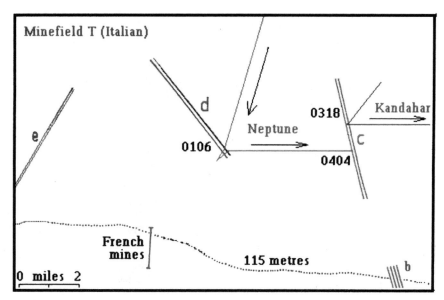

Italian Minefield 'T' showing detail of Minelines 'd' and 'c' and the drift of Neptune *and* Kandahar *after hitting mines. From* Mediterranean Minefield, *Adrian St Clair*

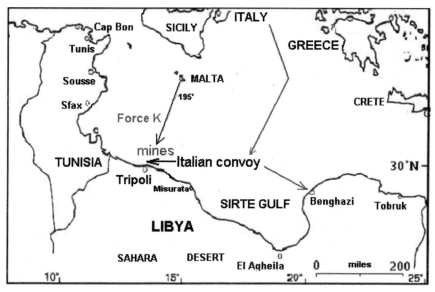

Central Mediterranean map shows the routes taken by Force K and Italian convoy on 18 December 1941. My father in a Carley raft had drifted for five and a half days towards the Libyan town of Misurata before being sighted by the Italians

laid a minefield across this hypothetical path. Because the Italian mines could only be laid in waters as deep as seventy fathoms they used special German mines which could be laid in waters up to eighty-two fathoms deep. Called minefield 'T' it consisted of five minelines named 'b' to 'f'; line 'a' was cancelled. They removed two existing minefields so that they did not interfere with the manoeuvrings of the warships while laying minefield 'T'. The Italians were right in their reckoning of a British bombardment, which occurred at dawn on 21 April 1941, before minefield 'T' was laid. The Seventh Cruiser Division began to lay minelines 'd', 'e' and 'f' in May. They were special German deep-water, antenna, six-horned, type GY contact mines, 420 in all laid ten to fifteen miles north of Tripoli. The British would not expect minefields in waters that deep. By June, the Fourth and Seventh Cruiser Divisions were laying minelines 'b' and 'c'. One hundred and seventy-six contact mines of the German deep-water type were laid in two parallel rows in mineline 'c'. Mineline 'd' was also laid in two parallel rows but these were 278 Italian contact mines of normal seventy-fathom depth. Minefield 'T' was first heard of by the British in an ULTRA decrypt in September 1941. This decrypt gave no details of where off Tripoli this minefield 'T' was but as Commander Simpson had commented earlier he had already lost two submarines on the approaches to Tripoli in August of that year.

It was the Italian decision to send convoy 'M42' with a battleship escort to Tripoli that prompted the urgent decision to mobilise Force K. The Italian convoy left Taranto on 16 December and by noon of 18 December had divided in two, branching off to Benghazi and Tripoli. At the same time the battleships turned back northwards to Italy. A Wellington bomber reported later that afternoon the Tripoli branch of the convoy approaching that harbour from the north-east.

Back in Malta on the evening of 18 December, it was estimated that the Tripoli branch of the convoy would reach the harbour at dawn on 19 December, so there was still a slender chance that it could be intercepted. It was considered imperative that the combined cruisers and destroyers that made up Force K should get underway quickly if they were to intercept this enemy convoy loaded with Panzer tanks, fuel and vital military equipment to support Rommel's desert war. Meanwhile Wellington bombers were immediately sent out to drop conspicuously a few mines off the entrance of Tripoli harbour in order to entice the convoy to remain at sea until these mines were swept, thus giving Force K more time in which to catch its quarry.

Several decrypted enigma signals gave progress of the enemy convoy but exactly what was planned in Malta is a matter of speculation.

In Valletta harbour each ship's captain was delivered a sealed secret envelope containing Vice Admiral's operational order sent at 17.30 on 18 December. The Force left harbour astern of *Neptune* and was soon steaming at thirty knots on the direct course to Tripoli as ordered by V-A Malta. Later reports of that night show that two midshipmen in HMS *Ajax* witnessed the anger and discomfiture of Rear Admiral Rawlings (the designated Commander of Force K) as he came on deck of *Ajax*, to see his ships exiting harbour without him. The flagship HMS *Ajax* had mechanical problems which prevented her from sailing.

Harry Jones, a seaman in HMS *Aurora*, had just arrived in harbour with his ship and described how the evening of 18 December unfolded:

> We were all tired after thirty hours spent continuously at action stations. We were to be given no respite however, and after completing refuelling we received an urgent signal to leave at once: this time reinforced by *Neptune*, *Kandahar* and *Havock*. During previous sorties carried out by Force K an A.S.V. (airborne surveillance) Wellington operating from Luqa had helped to pinpoint the convoys that we had set out to destroy. A.S.V., being one of the first airborne radars, was unfortunately prone to many early defects. The Wellington could guide Force K directly via an A.S.V. beacon fitted on *Aurora*'s masthead. However as Captain O'Conor of *Neptune* was senior to Captain Agnew, the A.S.V. beacon had been moved to *Neptune*, as her Captain had taken over command of the strike force: unfortunately it failed to function correctly in its new position. The Wellington had reported sighting a cruiser and six destroyers escorting a convoy of three merchant ships at 16.17 on the 18th. So when our cruisers left Malta Captain O'Conor headed toward the last expected position of the enemy, received by signal from Malta at 22.18. Although the A.S.V. Wellington was still in touch with the convoy and transmitting information, it could not make direct contact with *Neptune* by radio and so no further information was received. *Neptune* as senior ship, assumed command and led the force out past the boom. Heading south we had orders to find and destroy the four-ship convoy. Steaming line ahead at full speed we headed towards Tripoli, but the weather turned and the destroyer *Havock* was soon unable to keep station at those speeds and in terrible weather conditions, dropping behind the remainder of the ships.

Frank Brown, a nineteen-year old gunner on *Havock* at the time, described his memories of the night of the 18 December:

> *Havock* was not part of Force K, but through escorting *Breconshire* to Malta with Rear Admiral Vian's squadron had been deployed with *Decoy* to cover *Breconshire* on the final stage to Grand Harbour while the main force returned to Alex. Boiler repairs extended our stay while *Decoy* sailed to rejoin Vian. Thus *Havock* became part of Force K and that ill-fated sortie.
>
> We sailed that evening on a pitch-black night, the smallest of the four destroyers, into very heavy weather, *Havock* having some difficulty in maintaining her position at the speed set by *Neptune*.

The cruiser *Neptune* passed through the breakwater at twelve knots with the clock showing 18.21, then came *Aurora* at 18.26 and *Penelope* at 18.30. The destroyer *Kandahar* followed at 18.35 with *Lance*, *Lively* and *Havock* close behind at 18.47. *Havock* was being swept by cross-seas while cutting *Lance*'s wash at twenty-eight knots. To make matters worse, *Lance*'s single raked funnel was emitting dense clouds of smoke which, in the starless night, hid her small stern light so often that it became hard for the ships to keep the correct distance apart. When they cleared the safe channel *Neptune* altered course to 196 degrees, which carried the smoke away and made the going easier. *Neptune*'s wake boiled as she increased speed steaming south at thirty knots in single line ahead in very rough seas. Captain O'Conor signalled down the line for thirty knots and each ship adjusted her revolutions accordingly. *Neptune* signalled all ships to action stations.

There was the usual sense of urgency when action stations were called in a ship with everyone sidestepping dark shapes while finding their way to windswept stations. It would soon be time to change place with those recumbent bodies in corners out of the wind, but some not yet tired would let their sleeping opposite numbers continue. The ship slewed, its mast gyrating. My father swayed with the ship as it topped a large broken swell and shuddered down straight through the following one and so it would be throughout all departments. Asdic operation was impossible at this speed and my father was attempting to make his way to the upper deck, his mind momentarily drifting to his family. In a few days it would be Christmas Day with his Mam carving the roast for Dad and all his brothers and sisters in Swalwell. My father described the events as the squadron steamed full speed towards the danger line. The descriptive notes are written in a small brown Pacific memorandum book that

1 Norman Walton holds a model of a monument in the shape of a pyramid at his home in Pudsey, Leeds in March 2005.

2 The 837 sailors lost in HMS Neptune and HMS Kandahar in the Force K disaster were finally commemorated at a Memorial Service on 9 July 2005. Norma is attended by the Neptune Association Chaplain, Rev. Ron Peterson at the unveiling ceremony reading the exhortation on behalf of her father Norman who sadly passed away on 20 April 2005. The Memorial, a stone pyramid, stands in the National Memorial Arboretum, near Lichfield, Staffordshire.

3 Norman's grandfather William Walton (1866–1935) sits in his garden in Rowlands Gill, Co. Durham.

4 Norman's father John Norman (nickname 'Patsy') Walton born 1898, joining His Majesty's Royal Navy during World War I (1914–18).

5 John Norman Walton, born 15 January 1920, pictured at three years old.

6 The Miners Concert Party pictured left to right are: Ossie Gardner, Tony Morpeth at the piano, comedian 'Patsy' Walton and female impressionist Kit Robinson with concertina player George Morpeth. The Concert Party used to perform in villages around the north-east during the 1920s and 1930s.

7 Swalwell Presbyterian Football Team featuring 'Patsy' Walton Captain, middle row, second right and his son Norman, team mascot front left. A very successful team in 1924 as the prizes show.

8 Blaydon Town stretches along the River Tyne, showing the villages of Blaydon-Haughs and Swalwell to the south. Taken from Summerhouse Hill.

9 Irene Dodds born in Winlaton village, Co. Durham, 12 August 1922. Copy of a photograph sent to her sweetheart Norman Walton who was serving in HM Royal Navy when war was declared with Germany in 1939.

10 HMS Janus, a destroyer of the J Class Norman was proud to join in Jarrow on Tyne on 2 August 1939 serving until March 1941.

11 HMS Bittern (a sloop) hit and set on fire by German air attack at Namsos, where Norman climbed aboard with a volunteer party to trans-ship survivors onto Janus.

12 Destruction at Suda Bay – British ships under attack in the Battle of Crete.

13 HMS Orion. *The sister ship to* Neptune *and Norman's taxi out of Crete on 29 May 1941.*

14 Norman returns to Crete in May 1994. Shown here with his wife Irene in the Commonwealth War Cemetery at Suda Bay.

15 HMS Abdiel. *Norman joined the fast mine-layer in June 1941. She was used on the so called 'Tobruk Run' taking supplies from Alexandria to Tobruk aiding the fight against Rommel in North Africa.*

16 HMS Tetrarch *(Patrol type) submarine. Another lucky escape for Norman.*

'Cruisers that led Force K from Malta harbour on the night of 18 December 1941'

17 HMS Neptune *(Captain Rory O'Conor).*

18 HMS Aurora *(Captain William Agnew CB, later Vice Admiral Sir William Agnew).*

19 HMS Penelope *entering Malta harbour (Captain Angus Nichol DSO later Rear Admiral Sir Angus Nichol).*

21 *Rear Admiral Bernard Rawlings OBE*
(later Admiral Sir Bernard Rawlings).

20 *Admiral Sir Andrew B. Cunningham DSO*
(later Admiral of the Fleet).

22 *Captain Rory O'Conor (1898–1941) with his fellow officers aboard* Neptune *in the summer of 1941.*

23 Norman with his mates enjoying some light relief from action and a local beer in Malta. Note the black eye
− the result of a boxing contest in the Mediterranean Fleet Championships in December, 1941 before
Neptune*'s fateful sortie.*

HEENEY. Arthur John. (Darcy.)
E.A. N.Z. 31.

24 Arthur John Heeney (Electrical Artificer 4th Class) Petty Officer RNZN.
Norman's sparing partner and mate aboard HMS Neptune.

25 Leading Seaman Revell Brownie, RNZN, on the upper deck of HMS Neptune *resting on one of the*
two Carley rafts lashed beside 'B' gun turret. One of these Carley rafts saved Norman's life. Inside the raft
are paddles, one of which Norman snapped in half, using the paddle in an attempt to make it to shore.
Brownie was the coxswain of Captain O'Conor's motor boat. Reg Rushton who took this photograph left
Neptune *just before she sank.*

26 HMS Neptune *striking mines off the coast of Tripoli, on 19 December 1941.*
(Painting by Colin Wynn, on view at the Navy Museum at Devonport, Auckland, New Zealand).

27 HMS Kandahar, *Commander W.G.A. Robson, DSO, DSC, a destroyer escort to Force K who attempted to come alongside* Neptune *and take her on tow also striking a mine. On the morning of 20 December 1941 HMS* Jaguar *was ordered to sink the stricken ship and 170 crew plus eight officers were saved.*

28 Captain Rory O'Conor, who died in Norman's arms on the fourth day in the raft.

29 Able Seaman Ronald F. Quinn, RNZN, who left the sinking ship with Norman and died on day three, son of Mrs S. E. Quinn, Lower Hutt, New Zealand,

30 Able Seaman John Norman Walton, RN, the only survivor of the 765 men aboard HMS Neptune *when the Italian sailors came to the rescue.*

31 Acting Leading Seaman Albert Price, RN still with Norman at the end but pronounced dead by the Italians on the afternoon of 24 December 1941.

RMB/X.59 CORPORAL
H. R. GARDNER
ROYAL MARINE BAND
25TH FEBRUARY 1942 AGE 29

THOUGH I WALK
THROUGH THE VALLEY
OF THE SHADOW OF DEATH
I WILL FEAR NO EVIL

32 Hubert Gardner, a musician with the Royal Marine Band of HMS Neptune *was not aboard on 18 December 1941. While recuperating in the Naval hospital in Malta he heard the news regarding the annihilation of his friends and the realisation that he was perhaps the only survivor was sited as a possible cause of him taking his life.*

33 Eight bodies were recovered from the sea off the shores of Libya by the Italians after the loss of Neptune *and Kandahar. Six were buried in Tripoli – Able Seaman J. S. Brooks, Able Seaman W. Miller, Able Seaman C. W. Pugh, Ldg. Seaman R. C. Turley, Stoker R. F. Walton, Supply Assistant H. Walpole RNZN and two in Tobruk Lieutenant D. J. Wilson and Able Seaman Lloyd Lord RNZN. Frank Brown, a Force K Veteran with the destroyer HMS* Havock *escorting the cruisers on that fateful night and Geoff Staley, son of* Neptune *casualty Leonard Staley stand by the six* Neptune *named graves and the many 'only known unto God' at the British War Cemetery in Tripoli, April 2007.*

34 Norman and Irene's wedding photograph 13 November 1943.

he kept from all eyes for sixty years. He wrote the account of events whilst being held in an Italian prisoner of war camp and referred to his account when he was ordered to report to Admiral Cunningham in Alexandria and Admiral Creasy in London nearly two years later. He began to write, '11.50 Captain announces that we will most probably meet up with enemy convoy between 3 and 4 a.m. All hands are already at action stations and have been since 8 o'clock.'

Another seaman, Harry Bradbear, was the signalman on the bridge of HMS *Lively* and described what he saw around midnight:

A signalman was proud to be regarded as 'the eyes of the fleet' and was well placed to participate and observe all that occurred. We were by this time perhaps 10 to 12 miles from the harbour entrance as we could just make out land by about midnight. My position at action stations was on the starboard side of the bridge. I saw our navigator, Lieutenant Beale, RNVR, come out of the 'charthouse' on the port side of the bridge. He reported to our Captain Lieutenant Commander Hussey, 'We're heading straight for a minefield'. This information was sent to *Neptune* by blue aldis signal lantern. The reply came back, 'Follow me'.

On the bridge of the cruiser *Penelope* at that time was Ron Oakley, Sub-Lieutenant, who wrote:

I was on the bridge of HMS *Penelope*, being trained for my watch-keeping certificate. We were steaming in line ahead about 30 knots. At about 00.50, before *Neptune* struck the first mine, I heard our Navigator Lieutenant Morgan (very worried) say to Captain Nicholl 'If *Neptune* stays on this course and speed, we will run into a minefield in 10 minutes.' Nicholl replied 'Until we have other orders, we must wait and see.'

Ten minutes later *Neptune* struck her first mine.

Neptune continued south with an occasional glimpse of *Aurora* as she dug into a big one on the high seas. In *Neptune*'s navigator's office, Bill Brown logged successive changes of speed on his charts, entering the mean course, which had not yet changed.

Aboard *Penelope* Captain A. D. Nicholl had been deliberating about the minefields so at 00.55 he ordered the echo sounder to be energised. But as his navigator, Lieutenant Pat Morgan had expected, the machine would not operate reliably at this speed. He switched it on to phase one setting and only from past experience could he estimate that it was indicating depths in excess of 120 fathoms. He was told to switch it off after advising his captain that there had been instances of these machines activating acoustic mines.

The Captain would know that Italian mines were laid at a maximum depth of seventy fathoms and therefore the space between the eighty- and seventy-fathom lines (about five miles) ought to be theoretically safe. The convoy continued south before it was the probable intention to turn the force eastward together. This would put the already widely-spaced line ahead formation onto an extensive line abreast disposition for their interception search enabling the squadron to reduce the range by about four miles gaining what could be for them a decisive margin for success in the darkness of the starless night. Whatever O'Conor intended to do, *Neptune* was steaming directly into minefield 'T' onto mineline 'd'.

My father recorded the events on *Neptune* succinctly as he remembered them, 'Explosion off starboard bow. Captain stops both and goes astern hitting another mine and blowing the screws and most of the stern away. We were then hit in the port side abaft the funnel, time approximately 12.20.'

An enormous explosion lit up the night sky. It created a jolting whiplash that threw men against panelled bulkheads in the signal office of *Neptune* as all lighting went out momentarily. On the bridge men and officers staggered as *Neptune* lifted for'ard, the fo'c'sle illuminated in a massive flare of orange flame rearing high above the foremast. A black cloud stinking of explosives, salt water, steam and burned paint swept the upper decks. The flame was gone in an instant to leave blind darkness. But *Neptune's* engines were unimpaired initially, steering unaffected, lighting and electrical systems back on.

As their pointers swung to 'full astern' the Chief Stokers in the boiler rooms watched their gauges and hand-signalled in the overall roar for more sprayers to be flashed to maintain pressure. With her helm amidship, her turbines racing and her four propellers thundering in reverse, everything aft was vibrating violently and her whole stern shook with the drastic engine and turbine power necessary to draw the 7,500-ton cruiser to a standstill. Steam vents blew like gunfire and she gradually lost way. By this time damage control parties were busy assessing damage, rushing shoring timber below to strengthen buckled bulkheads, stemming the torrent of water gushing through separated plates below sea level and blocking exposures in the hull above water. A fire party began extinguishing flames in the paint shop.

The propellers' forward pressure had been thrusting water away from the hull, swaying mines out of her path apart from the one which had exploded with such impact on her port paravane. Paravanes are designed floats operating at preset depth connected by wires on port and starboard, to the ship's forefoot. They spread laterally with the ship's speed and mines are deflected along the wire and are cut free by 'teeth' on the paravane. Mines are then destroyed by small arms fire. Ships following require to keep a sharp lookout and to detonate floaters which can be unpredictable when loose.

But now that her propellers were racing astern, they were drawing water to her stern with terrific suction attracting the mines she had just passed. The next two crashing explosions wrecked her rudder and propellers, blew away a large part of her stern together with the helpless first-aid parties stationed aft, flooded compartment after compartment when bulkheads collapsed, and left her powerless, at the mercy of the wind and heavy seas, drifting aimlessly in the night.

There was no need now to keep men at their gun stations so they joined others, retrieving torn and broken wounded from the wreckage. Distorted steel watertight bulkhead doors and heavy hatches could not be opened to release men imprisoned in the transmitting station, X turret magazine and nearby sealed sections. Cries for help soon ceased as the men drowned. All power aft had gone and with it the lighting circuits, even the auxiliary lighting. Men struggled in rising water to find an exit, tried to help their injured mates, but died with them. On his bridge Rory O'Conor was receiving damage control reports. *Neptune* still floated with only a slight list but she had gone down several feet aft.

As the concussion of an underwater explosion reached her, *Aurora*, next astern, hauled out to starboard and the next moment she too lifted to a staggering detonation as her paravane exploded a mine. Arthur Walshaw, Leading Stores Assistant on HMS *Aurora* was in the shell room of A turret when he heard the explosions and immediately felt a tremendous explosion lifting the fore part of *Aurora* violently. The six-inch shells were lifted from the racks and fell to the deck. By great good fortune the five in the room were untouched. Orders were received to leave their posts and they made their way to the mess-decks where they carried hammocks to help in an attempt to confine the inflow of water into the damaged compartment. Harry Jones was thrown across the deck and felt the ship turning 180 degrees to reach safe water. She was listing heavily to port and was down by the bow. Royal Marine Frank Harvey was on watch on the port forward four-inch gun in *Aurora* when he saw the huge explosion from *Neptune*, then another. He yelled, 'Alarm port, *Neptune's* been torpedoed'. A wave from a terrific explosion under *Aurora* then swept along the upper deck, over the torpedo tubes and the pom-poms and along Frank Harvey's four-inch gun deck. It swept him down into a corner where he held on like grim death to the gun mounting beside him. He lost his coat, tin hat and shoes and it was only the bravery of his Corporal who grabbed him that saved him from being swept overboard.

Several hundred yards astern of *Aurora* Captain Nicholl of *Penelope* saw the big explosion on *Neptune* followed minutes later by one on the port side of *Aurora*, and under the impression that the Force was under attack by submarines, he turned away to starboard to present less of a target for torpedoes. At 01.10 an explosion buffeted *Penelope's* port side abreast of the bridge. *Neptune* had ploughed some miles into the minefield while *Aurora* and *Penelope* escaped by turning to starboard and reversing course.

The cruiser force had run into a minefield in a depth of water and at a distance from land which made it utterly unexpected. Captain Nicholl's steering gear and engines were reported to be working satisfactorily, so he brought the ship around to the north to get clear of the minefield. *Aurora* had now been seen doing the same and *Penelope* formed astern of her also at ten knots. Then at 01.16 Captain Nicholl saw the two successive mine blasts which blew *Neptune's* stern off.

After *Neptune* hit her third mine the immobilised cruiser began to drift slowly in an easterly direction. Messages began flashing between ships explaining what had happened individually, offering assistance and trying to re-establish some form of cohesion in the present predicament. The gale was listing *Neptune* to port beyond nine degrees and *Lively*, which appeared to be manoeuvring to come alongside on the low side and unaware of the increasing list, was asked by loudhailer to make her approach to starboard. Time was passing rapidly and visual signals were countermanding orders given only moments previously by various senior officers.

At 01.30 *Aurora*, who had assumed overall command, had signalled to *Kandahar*, 'Send a destroyer alongside *Neptune*.' *Kandahar's* skipper, Commander Robson, immediately ordered *Lance*, 'Take charge of destroyers', then started to approach *Neptune* himself until, with only part of the distance covered, he was signalled by Captain O'Conor,

'Keep to leeward until I have drifted clear of the minefield.' So Commander Robson, *Kandahar*, patrolled on courses 270 degrees and 90 degrees as best he could.

At this stage *Neptune*'s damage control, fire and first-aid parties were scrambling to get things into some semblance of order. There was no question of abandoning ship while the possibility of her being towed home existed. In any case, all her boats were rendered useless when the successive blasts thrust them up from their chocks to be splintered and crushed against restraining lashes. Four-inch gun mounts had disappeared together with their ready-use ammunition lockers and crews. Many other men in exposed positions had been thrashed against steel structures and killed. More had been killed by falling chunks of metal and steel ladders, and others were hurtled into space far from their twisted ship when her stern blew apart. There was some auxiliary lighting that had been restored in less damaged areas and even the wireless transmitter offices that were left were functioning on battery for a time.

Stretcher bearers were moving wounded men to the first-aid centres, laying the more serious side by side in the canteen and sick bay flats. After quick selection some would be shifted to the sick bay to be operated on, or have splints applied to fractured limbs under auxiliary lights and torches. All spaces were being filled with injured.

Nothing could be done in the wrecked and flooded boiler and engine-rooms.

Without power on the capstan, fo'c'sle cable parties worked in the dark, heaving on heavy ropes and coiling heaving lines in readiness for throwing when help arrived.

The immobilised cruiser continued to drift eastwards away from mineline 'd' but unbeknown to the Captain and his crew, towards mineline 'c'.

My father was on the upper deck by this time and made his way along the windswept, swaying fo'c'sle with about half a dozen or so more volunteers working at speed to prepare the ship for towing. His diary notes recorded a clear and factual account of what he did, without emotion or personal comment on the traumatic events surrounding him:

By this time I am on the upper deck, we have a pretty bad list to port, and are down in the stern. Commander Berry asks for a few ratings to go forward

and prepare to be towed. I was one along with another six, with Petty Officer
Evans the so-called Captain of the fo'c'sle in charge and two other Leading
Hands included, when *Kandahar* hit a mine. *Lively* came around our stern and
up on our starboard side but turned back again. Just as I had put a chain
stopper on a towrope and walked forward to assist Petty Officer Evans, we
were hit with a fourth mine. The Captain sang out 'abandon ship' when we
were lifted up and dropped back on the deck again. I caught hold of the
guardrails and looking round, saw Petty Officer Evans underneath the cable.
I found he had a broken back. Time approx 2 a.m.

Petty Officer Dick Barton, Captain of *Lively*'s fo'c'sle, was in the
bows of the ship where the wires and chains for the anchors and
cables were handled. He was preparing to take *Neptune* in tow from
the quarterdeck – stern to stern. *Neptune* was down by the stern and
they tried to come up close with Dick throwing a heaving line to her
when there was another explosion; *Kandahar* had also hit a mine. A
shout came from *Neptune*'s bridge, 'Keep clear!' but as they backed
off another explosion from *Neptune* shook *Lively*. All destroyers were
stopped. It was a moonless night and they rolled beam to the sea. All
ships crews realised they were clearly in great peril.

Two destroyers *Havock* and *Lance* were eventually ordered to escort
the cruiser *Aurora* back to Malta to try to arrive before daylight; they
couldn't afford to hang around any longer. The crew in *Aurora* was
busy trying to assess damage and attempting to rectify the list to port
by redistributing oil and water supplies. It was very close to dawn and
imperative that they leave the area and head for base to obtain air
protection against the enemy aircraft who would no doubt by now
be alerted and eager to finish the squadron off. They sadly left the
scene around 2 a.m.

As high waves rolled *Neptune* over onto a more intense list, the
fo'c'sle party clung to anything available to stop being swept
overboard. Others were swept away, some hitting the side of the
ship on their way into the sea. After the silhouette of *Kandahar* was
seen in the glare of the huge explosion a message was flashed to
Neptune from *Penelope*, '*Aurora* now not in company, has gone to
Malta damaged.' *Aurora*, escorted by *Havock* and *Lance* were already
on their way back to Malta, leaving *Penelope* and *Lively* to help if they
could.

Black darkness fell again over *Neptune* as those above deck had
watched *Lively* obeying *Kandahar*'s emphatic order, when their ship

staggered from a crushing explosion on her port side abaft the funnel. This fourth mine had delivered *the coup de grace*.

The ship steadied and my father let go of the guard rail to check on those around him but he could hardly move, the blast that shook his doomed ship had whipped the anchor cable onto his shin, smashing his leg. The hopes of being towed were now dashed. As the Captain shouted, 'Abandon ship!' he could only see his two mates Acting Leading Seaman Albert Price, an RN Devonport rating and New Zealander Ron Quinn from Lower Hutt. With them was a young midshipman, a Scots lad only about seventeen-years-old. They were making their way back along the guard rail. He found he could not stand and slid to the guard rail, clambered over it, climbed down the anchor cable and onto the great anchor which was swinging dangerously just above the surface. His diary notes continued:

> By now most of the crew were over the side, some hitting the ship's side. Leading Seaman Price, A. B. Quinn (RNZN), 'Middy' and myself then climbed down onto the anchor and prepared to jump in, but I wanted somewhere to swim to first, not just float around. I then saw a Carley raft and jumping in, made raft easily, took tow rope and swam back to the other three as 'Middy' had no life jacket. Then made the raft again, this time it was crowded. We got the midshipman aboard. The rest of us clung to the side, there was approximately 30 hands in and around the raft. The sea was like an oil sump.

When Rory O'Conor had given the order to abandon ship everything happened so fast that almost anyone still below was trapped as water deluged madly through her opened side. The telegraphists that were left would have died instantly as their second wireless transmitter office disintegrated when *Neptune* drifted sideways onto the last mine. So did everyone in the stokers' mess-decks and low power room. Men in the torpedo room, keyboard flat and officers' galley were hurtled into space by the eruption which also dashed men to their deaths against bulkheads in the gunroom and marines' mess-deck. There was no hope for those previously injured or for those caring for them in the sick bay. There was no hope for anyone. Many attempting to escape along passages, were coming up against the ghastly remains of their shipmates who had been hurled against bulkhead doors now impossible to open as the ship lurched drunkenly, so flooding these passages. As she heeled more and more to port, the regulating office flooded, all the port side mess-decks went under water, then the recreation space along the fo'c'sle wing.

Neptune was wallowing on her side with many unable to swim scratching for hand-grips or trying to maintain a foothold on the slippery hull but the pull was too strong. One by one they were torn away by the seas that crashed over her and taken down in the backwash and undertow as the ship slid into the depths.

By some inherent impulse the asdic officer on the Carley raft led the men in cheering as my father recorded how he joined them:

> We cheered the ship as she went down led by A/S Officer. We picked up Captain Rory O'Conor who was clinging to what looked like an anchor buoy. Then we secured the cork raft to the Carley raft. On the cork raft was the Captain, A/S Officer, Commissioned Gunner and one other officer I believe was Paymaster Lt. The other ships in company I could see flashing in the dark as we hit the top of the swells.

A strong gale blew up and the survivors could only watch as the other ships sailed further and further away from the scene. They were being thrashed about in the thick black oily water, struggling, vomiting, unable to breathe and many suffering from injuries sustained during the blasts. The majority of the ship's company had gone down with the ship as she heaved a long drawn-out sigh and disappeared.

The men in the water were oblivious to the signals being transmitted between the ships left in the area, *Kandahar*, *Penelope* and *Lively*. Commander Robson looked at the eastern sky from the bridge of the crippled *Kandahar* and made his last signal to *Penelope*, 'Suggest you should go,' he said bluntly. 'I clearly cannot help you,' replied Captain Nicholl, 'God be with you.' The message at 04.03 was meant to be relayed to *Neptune*, however it was too late as the ship could be seen through night-glasses to be rolling on to her side. He signalled *Lively*, 'Course 010 speed 15 knots.' But still *Lively*'s Captain, Lt. Cdr. Hussey, could not harden his heart, 'Suggest I go for *Neptune*'s survivors,' he urged. The reply came, 'Regret not approved,' and a little later, 'I hate to leave them but I'm afraid we must.' The cruiser *Penelope* and destroyer *Lively* headed for home at about 4.20 a.m.

Throughout the few hours before daylight many of the original thirty survivors that had climbed inside or were hanging onto the Carley raft and its tethered float, had perished, many quietly releasing their Mae West (life jacket), to slip below the cold sea. When the survivors topped the big south-east swells at daybreak, they could still see *Kandahar* about three miles down wind, but throughout the day the crippled destroyer drifted with the high winds further and further away. As the day wore on they could find no signs of other *Neptune* survivors.

My father wrote factually about those dying around him, the words in his diary did not reflect his true feelings of helplessness as the men around him hung so close to the margins of life. He, with the remaining few, began to release the bodies of their shipmates to the deep; the guilt my father suffered was overpowering:

> A few died around us that night and by daylight there were 16 of us left including the Captain, A/S Officer, Commissioned Gunner and the Paymaster Lt. We could see the bows of the *Kandahar* at times, it was pretty rough. The A/S Officer and Commissioned Gunner left the raft and tried to swim to *Kandahar*. Aircraft flew over during forenoon, 3 ratings died that afternoon including A.B. Quinn. We picked up an oar, I broke it in two and secured it to the raft and, working by the sun, tried to make headway but couldn't reach land. It was the 20th December, and what was left of us were either aboard the Carley or cork raft.

The raft was drifting in a south-easterly direction following *Kandahar* on the strong winds. There was still some hope for Commander Robson and those not killed in the mine blast on *Kandahar*, even though her situation was perilous. All day *Kandahar* waited, sending signals to Malta. With the darkness the sea rose. It had carried *Kandahar* clear of the minefield, but she had already begun to list ominously.

The lighting had failed when the after switchboard was flooded. Numbers 1 and 2 4.7 inch twin gun mounts were workable by hand, most of the light armament still operated manually, the ship was watertight for'ard of the engine-room's after bulkhead, but she had no rudder or propellers.

Only the whaler was considered serviceable so it had been lowered with all the rafts, but while it was being hauled around the bows, the line parted and it drifted away downwind with its crew bailing hard. Although hailed to make for the ship, it failed to do so and was not seen again.

Confidential books, charts and documents were thrown overboard in weighted sacks, three of her ten torpedoes still able to be fired were jettisoned, then at daylight all hands turned to making the bulkheads more secure with baulks of timber. Anything moveable was thrown over the side to take off as much top weight as possible.

At about 09.15 a JU 88 bomber approached from the south, came near the ship, then flew on towards Italy. Half an hour later a fighter with Italian markings flew low overhead and returned to the south. Within minutes a Maryland aircraft circled a few times and disappeared northward. A coded message was sent by Commander Robson, when de-coded it read, 'Any British man of war. Have been closed and inspected by enemy reconnaissance aircraft. Am prepared to sink ship on arrival of enemy. My position 33 degrees 8 minutes N, 13 degrees 38 minutes E sent at 10.04 on 19 December. The signal got no answer from Malta so Robson sent another, 'Am still afloat in position 33 degrees 8 minutes N, 13 degrees 38 minutes E. Easterly drift approximately one knot' sent at 10.16 on 19 December. Still no replies. The *Kandahar* was eventually found by the persistence of a Wellington aircraft on the 20 December, in a position some fifty miles down the coast east of Tripoli.

Cheers ran through *Kandahar* as the word spread that Vice Admiral Malta had signalled to say HMS *Jaguar* had been dispatched to their assistance. *Jaguar* appeared out of the darkness, having been guided to the sinking destroyer by a radar-equipped Wellington flown by Sgt. Dennis Reason from Malta. The weather continued to deteriorate as Lt. Cdr. L. Tyrwhitt contrived to nurse the ship alongside bow to bow, but in the wind and sea he could not hold her steady against the yawing, helpless *Kandahar* without grave risk to his own ship. Fifty men had jumped across before he backed clear and signalled, 'Can you swim for it?' 'We will swim,' came the answer. The captain ordered all sea-cocks, scuttles and water intakes to be opened and all watertight doors secured in the open position. Then he made to *Jaguar*, 'Intend to abandon and sink ship. Lie to windward to pick up survivors. Leave not later than 05.30'. As he gave the order to abandon ship, the ship's company jumped into the water, and as *Jaguar* drifted slowly down towards them a total of eight officers and 157 crew were pulled out. A. B. Maurice Forty of *Kandahar* was an excellent swimmer and used his skill and bravery to go back and rescue three sailors who were struggling in the high seas and sinking beneath the waves. They included Bill Young who retained vivid memories of the rescue. Maurice Forty returned to save a fourth man, but unfortunately drowned. He gained a Mention in Despatches for his bravery. With dawn breaking and because *Kandahar* remained afloat after the expected twenty minutes, it was decided at 05.45 to put her under with a torpedo. Only a few solitary swimmers were located after *Kandahar* went down, but with them being widely dispersed and it being about fifteen miles off the enemy coast with dawn breaking, those not yet found had to be abandoned. *Jaguar* left for Malta at 06.05 at twenty-eight knots in a sea driven by gale-force winds.

My father had been hanging onto the Carley raft throughout the day, swimming around her at regular intervals to keep from falling asleep. Eventually when night-time arrived he was able to climb inside but his Dad's words kept coming into his head, 'I feel really tired, I just want to sleep but my Dad keeps cropping up and I hear him, "Don't go to sleep bonny lad or you won't wake up again. Never drink the water no matter how thirsty you are. Remember what your Dad said".' He continued to swim around the raft at regular intervals throughout the third day with no one else in the raft speaking. His notes from his diary described 22 December, 'On the fourth day there were only four of us left including the Captain who passed away that night. The only words he spoke all the time was on the first night when he said we were only four miles off Tripoli when we got sunk.'

Neptune's survivors were suffering from the gales and high seas. Men had succumbed, one after another as the days dragged on. My father recalled many years later that by the time darkness fell on the fourth day and he had to let go of his Captain it was at that moment that he began to doubt they would survive. He was losing his strength and described how he fought to survive:

> I get off the raft and swim around it a couple of times as I had been trying to do at regular intervals each day but I find it too difficult, my leg joints and arm joints are not working. I can hardly see and I think how much longer before somebody finds me. I'm still hoping for the best although there are only two of us left by the 24th. It's getting a bit rougher and I'm thirsty, I can't swallow as my tongue is swelling up. After 5 days in the water I was starting to wonder, where were all the ships in the Med., British, German, Italian. I wasn't bothered by this time as long as I get picked up. As I watched my shipmates die around me the guilt and depression was over-powering, not being able to help them and letting them go.

By daybreak on Christmas Eve 1941 my father clung to his only companion he believed was still alive, Leading Seaman Albert Price. He wavered between periods of oblivion and the hazy recollections of being alive, dreaming of home, his family and his sweetheart. The records in his diary described how he was saved from certain death.

 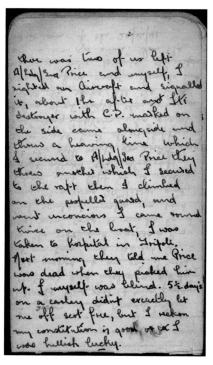

Norman's diary showing an example page of his handwritten notes from December 1941

An Italian reconnaissance aircraft had spotted the raft which had drifted some ninety miles east of Tripoli over the five and a half days. It was spotted near the port of Misurata. The Italian torpedo boat that carried my father to safety was called the *Calliope*. What an ironic twist in the tale. A nineteenth-century Comus class corvette called HMS *Calliope* was moored alongside the jetty on the River Tyne beside the Armstrong Whitworth's tank factory and was used as the RNVR Tyne Division drill ship. My father knew it well.

He floated in and out of consciousness throughout his journey to Tripoli hearing men speaking in a foreign language, he believed to be Italian, he thought he saw a bearded face peering over him. His diary notes described his experience at the hospital:

Christmas Day 1941 – I was blind all day and all I had to eat was a bowl of hot milk. I couldn't stomach anything. Next day, Boxing Day, towards night, my eyesight came back and I took a look through a mirror to see a face, which was un-recognisable to me. My tongue was swollen twice it's size, my lips were swollen and my nose was spread across my face which was black with oil. Due I suppose to exposure. I was treated very well by the naval ratings in the Tripoli hospital. I didn't know then that the food I was getting in that hospital was by far the best and most I'd ever get while I was a Prisoner of War.

As my father lay in his hospital bed a postcard was being typed up in a Tripoli office relaying hope to England. The postcard was posted in Tripoli on 25 December 1941. It was sent to inform my grandparents that he was safe and being treated well but the postcard was not received by the family until many weeks after they had been advised by an Admiralty telegram that he was 'missing on active service'.

The circumstances surrounding the loss of *Neptune*'s crew of 765 were kept secret, the next-of-kin merely received a telegram saying that their husbands or sons were 'missing on active service.' There was no publicity or public information issued.

Relatives clamoured at the Devonport Base gates for details of their loved ones but no information was forthcoming. Relatives of those deceased referred to the tardiness and total lack of sympathy of the original, and only, notification to those families who had lost fathers, husbands, brothers, sons, uncles, which affected them, as they remember, for years afterwards.

Of the crew, 150 or more were New Zealanders, there to prepare for taking over the cruiser, which was about to be transferred to the Royal New Zealand Navy. The disaster represented the greatest loss of life suffered by New Zealand in a naval action. There were also thirty-seven South Africans lost. My father was the only survivor from *Neptune*'s crew of 765 and the loss of HMS *Neptune* was one of the major naval tragedies of World War II. Seventy-three were lost in *Kandahar*, 178 were saved.

Commander G. W. G. Simpson takes up the story:

A few days later I found myself on a board of inquiry into the loss of *Neptune* and *Kandahar*, the president of the inquiry was Admiral Rawlings, who said to me: 'I feel rather stunned by the whole sad business. I was returning with my secretary from golf on a horse cab and arrived on the waterfront to see my squadron leaving harbour with my flagship in the van. Within 12 hours it was almost wholly sunk or damaged. It is difficult to accept the fact.'

So ended Force K as a highly efficient fighting squadron. I think everyone realised the dangers but decided to accept them. The prize was high; with hindsight I suggest the proper solution was to sail the squadron immediately the convoy was located, and send O'Conor and Force K their orders by cipher, rather than sending for O'Conor to headquarters, which must have lost forty minutes, which was perhaps a vital margin.

Many years later John McGregor, whose father Paymaster Commander Jack H. McGregor was a *Neptune* casualty, made calculations of the course – from naval reports, records, and diagrams – which shows the narrow channel between the laid minelines through which the convoy may have been attempting to pass. How narrow the space between glory and ignominy.

Only eight named bodies were recovered from the sea after the loss of *Neptune* and *Kandahar*. These eight men must also have struggled to stay alive, possibly on another raft, but unfortunately did not make it and were buried in Libyan cemeteries:

Tobruk   Lieutenant Donald Wilson
          Able Seaman Lloyd Lord RNZN
Tripoli   Able Seaman James Brooks
          Able Seaman William Miller
          Able Seaman Cyril Pugh
          Leading Seaman Reginald Turley
          Supply Assistant Henry Walpole RNZN
          Stoker Robert Walton

These are the only named graves identified from the list of those lost with *Neptune*. It may have been that many others were washed up on shore and having lost their identity tags would be buried in unnamed graves; tribute should be paid to all the brave men who must have struggled to survive the sinking of their ship. There were forty-four officers including twelve midshipmen, and 721 seamen. Amongst them were seventy-three Royal Marines, including fifteen Royal Marine Bandsmen. The average age of men aboard was twenty-five, including 109 teenagers. The different nationalities of the fatalities from Force K were spread as follows:

555   British RN, RNR and RNVR
150   New Zealanders
 37   South Africans
  8   Southern Irish

3	Australians
3	Maltese
2	Canadians
4	Civilians (Canteen Staff)
1	Rhodesian
1	Goanese
1	St Helena

A Board of Inquiry was held on 24 December 1941 to investigate the circumstances attending the loss of *Neptune* and *Kandahar*. The Board assembled as my father lay in the raft, clinging to life and the hope that he would be rescued, unaware that he would always bear the burden of being the only eyewitness to so much death and destruction; the only man who would survive to tell the story of the loss of *Neptune*.

The Board of Inquiry that assembled aboard *Ajax* in Malta was not aware of the existence of any survivor left behind in the water and so the following men began their deliberations without the sole surviving eyewitness from *Neptune*. Assembled there were:

Rear Admiral Henry Bernard Rawlings, OBE RN, Commander of the 7th Cruiser Squadron and the designated Commander of Force K, appointed as President of the Board, thus effectively silencing his evidence. Commander George Walter Gillow Simpson, Captain of the 10th Submarine Flotilla and Lieutenant David Grenville Clutterbuck (*Ajax*) were Board members. (The 10th Submarine Flotilla at Malta is the most famous submarine squadron in submarine history. Trident submarines based at Faslane took the name.)

Those who gave evidence were:

Commander Evans, Staff Officer (Operations) on the staff of Vice Admiral, Malta;
Captain Agnew, CB (*Aurora*);
Captain Nicholl (*Penelope*);
Commander Robson, DSO DSC (*Kandahar*);
Captain Wadham, Chief Staff Officer to Vice Admiral Malta;
Lieutenant McEwan, Navigator (*Aurora*);
Lieutenant Morgan, Navigator (*Penelope*);
Lieutenant-Commander Northcott (*Lance*);
Lieutenant-Commander Waymouth, Port W/T Officer, Malta;

Lieutenant-Commander Hussey, DSC (*Lively*);

Lieutenant Watkins, DSC (*Havock*);

Lieutenant the Marquess of Milford Haven, Navigator (*Kandahar*);

Lieutenant-Commander E. Havergal, Engineer Officer (*Kandahar*);

Temporary Surgeon Lieutenant Armstrong, Medical Officer (*Kandahar*);

Lieutenant-Commander Tyrwhitt, DSC (*Jaguar*).

The proceedings were secret and not released to public view until 1972. No other formal inquiry took place and no information was published or made available to relatives of all those who perished.

A quote made by a World War II Admiral relating to this Board was recorded as follows, 'Findings should be for the good of the Service. It's no good blaming people, we must get on with the war. We haven't time to go into details.' When reading this Board of Inquiry report, conclusions do not provide any clues as to how or why such a tragedy occurred; as the quoted Admiral stated, they did not go into details or apportion blame. Much material from those far-off days has now been released from archives, but it is somewhere within the untold, the conversations, arguments, debates, not officially recorded that the truth probably lies.

Vice Admiral Ford, who had done such a magnificent job in Grand Harbour, Malta, for so long, in his administration of the complexities of all shipping naval and merchant, the protection of the harbour, the competent direction of labour both in docks and dockyard repair, and his co-ordination and co-operation with Army and RAF together with the admiration of the Maltese people, was transferred from Malta shortly after the Board of Inquiry.

My father, over his remaining years, never questioned the actions of his Captains, he always fought for the good of the Service and never wanted to go into the details of action during the war years. He was trained well and even though he often stated that there was no glorification in death he did believe that no one during those war years died in vain – they gave up their life for the future of the generations that followed.

I, as his daughter, know that my father never entirely cleared from his mind the guilt he felt at leaving those men behind.

CHAPTER 6

A Family at War

THE CASUALTY REPORTING OFFICE was given the task of informing relatives when men were missing on war service. The C.R.O. Devonport was run by a team of Wrens led by Chief Petty Officer Muriel (Sandy) Holland – still alive and active in 2007 and living in Stoke-on-Trent. She remembers sending out the telegrams to the relatives of *Neptune* and *Kandahar* on Boxing Day 1941, delayed by twenty-four hours for obvious reasons. The news during that Christmas period was devastating. 'Missing believed killed' brought families to the barrack gates wanting more news but nothing came apart from a tiny press release weeks later to say HMS *Neptune* had been lost.

The C.R.O. team worked under the command of Commodore Victor Crutchley, VC. By May 1945, over 45,000 telegrams had been sent out on behalf of the Royal Navy.

It was Christmas Eve at Whorlton Terrace and the children were excited. The Walton parents were preparing for Christmas Day trying to make the best of difficult times with food shortages and the oppression of war that was never far away. Maud Walton was in the kitchen preparing for the roast dinner to be had next day. The six children living at home were bathed and sitting on the long wooden bench in front of the fire waiting for their regular cup of cocoa from Dad before he set off for his nightly jaunt at Swalwell Social Club. My father's brothers Leslie and Willy had now left school and taken up apprenticeships in the factories down by the River Tyne. Leslie was training as a precision tool-maker at the Vickers Armstrong factory and Willy was in electrical engineering joining his father at the Delta Foundry. Both brothers were itching to join their brother in the armed forces and did in fact join the Navy and the Royal Air Force respectively during the last year of the war.

The two elder lads left their younger brothers and sisters at home on Christmas Eve and set off with their mates. All the teenagers were out on Christmas Eve but the younger children were guided to bed by candlelight by their elder sister Isabelle, as she did every night, and tucked them in. Soon they would be asleep dreaming of what would fill the nine stockings hung on the brass rod that sat over the mantle-piece. They often had difficulty finding nine clean socks but there would always be one for each of the family and Santa would know by the size and colour of each who they belonged to. The parents sat silently with haunting thoughts of their eldest son who was not going be with them this Christmas and wondered when or if he would ever return. The children were out of bed too early, as usual, and crept downstairs before light only to hear their Dad's low Geordie voice, 'Geet back to bed!' On Christmas Day morning they all said a prayer for my father.

Isabelle, his eldest sister, remembers vividly when the telegram arrived:

All the children were in the bedroom when the telegram arrived. It was Christmas holidays and we were keeping warm under the bed covers. I remember it was very cold winter mornings then and we would stay under the bed covers at weekends and holidays as long as we could, at least until Dad lit the fire in the room. We heard the Postie come into the back yard and he was speaking to our Dad; it was just mumbles. It was scary if the Postie came to your door, we knew that from other families in the village who had lost their husbands and sons. We heard Dad walk across the room to the kitchen area next to their bedroom, then Mam made a noise that seemed to come from deep in her stomach, a loud moan.

I will never forget my mother's horrible scream, 'Oh, me bairn!' A horrible tone we never heard before and we all went quiet and looked at each other. Silence, silence then 'Norman where are you?' Mam was shouting and she started running around the house. Dad told us to stay in the bedroom. We were saying to each other, 'There's something wrong, there's something wrong,' but as children then, you were seen and not heard, and we were still not told what the matter was. We felt the trauma and the sadness as we heard both our parents sobbing.

Isabelle and the younger children were still in the bedroom afraid to come out. She describes what they saw when they did:

After a while Dad told us to come out for breakfast and Mother served us in silence, we could see she was upset. Dad was just a bundle of nerves and neither of them ate anything. That's all I can remember of the telegram coming. We were sent out to play. Most things were kept from the children in those days. I was the eldest there and would have been eleven years old. Leslie and Willy must have been at work; they worked nights then.

We picked up bits of information from hearing Mam and Dad talking as

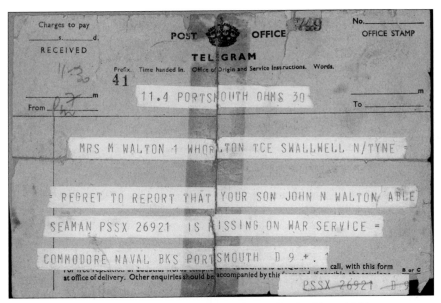

The telegram sent to Norman's mother on Boxing Day, 1941

the day wore on and worked out that Norman was missing in the war. The house was so sad and gloomy and my Mam kept crying all the time.

Isabelle, still living in the Whickham Bank area of Swalwell near Gateshead in 2007, was able to recall life in the Walton household during the war years. Many of the stories I had heard often through the years. She describes how they lived during the 1940s, when the family was stricken with the uncertainty of their brother ever returning to them:

The street, Whorlton Terrace, was in the village of Swalwell, which sits on the banks of the River Tyne, and with the other industrial villages along the river the villagers in the 1940s served the shipyards, foundries, factories and the railway that ran through the village parallel with the river. Whorlton Terrace was just one street of flats with shared back yards and the 'netties' were in the yards. They were three-bedroom flats upstairs, where we first lived at No. 1. Mam and Dad later had to move downstairs to a two-bedroom flat at No. 8 after 1941. Norman was away before we moved to No. 8 Whorlton Terrace. Being in the two-bedroom flat was very crowded, I know now, but it meant that when Mam went to the Council they would put us on the list for one of the family-size council houses on Whickham Bank which they did by 1943. We never thought life was hard because it was the same for all the families around us. Our house was always a warm and happy place and we never went short of food. Mam spent most of her days cooking and baking in the kitchen except on wash day which was always Monday and the whole house was given over to washing and drying the clothes.

Everyone knew each other, we had our own little community in Whorlton Terrace.

During the war years the families were making the best of difficult situations but one of the most feared sights at this time was when the Postie would deliver a telegram. Everyone began to ask us about Norman, it was very distressing for my Mam and Dad. Dad was always in the clubs and pubs bragging about Norman and now he had to tell them he was missing.

Isabelle describes another time they received a letter:

It was quite a while later that year when I opened the door to the Postie who had another letter. He said 'Give this straight to your Mam'. I was frightened in case it would upset her again so I tried to look, I didn't want to hear that awful scream again. Mam came into the room before I could see in the envelope so I gave it straight to her. She took it to Leslie who was in her bed after working the night shift. Mam would not have been able to bear any more bad news. Leslie struggled with the envelope and I remember that they saw 'England' printed on the envelope. We were all excited because we thought Norman must be in England, but then realised it was where the envelope was made. We let out a nervous laugh. He opened it and told Mam that the letter said Norman was safe and in Italian hands. We were all so excited and happy he was alive. She told me to take it straight to my Dad, who was working at the Delta foundry as a crane driver. I grabbed Tommy's hand. He was sitting staring into the fire, he had not spoken from the day Mam and Dad received the first telegram. The house was so clouded in gloom and sadness that our Tommy had become very depressed, he was only about eight or nine years old.

Anyway we ran and ran as fast as we could to the Delta works. I was dragging Tommy who I don't think understood why I was running. We stopped outside the gates to get our breath back and I said to Tommy, 'Let's put a big smile on our faces so Dad knows it's good news.' Tommy had not smiled since the first telegram. We went through the big gates and some fella there said 'Where are you going, you can't come in here.' We told him we have to take this to our Dad, he could see we were excited and let us go in. We saw Dad was sitting eating his 'bait' at the side of some corrugated iron. You know how they put the corrugated iron up against each other to make like a shelter? That was where the workers would eat their 'bait'. They had a tin with their sandwiches in, we called it 'bait' and a lad would bring them tea in a 'billy-can' that they heated on the fire. Dad had managed to get Norman the job of making tea and filling the 'billy-cans' for the men at the Delta, when he first left school. I remember Norman saying the job made him a good bit money, as the men always gave you a few pennies for bringing the tea and it would be on top of the small wage he had for learning his job at the foundry.

Anyway – when we saw Dad he was sat at the side of this corrugated iron. He saw us and we were shouting 'He's safe, he's safe.' We saw him freeze just staring at us. Then, suddenly, he tried to run up the corrugated iron, slipping down and running up again shouting, 'My lad's all right', his mates took hold of him and hugged him and we thought he'd gone a bit mad. We felt embarrassed that our Dad seemed so out of control. We were all crying again, but we were happy this time.

Tommy's mental health continued to deteriorate and he still wouldn't speak to anyone. Mam was always so busy looking after the younger children. Tommy was nine, Dorothy six, Lillian and Seppy were just toddlers and our new baby sister Ethel had arived on 13 February 1941. Mam had taken Tommy to the doctor and he asked her if Tommy could be taken on holiday away from the house if possible as he was suffering from depression. We could never afford a holiday but Mam sent him to live with her sister Ethel, who lived in High Spen, a village not far away. He got a lot more attention from Ethel and Mam could go see him regularly. Dad's hair had turned white virtually overnight when he received the news about Norman being missing at sea, we kids couldn't believe what we saw. He always had a head of silver hair from that day. It was a sad time. The younger children didn't really understand the roller coaster of emotions that were running through the house during those difficult years.

I do remember before the telegram, Aunt Bella had come to the house. Bella was Mam's sister, who lived in the railway cottages at the bottom of Swalwell village near the railway line. She was a regular visitor at the house, helping my Mam to look after us. Aunt Bella used to read the tea leaves and have vivid dreams and was known in the village to be quite a mystical lady that people would go to have their fortunes told. She came in the house one day really excited saying 'Maud, I've seen all this oil on the sea, I can smell it. Norman's hanging onto something. I see now he's getting lifted up and the man has a beard', she said. She went on to describe what Norman later said he thought could be the captain of the Italian ship that picked him up. She had told Mam that Norman was safe.

Soon after that visit the family received the telegram telling them that my father was indeed safe and in Italian hands. His closest brother Leslie, also recalls the episode with his Aunt Bella. Leslie was very close to Maud's sister Bella and spent a lot of time at her home staying with her many a night. He describes the day:

I used to spend at lot of time with my Aunt Bella, as you can imagine our house was always crowded. People from the area would come to her house to have the tea leaves read. She would also stare into the embers of the fire and talk of events in the future that would quite often come true. Aunt Bella had seen Norman in the oily sea and a man with a beard. I remember she also mentioned a red-haired boy that was with him. Until this day we are not sure who that may have been and only know that Acting Leading Seaman Albert Price was a fair lad and the sailor with Norman in the raft when the Italian boat picked them up.

Leslie remembers the telegrams, still with great emotion:

Receiving telegrams in those days was really hard and families feared the worst when the Postie would knock on your door. Being the eldest at home, usually meant my mother would hand me any official letters to open and I would have to read the news to my Mam. We were desperate when we thought Norman could have been lost to us, especially Dad as he was so proud of Norman. When we found out Norman was safe it was like a great cloud lifted. I remember the words on one postcard that have always stuck in my mind, 'They will always be friends of mine'. It wasn't Norman's writing but he was speaking about his Italian captors and I could not understand, at the time, how they could be his friends when they were his enemies.

The postcard that Leslie refers to was posted in Tripoli on 25 December 1941:

My dear father – I have survived the most unpleasant experience a man could ever wish for six days in a small boat with nothing to eat or drink. Sixteen of us started on this boat and they all died off leaving only me to be picked up by an Italian ship. Who have treated me very well? And they will always be friends of mine. Your loving Son John.

Isabelle recalls a postcard from her brother:

I only remember one postcard that came to the house at that time, Norman had written the postcard from the prisoner of war camp in Italy. I remember because it was in Norman's handwriting and had bits blacked out, that was the only postcard I can remember and I think we had received some official letter telling us he was in Italian hands.

The postcard sent from Campo 65 on 30 April 1942 still sits in my father's wooden ditty box along with the typewritten postcard from Tripoli. Much of his writing on the postcard from the camp is blacked out and what remains is difficult to read, worn with time, but it says, 'I've still not received any letter from you but I'm always hoping for some word and a few cigarettes or a parcel of some kind. Well, Mother I'm still going O.K. but I'll be glad when it's all over and we can all be united once again. Your loving son, Norman'

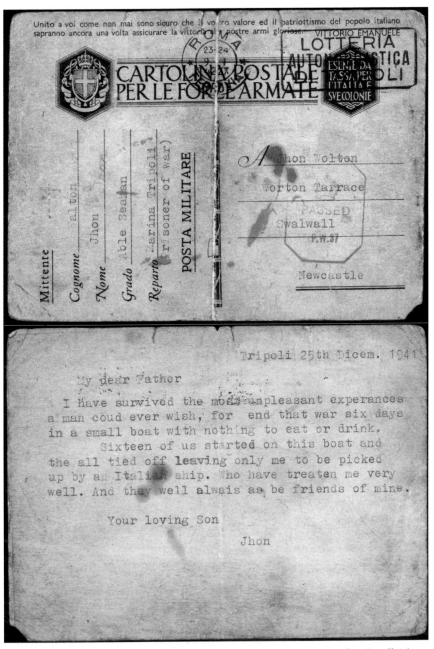

Unito a voi come non mai sono sicuro che il vostro valore ed il patriottismo del popolo italiano
sapranno ancora una volta assicurare la vittoria alle nostre armi gloriose.

VITTORIO EMANUELE

LOTTERIA

ESENTE DA
TASSA PER
L'ITALIA E
SVE COLONIE

CARTOLINA POSTALE
PER LE FORZE ARMATE

POSTA MILITARE

Mittente

Cognome ___ alton

Nome ___ Jhon

Grado ___ Able Sealan

Reparto ___ Marina Tripoli
(Prisoner of war)

A Jhon Wolton

Worton Tarrace

PASSED

Swalwall

P.W.37

Newcastle

Tripoli 25th Dicem. 1941

My dear Father

I have survived the most unpleasant experances
a man coud ever wish, for end that war six days
in a small boat with nothing to eat or drink.
        Sixteen of us started on this boat and
the all tied off leaving only me to be picked
up by an Italian ship. Who have treaten me very
well. And they well alwais as be friends of mine.

        Your loving Son

                Jhon

*The postcard received by Norman's mother and father many weeks after the official
telegram from the Navy stating he was missing on war service*

It is due to the careful protection of his letters, postcards and diaries by his mother and later by my mother Irene that they were still in his ditty box found in the loft at 90 Smalewell Road, Pudsey after he passed away in 2005.

My father's mother Maud was from a large family, as many were in the 1930s. She had six sisters and two brothers, who had survived; three children had died either at birth or in their infancy. His Dad had only one sister but five brothers. Maud was closest to her sisters, Bella, Ethel and Annie, who would all help each other during the difficulties of the war years. Neighbours were also very supportive then. In the flat below lived Lily Morpeth and her family. Maud, Lily and Lily's sister Betsy who lived at Rowlands Gill became lifelong friends of the Walton family.

Isabelle recalls the fun all the children would have in the street:

> The lads would sometimes 'find' an old leather football that would weigh heavily from being out in all weathers and play 'footie' in the street. Willy was the only boy that didn't like sport and he would patrol Whorlton Terrace to guard us all from the Germans. He once found a tin hat and he paraded up and down the street in the tin hat holding a big stick for a rifle, protecting the street from danger.

Isabelle laughs at the memory, 'He was real serious Willy, he probably thought he was responsible for the family, as he was the eldest boy at home with us most of the time during the war years.'

By 1942 after weeks of queuing and interviews with Council officers, the Walton parents were finally provided with the keys to a council house on Whickham Bank. The family were delighted with their new spacious home. My father did not know he had a new sister and would not know until he returned to Swalwell in 1943.

Isabelle describes the feelings of great responsibility when one day at the new house on Whickham Bank her mother had an accident:

> Mam was carrying our new baby sister Ethel down the stairs when she fell, very badly breaking her leg and fracturing her hip. She was taken to hospital and kept from moving, with her leg in traction for thirteen weeks. I was left to look after the five younger children. I was about thirteen years old by this time. My Dad and two older brothers were working and expected a dinner on the table when they came home from work. One day I tried to make a piecrust for putting over some meat a neighbour had stewed for us. Many of the neighbours would bring soups and stews to help us out. I set to making the pastry with flour and water, trying to remember desperately how Mam

would make it. Eventually with the addition of many piles of flour the rolling out of the piecrust seemed to be working. As I carried it over to the meat dish it fell on the floor. The kitchen floor was made of stone slabs and I had not had time to scrub it for weeks as I'd been so busy with the children, so you can imagine how dirty it was. The dirt was now ingrained into the pastry. I picked out most of the dirt and in went the pie to the oven. All the family were sat at the table at dinnertime and I presented the pie. I knew if Dad ate some we would all follow suit. No one could start till Dad took his first bite at the table. He just stared at the pie. The only one who attempted to try it was Leslie, he would never want to hurt my feelings. We watched as he chewed, then the rest of us just dug out the meat along with Dad. I don't know how everyone kept a straight face.

There were many similar stories told by the Walton family and I would listen intently to them all as a child. Isabelle's disasters in attempting to care for such a large family at the age of thirteen were always good for a laugh but it must have been a mammoth task. Of course the visits from the 'school-board man' were frequent. Isabelle describes one such visit:

A neighbour was at the house helping when Mr Foster, the school-board man knocked at the door. I still remember his name over sixty years later. I hid behind the door, listening to the neighbour tell the story that I'd set off for school. As I stood there I realised that there was a mirror on the wall and if I could see Mr Foster then clearly he could see me. He never mentioned it at the time but must have written to Dad and I remember my Dad going down to the school and I was really scared but when he came home he assured me everything was all right. Dad was a very even-tempered man he was never angry with us. When the man from the school-board came into the classroom one day the teacher asked me to read out a poem we had to learn and I read it perfectly for her. The teacher had made her point to the school-board man and we did not hear from him again.

The Waltons had taken my father's sweetheart, Irene, to their hearts. She continued to lived in Winlaton with her mother and father, brother Ronnie and sisters Hilda and Betty. It was 1942 when Irene and her family moved into Cromer Terrace in Armley, Leeds, where her father had gained a well-paid job as a furnace-man at Blackey's Foundry. All the villages around the River Tyne became targets as the enemy was being beaten back by the Allies and they desperately bombed the shipbuilders, foundries and factories producing the equipment that was being used so effectively against them.

On one such night, 1 September 1941, a lone German bomber dropped two high explosive bombs on Blaydon-on-Tyne. The warning air-raid siren wailed out into the night air and people were sent hurrying to their air-raid shelters. Every household had its own 'black bag' during the war which contained all the important documents connected to family matters: insurance policies, rent books, ration books, birth, death and marriage certificates and any other bits and pieces the family would consider irreplaceable. As the families emerged from the shelters the stink of cordite from the bombs was sickening and the sounds of people wailing and crying in the distance was dreadful. The people of Blaydon and surrounding areas surveyed the damage, smashed tiles, bricks strewn across the paths, splintered wood and broken glass everywhere. They peered through the smoke before them to be confronted with the devastation where houses had been completely destroyed. The huge crater left by the first bomb was broad and deep. The other bomb that exploded made no crater, as it detonated high up on the roof of Donald Brown's Engineering Factory in Tyne Street. Parallel on one side of the factory as with many other factories in the area, was the Newcastle to Hexham Road, and on the opposite side the Newcastle to Carlisle railway line. Then alongside the railway track was the River Tyne. The factory was demolished, taking with it jobs and livelihoods.

Irene was the eldest child, and by that time nearly twenty years old and desperate to see her first love again. They had not been together for nearly four years but the bond was still as strong as when they met when she was fifteen years old. Irene was a very beautiful girl with a bubbly and outgoing personality. She loved dancing, and had many friends in the area, but it was my father's family that she visited regularly and went to stay with when her family had moved to Leeds. She was always desperate to hear any news of her sweetheart. By the Christmas of 1942, the Walton family were still plagued by the sadness of my father being a prisoner of war and wondered how he would be spending his Christmas with little food and comfort. These feelings of sadness were very brief for the children, at home; they were looking forward with excitement to Santa Claus visiting the house.

The girls remember their mother making dolls for them from tea-towels and how they would put the blankets over the washing line that would be across the room, in front of the fire in the winter-time. The blankets acted as curtains for their theatre productions. The Walton family was famous for their concerts, when the children would write and perform plays, comic sketches and sing songs accompanied by their mother and they were particularly popular at Christmas time. The families, as all families across the country, wondered what 1943 would bring. My grandparents knew that my father would not be spending his twenty-first birthday on 15 January with them but hoped and prayed that he was at least safe and well in the prisoner of war camp in Italy, a comforting thought that they knew not all families were able to share and they felt very lucky.

CHAPTER 7

In Italian Hands

E VEN THOUGH CAPTAIN O'CONOR OF *Neptune* had, at one point, attempted to inspire those on the raft to use the oar and row to the coast they could make no headway due to the high seas and south-easterly winds. It was the last words the Captain had spoken and as each dawn broke the men lost strength and the will to carry on as the raft continued to drift in an easterly direction along the North African coast. It was too late for the Captain and Albert Price in the raft when they were eventually spotted by the Italian reconnaissance aeroplane and just in time for my father. The nurses on duty in the hospital in Tripoli over the Christmas period 1941 worked hard to save my father's shattered leg and restore his health after five and a half days in a raft on rough cold seas. He always spoke with gratitude in his voice when describing the care he received from the nurses and naval ratings in Tripoli and Italy. My father remembered one male nurse in particular who stayed with him day and night, nursing him back to health and often spoke of this man and his kindness many years later. My father must also have left quite an impression on the nurse, as many years later a letter arrived at his door from Luciano Bocchieri, Geneva, Switzerland. The letter took a long time to find him but eventually he was able to thank the man that nursed him back to health after his devastating experiences in December 1941.

Seven days of suffering passed and New Year's Eve 1941 arrived without celebration but he bathed in the relief that he was, against all odds, still alive and gaining strength by the day. The relief was tempered by a cold shadow of guilt that he could not dispel. He had watched his shipmates all die around him and those scenes of death were etched on his heart, he would never forget them. Two previous members of the ship's company were also experiencing feelings of guilt at escaping the fateful disaster on the 19 December.

Hubert Gardner, a musician with the Royal Marine Band of HMS *Neptune* was not aboard when Force K set sail on the 18 December. He had been taken ill and sent off the ship to the Naval hospital in

Luciano Bocchieri
    Büchler
chemin des Moulins
Vernier - Geneva
Switzerland

Geneva, juny 2nd, 1963

Dear Sir,

I write you lines by the motion of a long feeling, which is passing through my mind plenty of time. A long period of social mobility has halted me to write you before, but, as you can see, your name and your address have never disappeared from my head. I remember our evenings in speaking and writing my poor English to understand us, when you, unfortunated, was prisoner in my nursery of the Italian navy (in Tripolis). Do you remember? How big was always my desire to know about you. I can't explain you why now and only now I decided me to contact you or somebody for.

The first page of a letter received by Norman delivered to Swalwell, Co. Durham over twenty years after his memorable meeting with the Italian naval rating Luciano Bocchieri. Luciano had nursed him in the Tripoli hospital in December 1941. A photograph of Luciano is attached, the bearded man who worked so hard to save Norman's life

Malta. While recuperating he learned the fate of his comrades. In such a situation, realising he was perhaps the only survivor he became vulnerable to developing post-traumatic stress disorder. The annihilation of his friends and shipmates caused him to take his life, a kind of identification to be with his crew-mates.

Able Seaman Norman Stewart was called to report to his Commanding Officer on HMS *Neptune* on 18 December 1941, who told him that he was leaving the ship to get passage for some leave as he had not been back to England for three years and was the longest serving member on *Neptune*. Norman Stewart, still alive in 2007, living in his home town in the north-east of England contacted me after reading my father's obituary in the *Newcastle Chronicle* in 2005 and describes what happened:

> I pleaded with the C.O. to let me stay on board with all my friends and shipmates, but he told me to pack and leave, which I did and was sent to a lot of canvas tents at the HMS *Nile* holding pool for a few hours and then sent to the C-in-C's drafting office at HMS *Canopus* (Alexandria), which was the office in the transit camp used while you were awaiting passage to England. I left HMS *Neptune* three hours before she sailed off with other units in Force K.
>
> After the disaster I was informed at the drafting office that they knew who I was and was told about the *Neptune* and was given the task of putting the *Neptune*'s names of the ship's company personnel missing believed to be killed. These were all my friends – all 764 of them, it was a tear-jerking job.

Norman Stewart was put on a merchant ship that took him to Cape Town in South Africa where he spent a few days before being drafted to the cruiser HMS *London* for passage to England.

There are many similarities between the two Geordies, my father, Norman Walton and Norman Stewart. They were born in the same area near Gateshead on the River Tyne and both grew up in poor circumstances. Norman Stewart left school to work in Wardley High Pit but left the job as soon as he could to work at the Pattersons Miners Lamp Works making miners lamps. He joined the RNVR just as he turned seventeen and trained on HMS *Calliope* moored alongside the jetty on the River Tyne. On 25 August 1939, he was made an Able Seaman and after a short period with HMS *Furious*, an aircraft carrier, he joined *Neptune*. Many of his experiences during the war were in near proximity to my father as he describes his time with *Neptune*:

I was drafted to HMS *Neptune* in Gibraltar. It was a great ship with a great crew and a smashing Captain, Captain Rory O'Conor. We joined the 7th Cruiser Squadron with two of our sister ships, the cruisers HMS *Ajax* and HMS *Essex*. I can remember when we were off Crete seeing thousands of German parachutists jumping from hundreds of aircraft and bombers and landing on the island. We lost a good few ships during the battle for Crete and subsequent evacuation and a great deal of sailors were lost. I remember that some volunteers from our ship and other ships were given rum to help them get the bodies of dead sailors out of the bombed ships.

In July 1940, when escorting a convoy of ships sailing from Malta to Alexandria, we had a radio message to say the Italian warships were about at sea and we caught up with them and caused damage amongst their cruisers and destroyers – this was the Battle of Calabria.

My father was certainly involved in the action at both these events and by November 1941 became a fellow crew member aboard *Neptune*. By the time he came aboard *Neptune*, Norman Stewart was made Tanky (Rum Bosun), and with an officer it was his job to bring out the big rum casket and have it ready measured to serve to the ship's company. One sailor would get his turn to share out the rum to the men in his mess at around 12 noon each day.

There were no rum rations to be shared out in the hospital in Tripoli on New Year's Eve. On New Year's Day 1942 my father was suddenly transferred to a stretcher, loaded onto a truck and taken to the harbour. His diary notes described his journey to Italy and his subsequent experiences as a prisoner of war in the Italian prison camps:

I was boarded on the hospital ship *Gradisca* just before dinner and was told I was leaving for Italy. I didn't get anything to eat that day. We sailed from Tripoli about 5 p.m. I was the only prisoner of war on board, the rest consisting of Italian and German troops who were going back to Italy for leave. All I could understand was 'Andare Cassa', going home.

My father's leg had not responded to treatment in the hospital in Tripoli so he was transferred to Bari Hospital in southern Italy for further consultative care. He described his time in Bari Hospital and onwards to Bari transit camp:

4th January, 1942 – we arrive in Bari. I was put in hospital again, Bari Hospital, where I met up with some more prisoners who had been captured in the Libyan dessert. There were Tank Corps, Signals and quite a number of New Zealand forces. Turned 21 years old whilst in Bari hospital, my coming of age in more ways than one. I spent just over a month in there before I was well enough to be sent to Bari transit camp.

The hospital worked wonders on my shattered leg, five and a half days in the water did not help.

Back on my feet at last and learning to walk again, building up strength all the time.

I was still the only sailor among many soldiers. We were very tightly packed, in Bari transit camp. Our little hut was too tight to be healthy, on a piece of board about three feet wide for three men. The boards were hard up against each other right around the hut with a couple in the middle. The deck remaining was covered with men trying to sleep. If you had to get up in the night you had no chance getting back into the billet. We had to work every day and our daily rations were 400 grams of bread, 40 grams of macaroni or rice, 40 grams cheese, bread was cut to 200 grams.

23rd April, 1942 – some of us are transported north from Bari Transit Camp 75 to Campo 65. We arrive there late at night and got a bit of a shock as I had visions of better things. There was exactly nothing, the place was still being built. All that was there were six bungalows crammed with white-faced skinny looking blokes, in a bad state of health. The lads with me were pretty low in health, but not spirits. Next morning I met a few matelots from HMS Submarine *Tempest*. The first I'd seen since we were sunk. I spent a few day's with the lads I'd been in Bari with, then most of them got sent to another compound. After the lads I came from Bari with left, I naturally moved straight in with the survivors off HMS Submarine *Tempest* and stayed with them for the rest of my time. We were without doubt the most energetic and positive little mob in the camp.

HMS *Tempest* had been scuttled following depth-charge attacks. She had been sunk as a result of an attack on the Italian tanker *Lucania* by HMS *Una* (Lieutenant D. S. Martin RN). *Lucania* had been given a 'safe conduct' pass by the British because she was engaged on humanitarian work and thus the Italians were exceedingly angry that she had been sunk. Extra patrols were instituted to find the culprit but *Tempest* was the unlucky recipient of their attentions. At 03.15 hours on the 13 February 1942 the torpedo boat *Circe* (Capitano di Corvetta Stefanino Palmas) got an asdic contact with *Tempest* and then carried out seven hours of depth-charge attacks which reduced the inside of the submarine to a shambles. At 09.42 hrs, with No. 3 battery producing great clouds of toxic chlorine gas, Commanding Officer Lieutenant Commander Cavaye gave the order to surface. Machine gun fire from *Circe* prevented *Tempest*'s crew from bringing either the 4 inch gun or their machine guns into action so he gave the order to open main vents and set the scuttling charges before giving the order to abandon ship. The survivors were picked up by *Circe* but *Tempest* remained stubbornly afloat until 16.05 hrs when she

35 HMS Rowena, Algerine class minesweeper, in speed trials off Gourock in 1944. Norman served with her from October 1944 in the Mediterranean and Far East leaving her ranked Petty Officer in Singapore, December 1945. The Second World War was finally at an end.

36 HMS Rowena Football Team taken in Italy in the summer of 1945. Captain George C. Hocart seen centre back with Norman on his left.

37 Members of the sweep-deck crew, HMS Rowena in 1945. Norman back row second left, George Laidlaw second row extreme right. Front row kneeling extreme left Bill Duke and in the shadow fourth from left Jock (Shortie) McLean.

38 Members of the sweep-deck crew, fifty years on, ready for dinner at the Spa in Scarborough 13 and 14 May 1995. John Newton, Mr & Mrs Eric Cross. Barbara Newton, Norman & Irene Walton.

39 Norman returns to his family in England in June 1946 and is pictured with his wife Irene and son John who died in November 1946 having been with his father only five months.

40 Norman pictured outside Cromer Terrace in Armley, Leeds with his mother-in-law 'Lily' in the doorway, sister-in-law Betty and father-in-law Norman Dodds. Next to him are his brothers Leslie and Willy Walton.

41 Return to Swalwell in the summer of 1946. Left to right: Isabelle Walton and Ethel Walton with Norman's son John.

42 The photograph shows Billy Charlton's Gym in Gateshead, Tyneside.

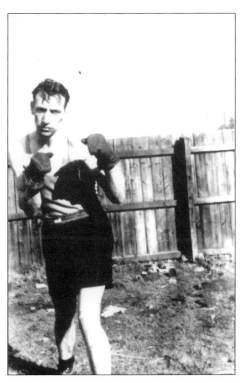

43 Norman the fighter. Professional boxing name 'Patsy Dodds', middleweight, 1947–1952.

44a Norman had 146 fights during his career in the boxing booths and on the professional circuit. Pictured sparing with his brother Tommy Walton at the gym in Gateshead, 1947.

44b Admiralty Floating Dock (AFD 22) pictured with a frigate inside her under repair. Norman served during the Korean War with her from 1952–55, moving on to minesweeping duties in the Pacific with HMS Chameleon. He was drafted back to HM Submarine Base in Gosport, England for the final two years of his naval career leaving in 1957 after serving a total of seventeen years in the Royal Navy.

sank. There were thirty-nine casualties with twenty-four survivors who were eventually sent to Campo 65.

> 29th April, 1942 – we received our first Red Cross parcel. What a godsend. I learn Italian and take advantage of it, anything to pass the time away. I talk to the Italian Officer in Charge of the camp about sport and he likes it, so I play on it.
>
> After we had been there about three months they allowed us to build a basketball pitch. Although there were very few who knew the game we soon mastered it and started a league and made a little shield. In the five finals we had in the camp our mob won it once and were runners up four times. I had picked up malaria, which laid me out for a while.
>
> About this time they gave me a job in the galley and I worked there for about three months, managed to get some grub down me, then they let someone else have a go. We struggled on more or less the same way all the time we were prisoners. The same thoughts all the time for me, freedom and food.
>
> February, 1943, – we received some sports kit from the Red Cross. Among it was boxing gloves so straight away we tried to make up a team. The naval ratings formed a team; two *Tempest* crew, one off a schooner and myself. We held an exhibition show of about 7 bouts. We challenged another compound but I left the camp before it came off.

In his diary notes my father has described his time as a prisoner of war through the positive events he experienced. This reflects the character of the boy and man. The bulk of recordings made during his time with his captors describe the friendships he made and the sporting events they organised and were involved in. The negative feelings and thoughts he most definitely had are never mentioned. It was his nature to play down the negatives in his life. His family and friends remember how he always found a positive in any situation, he never complained about his lot and saw the best in all those he met; 'to live and let live' was his motto. He had many friends and acquaintances throughout his life and they all describe him as a real character, a bit of a charmer with a kind spirit and someone to whom they instantly warmed. It was easy to love the man.

> 6th March, 1943 – I'm called into the camp office and asked, in Italian, if I wanted to go home. I learned quite a lot of Italian in the Camp, but I thought I must have heard him wrong so I asked him to repeat what he said. He replied: 'Anderra Cassa'. My brain started racing and I reply, 'Yes. Sir!' I leave the Campo 65 in darkness in the clothes I was provided with at Bari hospital and start to make my way through war torn Italy south to Bari for a second time. Kept my head down all the way till I met up with other released POWs

all headed for Bari. Eventually arrived in Bari hungry and exhausted when they took me back to the Transit Camp. It was there I learned some of us matelots were being repatriated in exchange for Italian soldiers. About 20 of us matelots, for how many Italians, who knows. Italy was on the verge of packing in then. We waited in the packed Camp to find out more news of what was to happen to us. I was searched about six times. I explained this diary every time and they let me keep it. Myself and the other matelots were despatched to the hospital ship *Gradisca* again on the 13th March, 1943, it was crowded and uncomfortable but we were happy to set sail on the 14th March and found out we were on our way to Mersin in Turkey, where the exchange was to take place. We eventually arrived in Mersin on the 19th and the exchange took place as they had promised. I was taken to the British ship HMT *Talma* on the 21st March, 1943 and handed over.

At last I was free!

Throughout his life my father expressed his respect and love for the Italian people who not only saved his life but helped him through and out of captivity.

My father continued to write in his little brown memorandum book that he kept so close to him since the prison camp and described his journey home to England:

We set sail for Port Said, arriving 24th March, 1943. When we docked I was put straight into hospital in Alexandria. I had another dose of malaria. I'd had a dose in the camp but came through it. On 13th April, I was taken to R.N.R.H. I was glad I had been able to keep the diary, which documented the disaster from my eyes and I read the details to Admiral Cunningham. I did not need a diary to remember the event, it would stay in my mind forever.

In Alexandria my father was interviewed by Admiral Andrew Bevan Cunningham who had recently returned from the United States of America. Cunningham listened attentively then finally spoke to him in a much more informal manner, concluding, 'Well, John Walton. You have either one hell of a constitution, or you were bloody lucky. I think that both apply.' There is no formal documentation of this interview in the public domain to support the official Board of Inquiry report. It was to be 1959 before Captain Francis Cyril Flynn wrote to my father to include his account of the sinking of HMS *Neptune* in Admiralty records. This is detailed in the *Official History of the Second World War*, Volume III.

On 1 May 1943 my father was allowed to continue his long journey home and described the ships he boarded as he crossed the world:

ONE SURVIVOR

765 lost in the cruiser Neptune

OF 766 officers and men, only one—a rating who is now a prisoner of war—is named as a survivor of the cruiser Neptune, mined and sunk in the Mediterranean last December, in today's Admiralty casualty list.

He is Able Seaman John N. Walton.

Casualties, listed as missing, presumed killed, included 47 officers. Among them was Captain Rory O'Connor, who at 37 was the youngest captain in the service when he was promoted in 1936.

Missing ratings include 148 New Zealanders, 17 South Africans, two Australians and four Naafi staff.

The Neptune, sunk while trying to intercept reinforcements for Rommel, was a 7,175-ton ship of the Leander class.

Western Morning News. *Public reporting during the war years was classified and placed on the second or third page of national and local newspapers. This press cutting dated 1942 shows how low key the loss of life in disasters of war was portrayed in the media at that time. (It is generally accepted now that there was a crew of 765 of whom only one survived.)*

I go on board *Sphinx* sailing from Alexandria and arrived Port Tewfick on 2nd May. Joined HMT *Ile de France* and began the long journey home down the Suez Canal, Aden, then the Red Sea and on 7th May, crossed the equator. By the 16th May, we arrived in Durban, South Africa, then on to Cape Town and across to the Americas. On 3rd June, we sail into Rio de Janeiro, Brazil, what a beautiful sight.

We call in port for the night at Freetown, Sierra Leone on 12 June, then set off on my final journey to the United Kingdom arriving on 21 June 1943: 'Home and free!'

He had been away from his homeland for four years (July 1939 to June 1943). The return to his depot in Scotland was swift and convenient as he described, 'Sent straight to our various depots from Glasgow. I was lucky, Asdic Depot was now on the Clyde. They give me three weeks leave. I'm apprehensive about going home but excited to see my family and Irene again.'

ALL COMMUNICATIONS TO BE
ADDRESSED TO
"THE NAVAL SECRETARY."

PLEASE QUOTE FOLLOWING
IN REPLY:
N.A. 13/33/12

DOMINION OF NEW ZEALAND

NAVY OFFICE,

WELLINGTON C.1.

Dear Sir,   10th June, 1943.

Further to the telegram sent to you by the Minister of Defence
in July, 1942, informing you that it was presumed that the death of your son
had occurred on 19th December, 1941, I wish to convey to you the following
information which was received recently from the High Commissioner for New
Zealand, in London, concerning the loss of H.M.S."NEPTUNE": -

"Only one man is known to have survived the sinking of H.M.S."NEPTUNE"
on 19th December, 1941, and he is a prisoner of war in Italian hands.
According to information received from this rating, the ship struck a
mine during the night of 18th/19th December, 1941, and sank in about
ten minutes.   A small party, including the Commanding Officer, were
adrift on a raft for five days before Walton, who is the prisoner of
war and sole survivor, was picked up by an Italian warship.   Other
members of the party are stated to have died on the raft.   In view
of this report and the absence of news of further survivors, the
Admiralty sanctioned, on 5th June, 1942, the presumption of death of
all missing personnel. "

Yours faithfully,

Mr. A. H. Button,
18, Henry Street,
Avondale,
AUCKLAND.

Naval Secretary.

*Telegrams informing relatives that the crew of HMS Neptune was missing had been
issued on Boxing Day. It was much later in 1942/43 that letters such as this one gave
some news to grieving families of the events of 19 December 1941, and information
about the sole survivor*

CHAPTER 8

Home and Back Again

DURING THE SUMMER OF 1943 the Walton family received notification from the Royal Navy informing them that my father had been repatriated. There was no explanation of why or any information about the exchange. The details were not important; all the family cared about was the fact that he would be returning to them. There was great elation in the household and the news travelled quickly throughout the local area with everyone talking about him coming home.

In 1941 the Dodds family were spending a lot of their time in the Anderson air-raid shelter in Whitehall Road, Winlaton, as all families in the area did during the latter stages of the war. Irene's family decided to move when her father found a well-paid position in Blakeys Foundry. He was previously the Head Furnaceman at Pattersons Foundry in Blaydon-on-Tyne. They moved to Cromer Terrace into one of the rented houses provided by Blakey's. Many of these terrace streets in Armley still stand today as private housing.

When my father was declared missing at sea, Irene had been working with my father's brother, Leslie, at the Vickers Armstrong Factory standing alongside the River Tyne. In Leeds in 1942 she continued to work at the Avro Aircraft Factory in Yeadon. It was hard work and long hours with little time to think about anything. Everyone worked hard and played hard with little planning for the future. Most women of working age were called to replace the men who had left the factories to serve in the Army, Navy and Air Force in the war effort. The work the women performed was considered at the time to be men's work producing the materials and equipment required for war in the shipyards, steel foundries and factories.

The Walton family had no idea where my father was or exactly when he would be home but they did get the news to Irene that he was alive and could be coming back to England. She was so excited that she left her job in Leeds and caught the train to the Newcastle area so that she could be near her loved one's family. They all waited expectantly for more news. They had to wait until June 1943 before they heard from him that he was at last in England.

My father now sprang, full-grown, out of his war experiences. He somehow felt he was an outsider after four years away from England and his home and his spirit had never settled in Swalwell even before the war, when he spent much of his childhood and youth with his granddad in Rowlands Gill. He had a new baby sister that he had not seen, and he heard that his sweetheart Irene had moved to Leeds with her family. In his time in the water and as a prisoner of war his thoughts were always the same, of being reunited with his family and the hope of being able to rekindle the love he had shared with Irene. Now that his hopes and dreams of the last four years seemed possible his excitement was laced with fear: the fear of what was awaiting him and the dread of what questions would be asked.

He had endured experiences that no man would wish to endure and did not want to bring them back to the surface.

In the train station at Newcastle my father had mused over his return, he felt nervous, almost afraid of facing those people he had dreamed about for so long. The last emotion he could muster was shame and curiosity – how could he be the only survivor, a fact that was finally and officially confirmed by the Navy when he arrived in Alexandria? He did not want to try to explain how he survived or describe the death of the others around him, he couldn't. He knew that his father would want to show him off; it was his nature, but he didn't want any fuss, he was no hero. He decided to wait till darkness fell before returning to the house. He studied the new address of his family home on Whickham Bank written down on a piece of paper but decided to stay in Newcastle when he left the train. He would have a drink or two before catching the bus to Swalwell. When he finally stepped over the threshhold of his home it was past midnight. His Dad was sitting in the darkness in his old armchair, where he had been since returning home from the Club. It was a comforting and familiar sight and my father now felt he was home. It was not long before the house lit up with love and laughter.

My father's sister Isabelle remembers well Norman arriving home to Whickham Bank:

We must have heard he was in England I can't remember how, maybe he wrote to my Mam but we knew he was back in this country. I remember that Norman arrived home in the middle of the night. We heard my Dad shouting and everyone ran down the stairs, excited to see our brother again. The village had put out bunting and the British Legion had booked a party at the Stores Hall, but he arrived too late at night to celebrate and everyone had gone home.

Plans had been set in motion once the village knew my father was home and no one could stop them. His brother Leslie also remembers clearly that time in June:

Norman came home during the night. When I got home from work that morning, I was working nights, he was there. There was lots of laughter and noise in the house so I knew he was there, before I even opened the door. Mam said he was waiting upstairs for me. It was very emotional seeing him again and we just hugged for ages. But the next night he went straight to the Miners Dance Hall in Winlaton, hoping to see Irene. She was there and Norman said to me as soon as their eyes met they knew the love and feelings they had for each other were still alive. She came to our house almost every day for the parties that were arranged for him. During the next few days the three of us, our Dad, Norman and me, went to all the clubs and pubs to see everyone. The next week or two, people were arranging all kinds of welcome home parties for him. Swalwell Social Club put on a big party, friends and family from far and wide were informed, the reluctant hero had returned to them. My Dad was the proudest man in the world, going around with Norman at that time. He then had to go back to the Navy pretty soon. We all thought it was awful that he had been through what he went through and only came home for a few weeks.

Isabelle continues to describe another aspect to his return:

After he was home for a while there were these sacks of mail delivered to our house. All the letters must have been from relatives of those who had died on the ships, wanting to know any news about their deaths. It really upset Norman and he was in tears every day. He used to say to our Dad, 'What can I say to them? How can I say I'd seen him go down and could not help him. I watched him die and could not save him. I don't want to think about it all the time!' Once a lady came to the house and upset our Mam because she wanted to know why the eldest of nine had lived and her only child had died. It was a very upsetting time and finally our Dad said, 'No more!' It was making Norman ill trying to constantly explain what had happened and why he had survived. There was no official news coming out at the time and a secrecy ban was put on the information and I think Norman was not allowed to talk about it. I remember he did have a brown memo book he brought back but we were not allowed to look at it. Norman said it was not for us to read and hid it away, we never saw it again. To us children it seemed simple, Norman's ship was bombed, he fell in the water but another ship saved him then he came home. We did not realise the horror he had faced. My Dad made the decision to keep any further letters away from Norman for a while. It must have been a traumatic experience and he did not want to keep going over and over it. I think he just wanted to push it from his mind. I remember one particular parcel our Mam opened had a cheque for £2 inside and a lovely blue blanket with a letter explaining it was from the person's yacht. It was from Freshwater in the Isle of Wight. I remember our Mam saying that it would be wrong to profit from another mother's loss and she never cashed the cheque and kept it all those years.

The cheque Isabelle refers to is still safe in Norman's belongings. Lieutenant Gunnery Officer David C. Cunningham was with *Neptune* on the night of 18 December 1941 and my father mentioned a 'Commissioned Gunner' who was with him in the raft. His parents lived in Freshwater, Isle of Wight at the time and were friends of the O'Conor family.

It was quite by chance that David Cunningham's sister-in-law Mary and his two nieces Debbie and Fiona decided to take advantage of a unique opportunity to visit Tripoli and the site where *Neptune* went down over sixty years previously. I had also made the same decision to visit the site and it was on this trip where the Cunninghams and I, as well as many other relatives involved in the commemorative visit, struck up a special friendship. When I mentioned that this cheque still existed in my father's belongings they informed me that it was likely to be from David Cunningham's

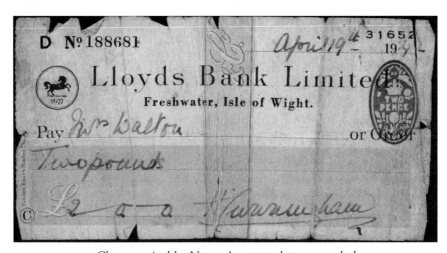

Cheque received by Norman's parents, but never cashed

parents, Hermione and T. C. Cunningham who, in 1942, lived at Shalfleet Manor. It was just one of the many coincidences that happened over the years since the tragedy that would link my family with the families of those men who perished with *Neptune*.

As my father's leave was drawing to an end his Dad was finding it unbearable that his son had to return to active service and in a desperate attempt to keep him home he had written a begging letter to The Right Honorable William Whiteley, MP, his local Member of Parliament. Unfortunately for the Walton family the following letter returned from the Admiralty explaining that my father had been repatriated by special arrangement between the Italian and British governments. Had he been sick or wounded and repatriated under the provisions of Article 68 of the Geneva Convention then he most certainly would have come within the provisions of Article 74, which prohibits the employment of repatriated persons on active military service. A negative response was received by my grandfather.

My father received a rail warrant and headed for London to attend an interview with Admiral Creasy. Again he was asked to report on the demise of Force K and his experiences in surviving the sinking of *Neptune*. He returned to active service with the Royal Navy after only three weeks of being able to rekindle relationships with his family and his sweetheart. Irene felt she had spent so little time with him after waiting so long. They were very much in love and decided that they would marry before he received drafts for overseas. On his return to the shore establishment at Portland he was drafted to ships that supported his re-training as a Sonar Detector. My father described in his diary his return to duty:

> I go back and pick up V & W destroyer HMS *Windsor*. An old destroyer built in 1918 and after a few weeks in training with *Windsor* I go on a week-end leave with Irene. My malaria recurs again and the doctor puts me to bed. I'm O.K. in a week and allowed to go back to the ship but I'm drafted to the Asdic Depot again as *Windsor* is in Dock.

There is a cryptic entry in his diary on the 25 July 1943, 'Had a very bad night, the nightmares will not go away.' It cannot be established exactly where he was on the night of 25 July, or whether it was another bad bout of malaria causing the nightmares but it is an unusual note, written by a man who had always played down the trauma and difficulties he faced in his life. The nightmares must have

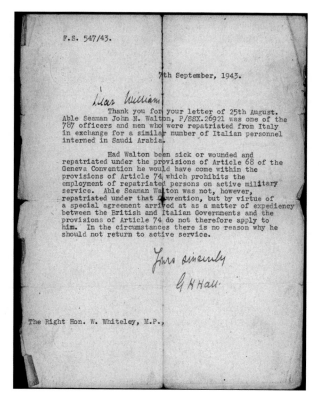

A letter from the Admiralty in reply to the request by Norman's Dad
to keep his son from returning to active service

been very disturbing for him to make such a special note in his diary
at that time.

Irene returned to Swalwell to arrange the wedding and again stayed
with my father's family. Isabelle describes what she remembers about
the wedding arrangements:

> Norman was away, but still in this country at first, and him and Irene had
> decided to get married. Mam had gone to Swalwell Vicarage to arrange for
> the banns to be read out in church. I remember because she had fallen again
> and hurt the same leg that had taken so long to mend at the end of 1942.
> Then Irene and Mam had to rearrange the date for November because
> Norman could not get home for some reason. In November 1943, Norman
> came on leave before being posted overseas and married Irene. The whole
> village of Swalwell seemed to be there. Irene's family came up from Leeds
> and her friends and family from Winlaton were there. The wedding was held
> in St Cuthbert's Church in Blaydon. Joe McBride was Norman's best friend

at that time and he was there with his wife and the maid of honour was Irene's friend Connie Blyth from Winlaton. My brother Leslie was Norman's best man and Seppy was a page boy. Irene bought him a lovely white satin suit to wear. All the families had been saving up stamps for the food and they had a car and an official photographer. It was one of the best weddings in St Cuthbert's for a long time and everyone was out in the streets waving. We had a great day.

Irene spent her married life alone and returned to live with her family in Leeds.

On 22 April 1944, Norman received orders to escort on Russian convoys, 'I'm drafted to HMS *Mermaid* a modified Black Swan class frigate built in 1943, acting as 1st Submarine Detector operator on Russian Convoys.' These frigates were designed for use as ocean-going escort frigates. They were larger and faster and were the last wartime escort sloops to be built. Ever since the Soviet Union was attacked by Germany in June 1941, Britain had been shipping munitions and war equipment into Russia through the Murmansk route and via Persia (Iran). It was able to do so because British industry had kept faith with Soviet Russia. Up to the end of May 1942, 11 per cent more aircraft were shipped than had been promised; even up to the end of June, 2,000 tanks had actually been shipped to Russia. The Merchant Navy continued to be escorted by the Royal Navy and had suffered comparatively few losses on the northern route and most of the supplies reached their destinations. The armed forces of the United Kingdom and indeed those of many other countries were dependent upon the British industrial workers some of whom my father had left behind in the foundries, factories and shipyards on the River Tyne.

My father described one incident when escorting such a convoy through the Murmansk route, 'Sub-detecting and picked up a submarine on my watch. (Watches were four hours on and four off). I request to stay with it, at my station for 24 hours before we finally drop depth charges and finish him off.' He was recommended for a good conduct medal and commended by his commanding officer. Unfortunately he then continued to describe another episode of his troublesome behaviour that jeopardised his commendations:

Put into port on the west coast of Scotland. We go ashore and have a good night ending with a brawl outside the dance-hall. All of us manage to get back on board but in the identification parade next morning I get picked out by the dance naval patrol. I get 30 days and serve 25 in Detention Quarters HMS *Spartiarte*. Back to HMS *Osprey* Asdic Depot.

It was the end of a chequered career on HMS *Mermaid*. The detention on 18 June 1944, is the only time forfeited that is recorded in his Certificate of Service. Whether other misdemeanours were ignored in the light of his war experiences or simply lost in the paperwork we will never know. He was deprived of his good conduct medal of which he was so proud. But this was restored again in January 1945 to be quickly followed by two further good conduct badges.

CHAPTER 9

Minesweepers

AUGUST 1944, 'I'M DRAFTED TO HMS *Rowena*, joining on 18th August, 1944. On going on board the Chief Coxwain is checking us in, I'm in charge of the Asdic Crew. I get up the gangway and I hear, "Not you Geordie!".' (British history records show that when King George travelled north to put down the Scottish Rebellion, he stopped at Newcastle where he was supplied with food and fodder. Before he departed the city numerous Newcastle men had joined his army and fought bravely in the subsequent struggle. From then on the men from the area became known as Geordie's men, meaning King George's men. Thus, all Geordies serving aboard His Majesty's ships were bonded by this heritage.)

My father continued to describe his reply to the Coxwain, 'We were A.B.s last time I saw him. All I say is, "I'm a married man now and the wife is expecting, I'm a good boy now".' This statement reflected my father's progress on the ship, being made up to Leading Seaman on 24 October 1944 then Petty Officer confirmed by 14 July 1945.

Minesweeping during World War II was essentially to make sure that the waters ahead of our following ships were clear of mines laid by Germany and Italy, either in advance of convoys, bigger warships or invasion fleets. Some such sweeping was done 'blind' as it was not known whether there were mines laid ahead. There were no minesweepers ahead of HMS *Neptune* to clear her path on 19 December 1941.

The other minesweeping was 'clearance sweeping' where it was known that minefields existed; a less demanding and dangerous job, but one that nevertheless required excellent seamanship skills and still resulted in ship casualties. The Algerine class fleet minesweeper was the biggest, both in numbers and tonnage, to be built for the Royal Navy, and HMS *Rowena* with the others was ordered to supplement the inadequate number of minesweeping vessels available at the outbreak of World War II. She was built by Lobnitz & Company in Renfrew and joined by my father on Clydeside in August 1944.

Another Able Seaman called George Laidlaw was already aboard having joined when the ship was being fitted out at the Lobnitz shipyard. He became a close shipmate of my father during their time aboard *Rowena* along with other mates including Bill Duke, Jock McLean, Fred Cross and the one New Zealander on board, named John Newton. It is from George Laidlaw and John Newton in particular, that many of the stories regarding my father's experiences during the war came to light. Over fifty years on they recalled their experiences and the stories shared between comrades in war serving on HMS *Rowena*. The Algerine class mineweepers quickly developed a reputation among those who served in them as being splendid seagoing ships, able to cope with bad weather, and with a number of comforts not previously found in vessels of a similar size. One particular benefit to the seaman rating was the upper mess-deck to use when the lower mess-decks were closed off during mine-sweeping. It was on these upper mess-decks that the seamen and their 'Killick' (the name for a Leading Seaman) spent many good times talking about home and the war.

Minesweeping was described as often complicated but exciting work where the seamen frequently worked through the night to replace or rectify damage to the sweep-gear and other equipment caused during the previous day's minesweeping. In addition to their minesweeping role they were fitted with the weapons and equipment necessary (radar and asdic) to act as anti-submarine escorts and this is where my father came into his own. He was by now highly skilled in asdic operation and had the advantage of speaking pretty fluent Italian having the ability to interpret for the officers and the crew during their time sweeping the coast of Italy. He often described the first Captain of HMS *Rowena*, Lieutenant-Commander George C. Hocart, RNA, as one of the best he ever served under. They formed a special relationship, which was rekindled in 1962 when my father, mother and I visited George Hocart after his retirement. We spent some time with him as guests at his home on Guernsey in the Channel Islands. Both men had a love for sport and my father had represented the ship many times during his service in the Mediterranean on the football team, in boxing bouts and at water polo.

The minesweeper HMS *Rowena* was operating off Portland until 12 October 1944, when my father received orders to sail for Malta minesweeping in the Mediterranean, and wrote:

We were sent out to the Mediterranean again and by the time we get out there I am rated Able Leading Seaman, 24th October, 1944. I now have a son. We call him John after Dad and myself. Irene tells me he is beautiful with blue eyes and blond hair. I really get stuck in now and pass for Petty Officer, confirmed 14th July, 1945.

HMS *Rowena*, together with her sister ships, *Regulus*, *Thisbe*, *Mary Rose*, *Moon*, *Providence*, *Seabear* and *Coquette* formed the 8th Minesweeper Flotilla. This was the fourth Algerine flotilla to spend time sweeping off Malta, which had become quite a training ground because of the many minefields which surrounded the island, and which now required clearing to make the approaches once again safe for shipping.

Early in December the flotilla were ordered to Taranto, southern Italy, where they arrived on 11 December and commenced sweeping three days later. On the first day thirty-six mines were accounted for. These were the first mines the flotilla had swept and there was considerable jubilation aboard the ships. The flotilla continued sweeping for the next week or so during which time a further nine mines were swept. It was a poignant time for my father, who only two years previously in December 1941, had fallen foul to mines not too far from this area. It felt good to scour these seas of the mines he had previously aimed to detect and avoid and that had eventually claimed the lives of so many of his shipmates.

On 4 January 1945, the flotilla was ordered to Corfu to clear a channel for vessels to enter the harbour to bring much-needed relief to the local population. The remaining four of the flotilla, HMS *Regulus*, *Thisbe*, *Rowena* and *Mary Rose* arrived the next day and immediately commenced sweeping. The area to be swept was a channel one mile wide between Paxos and Antipaxos islands, and leading into Corfu harbour. On arriving in the area the flotilla assumed formation 'K', (double Oropesa sweep) in order to give as wide a clearance as possible, although this meant that several of the ships would be in non-swept water. In all more than thirty mines were accounted for in this sweep which took the flotilla into Corfu harbour. Although several lost part of their sweep gear, *Mary Rose* detonating a mine by her sweep wire which had parted, and *Thisbe* and *Rowena* losing wire when detonating mines, all managed to reach harbour safely. It was on his return to the seas around the Greek islands that my father was once again involved in a 'dipping'. On 12

January, the flotilla was back in action. Several laps had been swept and about twenty mines accounted for when at 13.10 *Regulus*, the leading ship, hit a mine with her propellers. There was an enormous explosion and *Regulus* quickly came to a stop, settling at the stern and with a pronounced list to port. Able Seaman George Laidlaw, living in Motherwell, Scotland in 2007 and aged eighty-four years, described what happened:

> Norman, I and the others from the mess-deck went on board from *Rowena* hoping to save *Regulus* but in spite of shoring up the bulkheads and deck-head, it was to no avail and *Regulus* was sinking lower in the water by the stern and starboard quarter. We had to jump into the sea and swim toward our whaler and were taken on board. We made our way back to *Rowena* who also took transfers of survivors from the *Regulus* and steamed off to Malta the next day.

Although there were several injuries, there was amazingly only one fatality, the shipwright who had been working down in the tiller flat.

By 12 March 1945, the 8th Minesweeping Flotilla, with *Coquette* now as leader, were at full strength at Taranto, albeit only seven: *Providence, Rowena, Thisbe, Mary Rose, Moon* and *Seabear*. A check-sweep in the Gulf of Taranto was completed on 22 March and the next day they departed for Malta. The flotilla was check-sweeping around Malta and this continued on most days until 24 April 1945. My father had made a number of close friends whilst on the *Rowena* who remained mates on and off shore. Antics ashore tend to rise to the surface when matelots talk about their war service and the interviews with George Laidlaw and John Newton were no different. Both men described incidents in an area on the island of Malta they called 'the gut', often frequented by sailors in port:

> I remember one incident ashore in Malta when Norman, Bill Duke and Jock Mclean warded off several Maltese police who had attempted to arrest them down 'the gut'. The Maltese police came off worse in the episode and had to be transported home. The police came on board *Rowena* hoping to make an issue of the fight, but Captain Hocart quickly disposed of the whole issue by backing up Norman's side of the story.

John Newton describes another incident with the Redcaps (Military Police) who were not popular with the sailors:

> Redcaps stopped us as we walked down 'the gut' with our caps back on our heads, worse for wear from the booze. 'Geordie', as we all called Norman,

gave a rude reply and the Redcaps were quick to grab hold of him. 'Geordie' was a character, he pleads to the Redcap to let go of his arms they are hurting him, then throws a punch, whereupon we all go in and finish them off. Our hats then only had HMS on the front and not the name of the ship.

John Newton was the only New Zealander on board HMS *Rowena*. He was drafted from HMS *Colossus* in January 1945, in Malta, and my father was 'Killick' of his mess. John described when the flotilla arrived in Naples on 20 April and left port for Leghorn:

> We had only been in the Leghorn area for a short time before we witnessed an E-boat attack. There was some very colourful language on the *Rowena* as shore-based guns started blasting at the flotilla coming into port. The Italian E-boats, from their base at La Spezia, were driven off by the guns of the army on shore firing over the flotilla, fortunately without damage or casualties among the minesweepers. Asdics blip when U-boats are near and they knew they were attacking. The attack was described as 'more spectacular than successful.'

It was on one of their night watches, when all was quiet that John Newton recalled my father telling the story of surviving the sinking of *Neptune*. It was a story that was not mentioned again until fifty years later in the Nelson Yacht Club, South Island, New Zealand. It was at this time that commemoration services for the loss of HMS *Neptune* were being organised all across New Zealand by the Ex-Naval Men's Associations. John Newton was adamant that he had met a survivor from the *Neptune* during his service on HMS *Rowena* in 1944/45 and told members of the Associations that he had sailed with my father until he left the ship in Singapore in October 1945. HMS *Atheling* picked up approximately 200 New Zealand Naval men and took them home. They arrived on 24 December into Wellington, New Zealand. It was John Newton's dogged determination to bring his long-lost friend to New Zealand that resulted in my father and mother touring the Ex-Naval Men's Associations in 1990/91. They were able to meet many of the relatives of the 150 New Zealand seamen lost with *Neptune*, who had never until that time received a full explanation of what had happened to their loved ones.

Following the E-boat attack on *Rowena* in April 1945 there were severe gales hampering the sweeping programme. Whilst laying in port in Leghorn many sailors hitched lifts to Pisa, Florence and Rome. My father wrote that he stood in the square where the war-torn and disillusioned Italian people strung up their leader

Mussolini. He also made his first visit to the opera and was so excited by the spectacle he became a fan. My parents collected many long-playing records over the years of Caruso and Gigli. My father had developed a love of classical music sung in Italian that he attributed to this first visit to the opera that had made such an indelible impression on him.

VE Day on 8 May was a cause for great celebrations in Leghorn which my father and his comrades took advantage of. By 12 May the flotilla had dispersed for boiler-clean and refit. *Rowena* docked into the port of Naples and it was at this time that members of the crew were offered a short respite period on the beautiful island of Ischia. Minesweeping continued in Leghorn throughout June, with fifty-one mines being accounted for. By 25 June the area was declared clear and the flotilla left Leghorn. The flotilla was sweeping off Malta through to 14 August during which time thirty mines were accounted for. The next day was VJ Day and the sailors in port were allowed to relax and join in the celebrations. The ships were decorated and floodlit at night in their berths in Silema Creek.

Rowena had completed her refit by 18 August. The celebrations over, the flotilla received orders to prepare to leave the Mediterranean and set sail for the Far East where they were to be attached to the British Pacific Fleet. They then set sail for China, calling at Alexandria again, through the Suez Canal, Red Sea and on to Burma. My father sent my mother Irene regular letters always asking about his son and how he was growing; his first birthday was coming up in October 1945 and my father was hoping he could be there to celebrate with him.

The ships arrived in Singapore in the aftermath of war. Lieutenant Commander John Lamb, DSC RN, Captain of HMS *Moon* which was amongst the first naval vessels of the flotilla to arrive at Singapore described the scene vividly:

> Entering the port there was little visible damage to the city itself, but the port was in a very bad state. There were a number of Japanese ships lying sunk in the harbour, including a floating dock with a Japanese cruiser still in it. We were all greatly impressed by the bearing of the Commonwealth prisoners of war who were being released at the time. I was able to call on Bishop Wilson, whom I had known well since 1937, first as Dean of Hong Kong and then in 1941 as Bishop of Singapore. Before the war he had been a seemingly urbane, portly, Prince of the Church. I was staggered by his appearance now;

his jungle-green battle-dress was hanging round his tall, emaciated frame, and, with a remarkable light in his eyes, he looked like an Apostle of old.

My father described his arrival in the Far East, 'Been sweeping around Burma then onto Singapore. Manage to get my "dhobi" (cleaned clothes) from the locals on shore, as well as other services. We hear they've dropped a bomb on Nagasaki.' After a short period of rest at Singapore, the flotilla sailed for Hong Kong, arriving there on 19 October 1945. His mate, George Laidlaw, remembered the journey well:

> When we were making our way north from Singapore to Hong Kong one of our seamen developed appendicitis. We found a little horseshoe bay with palm trees, where we anchored. The operation was carried out successfully on board. It was an idyllic spot, where we basked in the sun and the sea, albeit for a short while. It was a spot never to be forgotten by many of us, in light of the circumstances of that time.

Shortly after their arrival they were put to work to sweep the Allied ground mines (magnetic and acoustic) and the Japanese moored mines (contact) in the approaches to the harbour.

As soon as the channel was clear the flotilla moved on to the Chinese port of Amoy. Working with a number of American minesweeping flotillas the *Rowena* helped to clear a large area stretching from the mainland to Formosa, enabling this to be declared safe for shipping. George Laidlaw described their duties:

> The Japanese mines that we were sent to sweep at Amoy were of an unusual, enormous size and were moored with massive chains. These chains effectively cut our sweep-wires and didn't allow us, as normal, to cut-release the giant mine float. We circumvented this problem by attaching explosive cutters to our sweep-wires, thus by explosion, parting the mine chain and surfacing the mines which we popped off.

A dangerous occupation where the men stood on deck with rifles, aiming at the mines and taking shots to explode them before they hit the ship. My father and his old shipmates recalled their experiences so simply without emotion, when in fact the events were traumatic in many cases and the work dangerous and complicated. He always tended to highlight the friendship and the humour in his experiences and the great admiration he had for all the men around him during the war years. He rarely mentioned any trauma, hardship or danger. Maybe those are the memories that he buried deep in his soul.

It was soon after leaving Amoy that the 8th Minesweeping Flotilla turned its attention to the minefields in Bias Bay, Hong Kong, the renowned pirates' lair. Leading Telegraphist Geoff Race of HMS *Moon* described the scene:

> During the time in Bias Bay it was necessary to be armed when on duty watch when we were anchored at night. The pirates were notorious and would have had no hesitation in slitting our throats and stealing all they could carry if they had been allowed to board us. On one occasion they tried it but the alert Quartermaster spotted them and raised the alarm. When we were with the Americans we hit the edge of a typhoon, which was a really terrifying experience, with waves sixty feet high. Once when we were sweeping, a big junk sailed across the path of the flotilla and despite being warned over the loud hailer to get clear they took no notice. The junk ploughed on and even fired a cannonball at HMS *Moon*. A few minutes later she hit a mine and along with her crew completely disappeared.

George Laidlaw described another incident involving the pirates:

> When we were sweeping at Bias Bay we were aware of the presence of Chinese pirates near to our anchorage. The pirates overpowered the ferry-boat as it left shore, robbed the passengers and turfed them off the ferry-boat. All this was done under the eyes and guns of the Allied ships lying in Hong Kong harbour. Some nerve!

The operation to clear Bias Bay was completed just in time to allow the flotilla to spend their first peacetime Christmas in harbour. An extra special event for my father who had been fighting for survival during the festive seasons over the past four years. He wrote his last entry in his diary notes from HMS *Rowena*, 'We went on sweeping the China coast from Hong Kong up to Island of Amoy. At last I spend a Christmas in peacetime, all of a sudden the war is over. We can go home!'

He had kept up his boxing throughout the war and although still amateur status he fought professionally under various pseudonyms in Italy and China in matches organised by the American occupation forces. He loved the Navy and his sport:

> I want to re-engage to qualify for pension at 22 years but I have a son nearly 2 years old I haven't seen. The wife's only had me home a few weeks of our married life. I decide to give in to her wishes and take my leave from the Royal Navy. I regretfully leave the *Rowena*, for release from the Royal Navy, in December, 1945.

By the end of January 1946, all the ships except HMS *Mary Rose* had left Hong Kong and the flotilla, with which my father had spent such exciting times, arrived back at Malta. Since leaving Malta for the Far East on 25 August the flotilla had steamed a total of 19,895 miles. My father, meanwhile, was drafted to the parent ship whilst in Hong Kong for his passage home. He described the journey home:

> HMS *Challenger*, a survey vessel, comes into harbour on her way back to England. I reckon I'll go the short route home; I volunteer to go on her as Chief Bosun's Mate, a big mistake. Instead of going straight home, we go to do a survey of the Borneo Rivers. I end up with a bout of Yellow Fever and we don't get home till 16th June 1946.

While aboard HMS *Challenger*, my father became friends with Edward 'Geordie' Gallagher, who was also from Newcastle. Gallagher claimed that when they returned my father took him into his mess. In the mess was a bag of letters waiting. They were letters from hundreds of people asking if it was possible that their sons, husbands, uncles, nephews, had any chance to survive the *Neptune* tragedy. All the letter envelopes were addressed to: 'Petty Officer Walton, Only Known Survivor HMS *Neptune*.'

CHAPTER 10

In for a Penny . . .

THE YEAR 1946 BROUGHT WITH IT the hope that there would be no more sleepless nights and an end to living with the daily fear of injury or death. The Second World War was finally at an end and families the length and breadth of Great Britain were celebrating and waiting anxiously for their loved ones to return to them but there were many who mourned the loss of their menfolk. The towns and villages joined in celebration, as it was a time to look to the future with hope.

After a couple of weeks in his barracks in Portsmouth, my father finally took his leave of the Royal Navy in June 1946. He began the journey north back to his wife, with whom he had spent so little time and the son he had not yet seen. My mother Irene had moved down to Leeds again to her family after my father left England to serve in the Mediterranean and later the Far East. She wanted to be with her mother when her son was born. My father could not wait to see them both and when the train arrived in Leeds railway station Irene was standing there with a beautiful blond-haired, blue-eyed, healthy-looking boy by her side: John was nearly two years old. They embraced hard then noticed John looking at them strangely, wondering what his Mammy was doing hugging this man who he did not recognise. My father picked him up and introduced himself to his son who immediately looked at his Mammy for reassurance. As they huddled together tightly a flood of emotions which the couple had kept under wraps for so long, was now released. The new family unit began to plan their future. My mother had been working at a munitions factory near Leeds while her mother had helped look after John, so she had some money saved. There was very little housing available to buy even if they could have afforded it. Her savings and my father's small gratuity would not get them far. Most of the housing available to young married couples was rented accommodation. My parents hankered to go back to their roots and decided to make a life back in north-east England. My father described the move back to Swalwell:

What do I do now in 'civvy street' (a term for civilian life). I've never worked long enough for anyone and have no trade. I've a wife and child to look after and bills to pay. We move back up to the North East, to where we come from. I find a job doing piecework where you get paid for what you make. I'm doing all right 'till the Union tells me I can only do so many hours, I tell the management I need the money but the Unions seem to rule the factories now.

I go back to the Foundry where I started at 14. They take me on but I'm not making enough money to keep my family the way I want to.

His words reflect a sign of the times for many men who returned from the war. Most of the essential work for the war effort had been taken over by the women, who worked in the factories and foundries in the area right through the war years. Many of the men returning to work were put on 'piecework' with restricted hours to enable as many men as possible to gain employment. Some men returning from the war felt lost and unskilled, they described feelings that they had no place in the society to which they now returned and had lost their identity. Many of the men returning from the war came home to a wife they hardly knew who, through necessity, had been living with their families until their new husbands returned, some wounded, some did not return at all. Housing, even rented property, was at a premium. My parents were living with the Walton family, who were delighted to have my father home but were, even in their new house on Whickham Bank, pretty crowded in 1946 with Isabelle, Tommy, Dorothy, Lillian, Seppy and Ethel still at home. The three older boys, my father, Leslie and Willy had all made a new life for themselves and married.

The green fields that rolled across the Whickham area at the time had proved an ideal site for the location of an Army training camp. It was here that they trained the many new army recruits before being sent into action during the latter years of the war. By the middle of 1946 the Army had left the camp and it stood derelict. My father's eldest sister Isabelle described when my parents returned to Whickham Bank in the summer of 1946:

We heard that squatters were making claims on the huts at Whickham Camp so my younger brother Tommy and I went up and chalked the name 'Walton' on one of the huts, later we went back and painted it on. They were just big wooden huts that the Army had left but eventually the council took them over and put drainage in with plumbing for sinks and toilets in each of the huts. When Irene and Norman arrived at our house we were all celebrating Norman's return and Tommy and I were so proud we could not wait to tell them about the hut. We took them up to show them and I think they decided on another one in a better position but they were really pleased. We all worked to make some curtains and rugs. We had a wooden mat-making frame and prog. Irene bought the woven hessian backing that would be stretched tightly across the rectangular wooden frame. In those days many families had these mat-making frames and the neighbours would come round with their own progger, have a cup of tea and join in the mat-making while they chatted. We used clippings, old clothes and bits of material that people in the street had finished with. We cut them into strips that were woven into the hessian to make mats for the floors. Norman managed to get a wood-burning stove and fixed it in the middle of the room with the chimney going out of the roof. Irene sectioned off areas of the hut with the curtains to make a kitchen living area and a bedroom. It was really warm and cosy.

My parents and John were finally together in a home of their own. My father fitted a bath into the hut to replace the tin bath they used to bring in at night and my mother created a beautiful nursery area for her growing little boy, from the gifts and 'hand-me-downs' she kindly received from friends and family. John had the run of the open fields.

The Camp was a happy place filled with young families who helped each other get by and joined together in celebrating the beginning of a new era of peace and hope. The views from the Camp were magnificent, looking across the rolling hills and wooded valleys to Winlaton in the east and further towards Hexham and the north. The walk from Whickham Camp south was all downhill to Swalwell and Blaydon, and the views down the valley stretched across the River Tyne to Newcastle and beyond. The site was quite idyllic and so seemed life for my parents as they spent the next few months getting to know each other as a family, sharing stories of their time apart and rekindling their undoubted love for each other. Planning their future was exciting but my father realised he needed to find a way to make more money to support his family. My mother had given up her job when they moved back to the north-east and now spent her time home-making and looking after their son. During the first few months at the Camp she had witnessed first-hand my father suffering from the guilt, the malaria attacks and the nightmares but as the weeks went by he grew stronger and he again turned his attention to sport, an area in which he had always excelled.

My father decided to play football again and gained a place in a team playing in the local district league but he was paid expenses only. He decided to return to the local gym to do some fitness training and sparing with the local lads. His brother Tommy had recently left school and followed his brother to the gym. He idolised him and his sisters told how he stuck with him like glue when he returned from the war. My father always maintained that Tommy was the more technical and superior fighter. According to my father he could have gone on to be a great fighter but he married and had a child, deciding not to continue with the sport. Tommy was very happy with his wife Dorothy and his lovely daughter Linda, with no ambition to overtake his brother in the boxing arena.

My grandfather talked to my father about the possibility of making some money out of the boxing game as he had a few contacts. A local boxing manager called Billy Charlton had contacted my grandfather to ask if he might be interested in turning professional, so my father went to see him. Billy Charlton was from Gateshead where he ran a popular gym frequented by a number of local fighters including my father and his friend Billy Farrell from Whickham, who fought in the Featherweight Division with Billy Charlton. My father fought in the Middleweight Division. Billy Charlton also ran a gym in Blaydon and was well established in the boxing circles by 1947. My father signed up with Billy Charlton and began training with his gym for contests in the Middleweight Division.

It was in 2005 when my father died and his obituary was posted in the *Newcastle Chronicle* that many of his boxing associates from the 1940s/50s contacted me. Billy Charlton became President of the Tyneside & District Ex-Boxers Association and remembered my father well, sadly he passed away not long after my father but had lived to the ripe old age of ninety years. Maxie Walsh, Chairman of the Association and Malcolm Dinning, Vice-President and Treasurer kindly published my father's obituary in the July 2005 edition of *Ringwise*, which has a wide distribution network prompting many fans of 'Patsy Dodds' to write to me with fond memories of my father. It was with the help and support of boxing associates, particularly of Malcolm Dinning that I was able to gain photographs, posters and records that helped in the writing of this book. Malcolm Dinning, now sixty-nine years of age, started the Tyneside and District Ex-Boxers Association with Billy Charlton in 1970 and my father came up from his home in Leeds to visit with ex-boxing friends Joe Thompson and Billy Farrell in the 1970s.

In 1947 he was just starting out on his boxing career and described his entry onto the professional circuit:

> I turn professional and register with the British Boxing Board of Control under the fighting name of 'Patsy Dodds', Patsy after my Dad and Dodds after my father-in-law and with Billy Charlton as my Manager soon the money starts to get better. I win a few, lose a few but getting plenty of fights, not many top of the bill yet. I still work my job in the foundry during the day and train after work. Meet my first big contender Bert Ingram. We put on a show at New St. James Hall in Newcastle on September 5, 1946. It's a hard fight of eight rounds but we manage to draw.

The promoter at New St James Hall in Newcastle was Fred Charlton who went on to promote a number of championship fights. The Charlton families were well known for sport in the area, as were many large families in the north-east at that time. My father knew most of the lads including Jackie and Bobby Charlton who lived in Ashington and went on to play professional football for England. His friendship with Jack Charlton continued into later life when they would attend sporting functions along with other sporting celebrities of the time.

Three fights came in succession with Bert Ingram. They fought again in New St James Hall on 14 November, where my father was knocked out in Round 3 of a six-round bout, then they put on a contest in Darlington at the Baths Hall but the referee stopped the fight in Round 4 of an eight-rounder. They had put on a great show with Bert winning the day. The two fighters became good friends and my father often talked about Bert Ingram in later life and the annoying fact that he never managed to put him down. When my parents moved to Leeds in 1960 Bert came to visit my father and they attended the Leeds Ex-Boxers Association where the President was Johnny Durkin, spending many happy hours talking about their boxing days. Bert died in the same year as my father. These fighters all worked hard and played hard but had good long lives. My father would always say that his priority in the boxing ring was to stay safe and please the paying crowd. He was of the opinion that he had not been blessed with a natural ability to fight and wished he had a greater talent rather than sheer guts and determination.

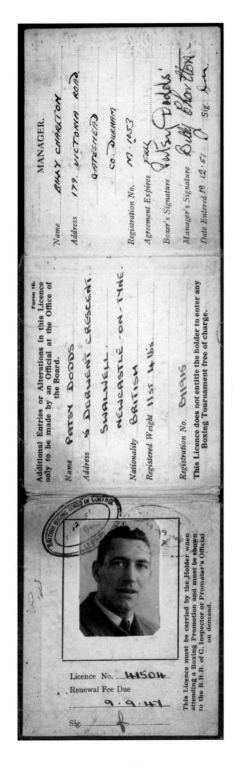

My father's Professional Boxing Licence issued by the British Boxing Board of Control under his fighting name 'Patsy Dodds'. He fought professionally in the Middleweight Division in the 1940s and 1950s

My father saw the boxing booths as a good way to earn extra money for his family and he joined the booths whenever he could, they were a good training ground as he worked his way up the professional ladder. My father became what was called a 'journeyman'. He travelled the country following boxing tournaments to put himself forward as a substitute fighter. This meant that if a fighter 'cried off' a fight for any reason the promoter would offer my father the fight for an agreed purse. Of course, these fights were not recorded. According to boxing fans that knew my father he was known for putting on a good show and was therefore very successful as a 'journeyman' with over a hundred show fights and exhibitions to his name. As well as developing his professional boxing career, he was now working full steam to keep his family happy and bring home the pennies. The summer of 1946 had been very nearly perfect for my parents who were now preparing excitedly for their first Christmas together. My mother was busy with the usual Christmas preparations, winter clothes shopping and looking for a special present for their son.

By the end of November the winter began to take a grip and my brother John was taken ill. He had been such a strong and healthy boy with never a sign of illness since he was born so my mother was naturally worried when John developed a temperature and had difficulty breathing. She rang from a telephone box for the local doctor to visit but he only advised her to keep him cool, give him some aspirin and Vick's rub could be good if he was chesty. As a new mother she did as the doctor advised. Isabelle describes the events when she visited John in November 1946:

> My Mam and me went up to see Irene at the Camp, because she was so worried about John. I remember he was in his cot and we took him some sweets but he just passed them back to us. John was always sharing his sweets with the other children, he was such a kind little boy. He looked really poorly and couldn't be bothered with the sweets. When Norman came home from work he went straight down to the doctor to tell him to come but the doctor said he was too busy and would come in the morning. Irene and Norman sat up all night with John who seemed to be getting worse, when eventually the doctor came and he sent straight for an ambulance. When the ambulance finally arrived they took John to the hospital in Newcastle. In those days you were only allowed to visit hospitals at visiting times so Irene and Norman had to stay at home and wait.

Leslie also heard that John was poorly and he and his wife Ethel walked to the Camp to see John and he describes what happened the day they took John to hospital:

I went with my wife Ethel and Norman's friend Joe McBride and his wife with Irene and Norman down to Blaydon to the telephone box. John was in the hospital for diphtheria and they wanted to telephone to see how he was, they couldn't wait till visiting time. They used the telephone box in the square to ring the hospital and check on John. They came out of the telephone box and we knew something was wrong, the hospital had told them he was dead. They were devastated. We took them straight to the hospital and they stayed with John. It was very emotional and one of the most horrible days I have ever experienced. When we eventually left it was very distressful as we went back to the Camp hut and all John's toys were all over the house. Irene and Norman were just clinging on to each other.

John was just over two years old when he died and my father had only been with him a few months. It was a day never to be forgotten by my parents. They ploughed through the funeral at St Cuthbert's Church in Blaydon, where they had only four years previously spoken their marriage vows. They spent the next few weeks in a daze trying to comfort each other for their loss. They were never able to describe the feelings they had at that time; no words could describe them. My father asked the same question many times over the years, 'Why did He take my son, when He had the chance to take me?'

How he survived was a question my father was never able to answer but in 2005, nearly sixty years later and just before he passed away, he wrote the following dedication in *Mediterranean Minefield* by Adrian St Clair in tribute to those who perished with Force K, 'Many times I have asked myself "why me?" There is no answer, only the realisation that we all survive in the hearts and memories of those left behind.'

The memory of my brother John remained in the hearts of my parents till their passing away. They struggled on over the Christmas period comforting each other as best they could. My mother spent most of her days at her son's graveside in Blaydon cemetery; she found her loss very difficult to bear and excluded my father from her insular world of sorrow. My father explained many times how again he felt so helpless. Unable to make things better for his wife he ploughed his energies and anger into boxing, undertaking more and more fights with the boxing booths and travelling to all the boxing tournaments to gain more fights.

He was emotionally unfit but returned to the professional ring on 24 April 1947, in a contest with Jack Richie from Wallsend. The contest was again at New St James Hall in Newcastle but my father lost an eight-rounder on points. On 5 June he fought George Casson from North Shields at New St James Hall but was knocked out in the first round of a six-round contest. His heart was not in the game and he knew his head was not in the right place to win contests. The fight was George Casson's professional debut and he went on to win the vacant Northern Area Middleweight title on 20 February 1950. He won the title on points against my father's greatest rival Bert Ingram. George relinquished the title on his retirement eight months later on 30 October 1950. My father did not go into the professional ring again that year.

My father had 146 fights in all with the main bulk of his shows being in the boxing booths and exhibition fights, which in the 1940s and 1950s could earn a fighter some good training opportunities and decent money. He described the reaction of his wife when he fought on the boxing booths:

> Irene would call the boxing booths blood money. She would take one look at my face, if I'd had some hard fights, then throw the money back at me saying 'I won't touch blood money,' and she didn't for a long time. We had opened a joint post office account when I came home in '46 and I would stick the money in there. It was only when I returned to the Navy in 1952 and we had moved into a new house on Hazel Road that I noticed she would draw money out to buy things for the home.

Boxing booths had been a popular training ground for young boxers in the 1920s and 1930s and my granddad had some experience of these when he would join with the boxing shows on the local fairgrounds as they travelled in the area. One champion boxer that my father said he admired was a famous Scottish fighter called Benny Lynch, 'The Kid from the Gorbals', who emerged from the boxing shows and became the World Flyweight Champion in 1937. Jimmy Wilde in his autobiography *Fighting was my Business*, wrote, 'Little known, hard working, certainly not wealthy, it is Jack and his fellow booth owners who prepare the champions of the boxing world. I have always believed the booths get too little attention and that many world beaters in the making never got more than a pound a fight.'

By 1947 there was a decline of the boxing shows on the fairground, which was linked to the decision by the Boxing Board of Control to limit and partially restrict the use of licensed boxers in the booths. The Boxing Board of Control made their initial decision in January 1947 where they announced that the boxing booth would be out of bounds to all licensed members of the Board. This ruling meant that licensed boxers were now restricted in their use of the booth as a training ground. This was despite the fact that Randolph Turpin, a former booth fighter who appeared on the front of the Hickman and Parkin family shows, won the Middleweight Championship of the World in 1951 by beating Sugar Ray Robinson. Eric Bell of Gateshead who was also a Royal Navy champion describes how he fought my father in an exhibition bout, 'I fought your Dad as a warm-up for the top of the bill between Randolph Turpin and Dave Sands of Australia. We put on a good show for them.'

My father realised there was still money to be made and experience to be gained with the booths and as a 'journeyman'. He could also take on challengers at the local fairs for the three-round challenges. He did take on a number of fights in the booths travelling around the Tyneside area and especially when the fairground boxing shows visited Newcastle Town Moor, a vast fairground event held just outside Newcastle city centre. One of the many misconceptions about the boxing shows was that they were often the unsavoury side of the fight game but Michael Herbert in his biography of Len Johnson gives greater credit to the fairground booth and writes, 'A boxer had to be fit, strong and healthy to make a living on the booth . . . It offered an unrivalled opportunity to acquire good experience in a short space of time and to develop his skills.'

My father recalled how lads in the crowd would particularly enjoy getting in the ring with local fighters and trying their luck. When a fight was especially entertaining, some men from the audience would throw money into the ring. It could be a high earner, although risky and exhausting. Certainly not the kind of boxing that would adhere to the health and safety standards of today.

During the fairground boxing booths' illustrious history, fighters such as Jem Mace, 'Kid' Furness, Jimmy Wilde, Freddie Mills and Tommy Farr all fought, exhibited on or ran boxing shows. Indeed the greatest champion and showman of them all, Muhammed Ali, displayed his skills for charity on the front of Ron Taylor's Boxing

Emporium at the Amusement Park in South Shields on Saturday 16 July 1977. My father was an avid fan of Muhammed Ali admiring his skill and fancy footwork in the ring.

Alf and Billy Stewart travelled a boxing show and would run the show on Newcastle Town Moor together, as Polly Stewart explains:

> My uncle Billy Stewart and my father would work together and they would do Newcastle together. The family boxing shows travelled the length and breadth of the country and appeared at all of the major fairs, doing what they used to call the Cumberland Run, the West Country Regattas, Newcastle Town Moor, Durham Miners Gala, Cambridge Midsummer Fair and nearly every premier fair in the country during the 1940s and 50s.

Alf Stewart was involved in promoting fights in the London area where as well as staging contests between George Cook and John Anderson, he also promoted Eddie Phillips, a fighter with whom my father topped the bill at Portobello Town Hall. My father described to me his most memorable top of the bill performance:

> It was a Dick Hamilton Promotions Contest fighting at Portobello Town Hall in Scotland on 8 April 1952. I was top of the bill with Eddie Phillips from Edinburgh. We both weighed in over eleven stone and the fight went the full eight rounds. Even though I lost on points it certainly pleased the customers as we both gave our best on that night.

Earlier in my father's boxing career he picked up extra cash fighting in the exhibition bouts with the Stewart's Boxing Show when it visited Newcastle Town Moor. Local fighters were called in initially to bring in the punters. It would be about one shilling to enter the brightly coloured frontage of the boxing shows. The fighters would be supplied either by the local manager or through an advertisement. The promoter would bring a number of the local fighters to the booths to perform exhibition bouts out front and attract the crowds and my father fought in many unrecorded exhibition bouts as a 'journeyman boxer'.

My parents continued to struggle on into another New Year and were gifted with a daughter, me, born on 24 May 1948, they called me Norma after my father but there were too many memories of John in the home they had so lovingly made at Whickham Camp. They moved to rented accommodation in Scotswood Road, across the river, but did not settle. Then eventually they were offered a rented house in Blaydon-Haughs back on the other side of the river.

45 Norma Walton born 24 May 1948 and named after her father Norman, attending Blaydon Infant and Junior School on Blaydon Bank.

46 Norma with her husband John Hudson at their wedding.

47a Glendennings Containers Limited retirement party for Norman Walton, Works Director in 1985. Left to right is Mick Spivey (a competitor), Barry Glendenning (Director), his son Ian Glendenning and Norman.

47b 'The Boys at Christmas'
Back row: John Hudson, Tony Ruane, Simon Glendenning; front row: Norman with his grandson Michael Hudson and Barry Glendenning with Tony's son James Ruane.

48 Norma with her husband John, children Nicola and Michael on her right and step-son Paul on her left in 2001.

49 Norman supporting his granddaughter Nicola Jane on her wedding day in August 1998.

50 Norman practising his swing at Fulneck Golf Club, a member for twenty years representing the Club as President from 1979–81 and Captain in 1984.

51 Norman's great-grandchildren Alice and Thomas, pictured on holiday in Cyprus in 2007.

52 Fiftieth Anniversary Ceremony in New Zealand to mark the sinking of HMS Neptune with the largest loss of life in a single naval disaster for New Zealand. Norman is pictured at the Ceremony in Anzac Park, Nelson, N.Z. on 22 December 1991, with Rear Admiral Sir Ian Hunter on his right and the then Mayor of Nelson Peter Malone on his left.

53 Jean Tapper of Christchurch presenting the Neptune Cup Trophy awarded in memory of her brother Trevor McComish, a Neptune casualty. Norman, helming the Politeia to victory in the annual Neptune Cup regatta stands with the crew including Mike Heath (owner), Norm Bryant, Ron Parkin, John Newton and Peter Harley in December 1991.

54 Norman and Nattalea O'Toole with a photograph of Mrs O'Toole's son Bill Gibbs, a Neptune *casualty who with L. N. Nalder, RNZN and T. J. McComish, RNZN were members of the Nelson Yacht Club. The photograph was taken on Norman's visit to New Zealand in 1991/92 and represents one of his treasured meetings with the relatives of the New Zealand sailors.*

© Nelson Evening Mail.

55 Norma with her daughter Nicola aboard the keeler Politeia *with owner Mike Heath in the background, competing in the Nelson Cup Yacht Race in 1996, following in the footsteps of her father who had steered the* Politeia *to victory in 1991. The Neptune Cup, competed for annually by ex-servicemen members of the Yacht Club was donated by Mr P. J. McComish in 1952 in memory of his son Trevor, who lost his life with* Neptune.

56 The memorial that stands in Nelson, commemorating the loss of 150 New Zealand sailors in HMS Neptune. *John and Norma pictured visiting the Memorial in December 2006.*

BARFLEUR   1692   QUEBEC   1759
TRAFALGAR   1805   MARTINIQUE   1809
BALTIC   1854   JUTLAND   1916
ATLANTIC   1939   CALABRIA   1940
MEDITERRANEAN   1940   'Bismarck'   1941
MALTA CONVOYS 1941

57 Her Majesty's Naval Base Clyde (HMS Neptune) Faslane, Scotland. Pictured are Norman and his wife Irene with Captain Kerr RN. The Battle of Honours Board for HMS Neptune in the background.

58 Commander John McGregor, OBE, RN, (left) Chairman of the Neptune Association founded in December 2002, becoming a close friend to Norman. Seen with his brother Richard wearing the medals of their father Paymaster Commander J. H. McGregor (right) a Neptune casualty.

59 Norman pictured with Nixie Taverner, the niece and adopted daughter of Captain Rory O'Conor, RN (HMS Neptune), who died in Norman's arms on a Carley raft on 22 December 1941, sharing a moment together at the inaugral meeting of the Neptune Association. Nixie wrote the story of the loss of Neptune in her book Neptune's Legacy.

60 Neptune Association members who were able to make a special pilgrimage to Malta and Tripoli in April 2007 to pay tribute to relatives and friends who were lost in the two ships HMS Neptune *and HMS* Kandahar *sixty-four years previously. The group sit below the Seige Bell in Malta after which they attended the unveiling of a memorial plaque in the Maritime Museum in Vittoriosa and presented a parchment scroll with the names of the 837 who died to the President of Malta Fenech Adami. (See page 163.)*

61 *The Neptune Association party in April 2007 boarding the dredger Jarif in Tripoli harbour.*

62 The Neptune Association's sixty-sixth Anniversary Memorial Service for HMS Neptune *and HMS* Kandahar, *held at sea sixteen miles off the coast of Tripoli at the approximate site of the mining of both ships. Descendants of those 837 who perished in the sinkings prepare to cast a floral tribute whilst the White Ensign is being lowered into the sea.*

63 As the Neptune Association group stand in silence, Norma casts her father's ashes into the sea, returning his soul to the deep to join again his mates as he requested.

64 Congratulations for the Captain of Jarif for making possible the final incredible journey.

65 'Counting the Cost' – Royden Thomson, whose father Bruce Thomson RNZN was a Neptune casualty stands with his wife Sandie beside a display in the War Museum, Malta which provides an account of the demise of Force K and details the tragic loss of life. Royden and Sandie remain very close friends of the family and represent the many relationships formed between descendants of the crew of HMS Neptune and HMS Kandahar some sixty-six years after their passing. A unique group evolved from a World War II disaster and one that cannot have been imagined by the sailors that served and died in the two ships in December 1941.

66 Tripoli Central Hospital. The photograph shows the Nursery Section under refurbishment in April 2007. The arched balconies were Norman's only memories of where he was taken by his Italian rescue party on Christmas Eve, 1941.

67 The final goodbye. Norma in reflective mood looking out on Libyan waters by an anchor chain similar to the one Norman had made his way down from HMS Neptune to the Carley raft on that fateful night when Neptune slipped beneath the waves.

My mother's uncle, James Wears, who managed The Tavern public house in Blaydon-Haughs at the time, had been asked to manage the Conservative Club in Blaydon Town, which came with family accommodation. My father had managed to move to a well-paid position as furnace-man at Patterson's Foundry located in Blaydon-Haughs so they jumped at the chance to take over the tenancy of 7 Douglas Terrace, in which they hoped to rebuild their lives. My mother took the long walk up from the village of Blaydon-Haughs through Blaydon to the cemetery to visit my brother's grave as she had done almost every day since his death. She said my pram was a regular sight at the cemetery and friends and neighbours remember my mother spending a lot of her time there but she described one day when her life began to change:

> I visited John every day in the cemetery. One day I parked Norma's pram on the corner where the cemetery path ran down towards the entrance and I went over to John's grave. An unusual wind passed over me, the trees rustled overhead and I saw from the corner of my eye the pram holding my daughter slowly moving down towards the gates. I jumped up and ran to stop the pram. The wind seemed to suddenly stop for no reason. I took it as a sign and decided that day that I had to let go of the past and concentrate on the future with my daughter. John was always with me though.

My parents finally opened the door of their home in Blaydon-Haughs that was to be their new future. This door opened onto a long corridor with two spacious bedrooms which ran off either side. A lounge with a big fireplace was at the end of the corridor with a little kitchen at the side containing a large stone sink, stone-shelved pantry, and a back door opened out onto a yard enclosed by a high wall and the 'nettie'. Their uncle had kindly left a new gas-burning ring and large wash-barrel with a 'posser', for washing the clothes which they were grateful for. When they opened the yard door they could see Patterson's Foundry and a lane that led down to the River Tyne. There was a Methodist chapel on the right and the gaslight that indicated the end of the village.

I would often watch my father as he skipped and trained in the back yard, sitting patiently on my 'cracket' (a three-legged wooden stool). He would be up and out before dawn completing his daily run along the river path under the many bridges that now crossed the Tyne. Many years before, the residents of Blaydon-on-Tyne and surrounding villages would cross the river by ferry to reach Newburn and the Newcastle area. The industrial era brought with it great engineers that used the local steel to construct some wonderful crossings over the river including Scotswood Bridge, the Swing Bridge and Redheugh Bridge. Since my parents' house was the last in the terrace and the village, it had one of the few gas lamps outside the front door and my father would return to the house just as the gas lamp was doused and daylight peeped over the horizon.

Out of 146 fights my father fought, he won eighty-two, lost sixty-one and drew four. The bulk of these fights were with boxing shows but he described some of his most memorable professional fights in the Middleweight Division, 'By 1 March 1948, I'm back in the professional ring fighting Jim Cairns from Kelso in six three-minute rounds. I'm K.O.d in round four.' New St James Hall in Newcastle was a venue my father was always keen to win at in front of his home crowd. My granddad was often there and took up a position in his corner throwing in the towel when he thought his son was taking too much of a beating. My granddad was well known with the trainers and managers in the area having taken to the ring a number of times himself during the 1920s and 1930s and my father recalled one boxing event he witnessed as a boy when he travelled with his father to Scotland:

> Old 'Pop' was playing football in Scotland and I went up with him to watch the game. After the game some bloke in the Club told 'Pop' there was going to be a couple of boxing bouts in the Football Club later that day but one of the fighters had backed out. The money was pretty good so 'Pop' agrees to fight. I watch him complete a six-rounder after playing football and still fit enough to drink at the bar after. I think this is where I get my inspiration for keeping fit and making money.

My father recalled one of his hardest fights being part of the William Little's Boxing Promotions when he fought at the Drill Hall, Strand Road in Carlisle on 31 March 1952. His opponent was a Jamaican called Reuben Blairs. The fight was described in the *Boxing News* as a hard but entertaining fight that went the full six rounds, being judged as a draw. Only three more professional fights were recalled by my father in 1948. On August 29 he fought Gene Devlin from Seaham Harbour at the Ryhope Arena. Six three-minute rounds and he was knocked out in the third. Devlin was to go on to box in a final eliminator for the Northern Area Middleweight title but lost to the title-holder Bert Ingram in a ten-rounder. Bert's career had turned out pretty successful. My father continued his string of losses fighting Joe Elliot from Sunderland at Houghton-le-Spring on 15 October and losing a six-rounder, then fighting Tommy Crinley from Seaham at Hetton-le-Hole losing another six three-minute round bout on points.

My father described a disastrous contest on 2 April 1949 at Glasgow Grove Stadium:

> A promoter offers me a contest with Dave McLaren from Comrie up in Scotland and my Dad decides to come with me, taking on my corner. I weigh in at 10st. 5lbs. and McLaren at 10st. 3lbs. It's a six three-minute rounder but by the fourth Dad throws in the towel and I retire from the fight. Not a fight I was particularly proud of.

He returned to his home ground to fight Mike Cassidy from Sunderland at Ryhope Arena on 28 May and won the bout on points and in June he was offered a profitable contest at the open-air arena at Hendon Cricket Ground, Sunderland with Alf O'Neill from Chopwell. They put on a good show but my father narrowly lost the fight on points. O'Neill went on to have a further twenty-five bouts, winning seventeen, drawing one and losing seven.

On 18 June he fought Eddie Parsons from South Emsall at West Stanley Greyhound Stadium, another good venue with a large paying crowd but again he narrowly lost on points. My father completed his well-promoted contests for 1949 with a win on points when he fought Don Matthews from Manchester at Carlisle Drill Hall. By 1950 he was winning more than he was losing and described his next three fights in detail:

> On June 10 I win the contest convincingly fighting George McDonald from Langley Park. It is a six three-minute round contest at Ryhope 'The Arena' and we both weigh in at just over 11st. I returned to Hendon Cricket Ground on July 5 to fight Bob Conway from Stockton on Tees. The Ref. stopped the fight in the fifth of a six round contest as Conway had a cut eye. Dick Miller was the only southpaw I remember fighting. I fought Miller on November 28 at Kendal Market Hall. He was from Blackpool and I won the six-round contest on points.

My father fought against Benny Woods from Leeds whom he met again in the 1960s at the Leeds Ex-Boxers Association and they became friends. The venue for the fight in March 1952 was The Baths at East Hull. In a six-bout contest my father lost on points with both weighing in at 10st. 11lb. On 7 May 1952 he remembered fighting a highly-rated fighter and being lucky to be saved by the bell. He was fighting Peter Cain from Dundee in Scotland at the Dundee Premierland Stadium. There was a big crowd and this fight was a big earner with his Dad minding his corner again. My father said he left his corner and took a punch 'sweet on the chin' in the first round, taking three counts of seven before he was 'saved by the bell'. He had to be assisted to his corner by seconds and his Dad wanted to leave it there but my father carried on into Round 2 where he was knocked out and this time stayed down. He took home a good purse from that fight. My father went out in style with knock-outs in his final two bouts in 1952, winning against Bobby Foster from Throckley and Billy Parker from Sunderland, both at the Sunderland Park Lane Arena, the last recorded fights of his career as a professional middleweight before his return to the Royal Navy.

As his daughter it was difficult to keep up with my father's sporting life but I became a regular visitor to the boxing gym and was used to seeing my father with what I called his 'funny face', the morning after a fight. I was only four years old but followed my father everywhere I could and was described by family and friends as a real 'Daddy's girl'. When my father would sit me on the cracket in our home in Douglas Terrace I loved to watch him do his fancy skipping and shadow boxing and then he would kneel down and play-box with me. When I went to the gym he would sit me on the long wooden forms that ran around the walls while he sparred and trained with the other boxers but the highlight for me was when he finished and would pick me up to reach the punch ball and practise my punches. On Saturday mornings we would go to my granddad's and he would take the opportunity to visit Swalwell Social Club with Granddad and his brothers, while his sisters took me to the local picture house to see the matinee, a regular weekly activity that I enjoyed with his sisters for many years.

Things were beginning to get back to normal for my parents and they were enjoying living in the village of Blaydon-Haughs. They made some good friends in the village and my mother's grandmother, Matilda Wears, 'Tilly' as she was always known, only lived a couple of streets away. An Italian family called Perna moved into the house opposite. My father was able to practise his Italian once again and the Perna family were pleased to be able to converse in their own language. My mother learnt to cook some traditional Italian recipes from Mrs Perna and my father enjoyed a pasta meal that contained meat and tomatoes. A far cry from the Italian food he had experienced in the prison camps. The Perna family fled to England after the war, they had been unhappy with their existence under the reign of Mussolini and wanted to make a new life in the new Europe.

Italians certainly knew how to make delicious ice cream and the family decided to set up an ice-cream business. Their brightly painted two-wheel hand-cart was pushed around the streets of Blaydon-Haughs and up to Blaydon, the vendor shouting their wares. To help prevent the ice cream from melting, the churn containing the product was lifted into a container of bigger volume, then the space between the two cylinders was packed with chopped-up ice. The whole lot was then placed in the middle of the cart, wedged and was ready for dispensing. They did a roaring trade on hot summer days, especially when considering the large number of children living down the streets of Blaydon and Blaydon-Haughs at the time. Of course, as their neighbour's daughter I was given my share of the left-overs after the daily rounds. Rifle Court was the place where the Perna family had premises where they made the ice cream. It was an unusual jumble of buildings inside a big yard, Dickensian in style and character, mostly stone buildings and all designed differently. With its cobblestones, gas lamps and the higgledy-piggledy nature of the structures it was the essence of quaintness. Rifle Court was accessed from Church Street in Blaydon. Alas, it was never preserved, along with much of Blaydon and its little suburb Blaydon-Haughs. There was major demolition work in the area in the 1970s to make way for modern industrial estates and shopping precincts.

Sometimes at weekends my father's sisters would babysit and my parents would walk up from the river and take the footbridge crossing the mineral railway line when the crossing gates were closed, into the town of Blaydon which was thriving in the 1940s with plenty of shops and entertainment. Their favourite night out was to go to the Empire Theatre and afterwards call at one of the great selection of fish and chip shops that Blaydon had to offer, their favourite being Pinch's. They would sit in a cubicle where Harry Pinch had hung an amplified wireless that played music while they ate. It was a very popular shop with lots of laughter and banter that would keep the customers entertained and Annie, the shop assistant, busy.

Our family was very happy at that time and everything looked well for the future with the worst appearing to be behind them when a letter arrived from the Admiralty in August 1952. My father described that day, 'A letter arrives from the Admiralty. I think it is my Reserve pay but it's a call up for the Korean War. I'm happy to go but I'm worried for my wife and daughter.'

CHAPTER 11

Korean War Call Up

O N RE-ENTRY TO THE ROYAL NAVY in 1952 with the ranking of Petty Officer, my father was described as 5 feet 11 inches tall, chest measurement 42 inches, with light brown hair, blue eyes and a fresh complexion. He had grown two and a half inches and increased his chest measurement by six inches since his first advancement to man's rating in 1939. A severe wound on his left leg was also recorded, his only injury remaining from the disaster in 1941. This time he left behind a fragile wife and a precious new daughter and he was worried for them but for himself he was pleased to be back with the Royal Navy and full of anticipation at returning to the service he loved. Initially he did not need to travel far as he executed his re-training programme at HMS *Vernon*, the Portsmouth shore training base, training in torpedo and underwater detection from September 1952 to April 1953.

My mother and I were able to stay in Portsmouth with my father in rented rooms near the base until I began primary school back in Blaydon. My father had lots of friends and colleagues in Portsmouth and as they were a couple who enjoyed a full social life I was often looked after by some handsome young sailor that my father had volunteered in for the job. Unfortunately I was much too young at the time to appreciate their company. A photograph of my father and mother kissing on the beach near Portsmouth is one of my favourites as it always reminds me of how much in love they were. I was very lucky to have childhood memories full of love and laughter. They were certainly a fun couple to grow up with and be around.

In April 1953 my father was drafted to the Admiralty Floating Docks based in the Mediterranean and then the Far East. Another long stint away from my mother and me, who returned to the north-east. He served as bosun on HMS *Montclare* and then HMS *Adamant* in Singapore. Admiralty Floating Docks sailed into the various Royal Naval dock yards to lift and execute repairs to Royal Naval ships in service during the Korean War. He revived his sporting activities boxing for the Navy at home and in the fleet clubs in the Mediterranean and Singapore and was a successful player for the Admiralty Floating Dock 22 Soccer Team.

In February 1955 he was drafted to another Algerine class minesweeper, HMS *Chameleon*. Again he was involved in sweeping clear of mines the harbours and channels along the coasts of Malaysia and China and particularly around the Japanese islands, where much of the Korean War had been fought by the American and Combined Forces. He was involved in a number of Naval shore parties on the Japanese islands carrying out what they called 'mopping up' when the Korean War ended. He recalled a story when he and another Petty Officer were sent ashore with one such Naval shore party where there was a building occupied by some Japanese troops left behind. They were called upon to surrender. A white flag was shown from a window but my father remained very cautious; however, the other Petty Officer stepped out from cover to accept the surrender but was met with a hail of gunfire and fell to the ground mortally wounded. My father and the patrol then opened fire on the building, letting go of a few hand grenades. The Japanese troops that were left ran out in surrender and were lined up in front of the patrol whereupon one soldier began to protest and shout about their rough handling by the seamen. Tempers were high on both sides. Such were the fortunes of war.

Back in England the family was then smitten with another blow when my mother was diagnosed with breast cancer. She was only in her early thirties and my father was away. I had not spent very long at my new primary school when I was sent to Leeds to stay with my grandparents where I attended Swinnow Primary School for three months to allow my mother time to recover from what transpired to be a full mastectomy to rid her of the malignant tumours. It was an anxious time for my father who felt he could not bear to lose her and again he felt helpless not being with her. After a very lonely and worrying time for my mother she happily made a full recovery and by June 1955 when my father returned to England on leave the couple were able to rejoice again at the news that she was in remission. For me it was a confusing and unhappy time being without my parents but I do remember being ecstatic when Daddy came home again. My mother used to tell the story of the day the doctor came to the house and asked me if I was pleased to have Daddy home. I replied that I really enjoyed watching him play with Mummy on the floor. The doctor found this very amusing. I fondly remember him bringing home presents, a Japanese kimono for my mother and a doll in traditional Japanese dress for me, which I cherished and showed off to the other children who lived on the estate in Blaydon-on-Tyne.

On his return my father was pleased to be drafted to HMS *Dolphin* Submarine Base in Gosport where he spent his last two years in the Navy in charge of torpedo recovery vessels. It was at this time that he received another commendation for his seamanship. He was engaged in the recovery of a spent torpedo during training off the south coast of England and put himself in danger, ignoring the advice of those around him, to recover the lost torpedo. Another example of his dogged determination to finish what he had started. My mother and I spent many happy holidays in Portsmouth and I have very fond memories of swimming and sailing with my father at the beaches along the south coast of England, the seaside resort of West Wittering being our favourite weekend retreat. Water was not a favourite for my mother who could not swim and preferred to stay on dry land. My father was enjoying life in Portsmouth and had taken on the role of instructor in underwater detection but when his date to leave the Service was drawing near my mother made it quite clear that 'home' was where she wanted him. He desperately wanted to sign up for further service but gave in to my mother's wishes and on 9 September 1957 he was released from the Royal Navy to RN Emergency Reserve having served seventeen years in total.

Home was now 45 Hazel Road on a newly-built council estate in Blaydon-on-Tyne. My mother had decorated and furnished their semi-detached home to perfection, she had very good taste. She worked in a local bakery called Carrick's and became the manager enabling her to save money to buy furniture, and even bought their first car after she passed her driving test first time. When my father returned home from the Navy he was offered a position at the Post Office sorting office in Newcastle and accepted even though it wasn't his 'cup of tea'. Royal Mail did not have the pleasure of my father's company for long since he decided to return to Patterson's Foundry where he was soon made up to Head Furnaceman, the best paid job on the factory floor. It was the position that his father-in-law, Norman Dodds, had held for many years until he moved to Leeds in 1942.

Tilly lived near the foundry in Blaydon-Haughs and relied on my father to call in at her home regularly and supply her with coal and firewood. She was a formidable woman even in her old age and had no fear of walking into a factory working at full swing to state her case. She was well known in the area and no one ignored Tilly. It brought my father down to size when one day she marched into the foundry and told the men working to pass on a message for my father that her firewood had run out. He made sure he was round to her house with the firewood post haste as soon as he finished work at the foundry. She would be in her eighties by this time and could be seen each day by the river as she marched her usual path on the riverside taking her daily constitutional. It was in the River Tyne that she met her end. When they found her drowned the death was recorded as an open verdict. Our family was blessed with strong women and charming men.

My parents continued with their life in the north-east of England, visiting my mother's family in Leeds whenever they could. It was on such a visit that they met Barry Glendenning who was to marry my mother's youngest sister Betty. The Glendenning family owned a coopers (barrel-making) business in Armley Road, Leeds. Barry regularly visited the Newcastle and Gateshead area on business and stayed with my mother and father in Blaydon. I would often return with him to stay with my grandparents in Leeds for school holidays. The journey was a long hard ride as I travelled in the lorry cab perched on a steel barrel; no seat belts or safety regulations in those days. The company had progressed into reconditioning 45-gallon steel drums and was a thriving business.

In June 1957 our family travelled to Leeds to Betty and Barry's wedding staying with my grandparents who lived in a large rented house on Troydale Lane that was owned by Troydale Woollen Mill. My granddad was employed as groundsman for the Mill taking care of the gardens and the bowling green attached to the Mill's Social Club, which many commented was the smoothest and best kept bowling green in Leeds. My grandmother worked in the Mill canteen. It was only two years later in 1959 that Barry's father passed away followed by the death of his mother soon after. It left a young innocent 24-year old with a business to run. He wasn't too experienced in the management of men or business. My father had never been to any business college or had any experience running a business but he did know how to manage men. His experiences in the Navy and in life had taught him a great deal and he thought this might be of value to Barry. The pair discussed working together and my father came to work in the business for a trial run at the end of 1959. It was a working relationship for Barry and my father that was to last over twenty-five years, until my father's retirement in 1985. Barry and he were friends, work colleagues and brothers-in-law all rolled into one.

My mother wasn't too happy to leave the north-east where she always felt her roots lay but my father saw that they had the opportunity for a better future in West Yorkshire, and by 1960 we had moved to Pudsey near Leeds where they happily lived out the rest of their lives together. Their first house was in Valley Road near Troydale and my mother took up a full-time position in the offices at Troydale Mill. I had spent many long holidays with my grandparents in Troydale and knew the Mill well. I would often help my grandmother take the tea trolley through the weaving sheds twice a day. The noise of the looms was deafening as the shuttles would whip across the loom threaded with the weft (wool woven horizontally) weaving the cloth. This was at a time when woollen mills and sewing factories were the major employers in Leeds and the woollen cloth was world-renowned. My grandmother was highly skilled in lip reading as the tenders at the looms would shout and sign their orders. When my grandfather passed away my grandmother Lily Dodds came to live with us and was a regular sight behind the counter of our grocery shop. My father and mother had decided to buy a grocery shop in Pudsey during the late 1960s and became very well known in the area, my mother running the shop as my father continued at Glendennings (Containers) Limited.

My father became Works Director with the company and lifelong friends with all those who were connected with the company. His colleagues recalled many events which described my father's time with the company but most tend to focus on how he 'sorted out' troublesome characters They said he never looked for trouble but trouble often found him. His nose would flare and turn white and this was the warning they all recognised, making a point of getting out of his way as soon as possible. Barry recalled one such story when they took on Mick Cleary, a young lad who came to the company for work from Ireland. On one occasion he had apparently tested my father's patience to the full, as Barry describes the incident:

I heard the noise of a scuffle from the office and ran out to see Norman holding Mick up against the wall. I had never seen anything like it before and tried to pull Norman off him, he turned fast as lightning and I feared for my life. We all calmed down and Mick stayed with the company for the rest of his working life. The men rarely stepped out of line with Norman about and respected his leadership.

Another incident the workmen at Glendenning's remember again involved Mick:

It was his job to clean the water jets on the conveyor belt that cleaned the steel drums as they went through the tunnel washer. Unbeknown to Norman, Mick was in the tunnel completing the job late one morning. Norman started up the machine, luckily Mick had not added the caustic soda yet, and to the sounds of the young lad's shouts Norman quickly turned off the machine. Another time the joke was on Norman when, as an ex head furnaceman he believed himself to be quite skilled at the art of bricking out a furnace, he set to, to mend the works boiler during a holiday break. He squeezed inside the opening of the coke boiler and steadily replaced the fire-bricks around the base. Eventually he realised that he had bricked himself in and had to break out to the great amusement of the men in the yard. Thank goodness for progress in the Health and Safety department.

Norman was always in the yard with the workers even at lunch breaks where he would spar with a lad they called 'Bowey' and started them playing football on the spare ground near the units. Unfortunately this lunchtime activity was curtailed when Norman accidentally kicked a long ball through the windows of the Electricity Board building which backed onto the site.

Both my parents worked hard and played hard all their lives. When I completed my full-time education in 1968 I left the area to spend some time touring Europe and working in the United States of America; I appeared to have inherited my father's wanderlust and very much enjoyed travelling. When I returned my father proudly escorted me down the aisle at Pudsey St Lawrence Church where I married my first husband, and by 1972 he held his first grandchild, Nicola Jane, the first visitor to see her at the Four Gables Nursing Home in Horsforth, Leeds. My father was the first visitor again to see his second grandchild born Michael James in October 1979. He enjoyed his grandchildren immensely spending many great holidays as a family with my mother, my second husband, John, me and the children. He was also very lucky to still be alive and see his great-grandchildren Thomas and Alice.

My father continued to be involved in sport throughout his life in Yorkshire. Around 1972 he started to consider a less energetic activity. Barry Glendenning had taken my father to Sandmoor Golf Club, where he was then a member, to try his hand at the game of golf. He took to the game and joined the local golf club in Fulneck, Pudsey. It is a small friendly club, still standing, set in the ancient Moravian settlement in Fulneck Valley. The clubhouse is set high on the hillside next to Fulneck School, and both look out across the green valley to Tong village. The golf course is very picturesque with a stream, or 'beck' as they call it in Yorkshire, meandering through the valley, with a famous ninth hole on the top of the hillside testing the fittest of golfers.

My father was a popular member being elected President of the club in 1979, serving for two years to the end of 1980. In 1984 he served as Captain of the club. Fulneck Golf Club formed a Centenary Committee in 1989 and my father and mother served with other committee members to provide a programme of events to celebrate the first hundred years of the club. My mother was also a good golfer serving as President (1989) and Captain (1986) of the Ladies Section. It was a thorn in my father's side that my mother managed to strike a hole in one on two occasions and was a very competitive partner, although I know he secretly admired her talent and determination. My parents spent a great deal of their time at the club during their retirement years, making many friends and representing Fulneck at matches throughout West Yorkshire. They had many happy holidays playing golf with other members of the club in Scotland, Spain and Portugal.

My mother was also renowned for her skills in the kitchen, providing meals after matches and sumptuous buffets that were remembered well after she left the club due to ill health. As well as being heavily involved socially the couple were remembered for the significant contribution they made to the development of the club over the twenty years of their membership. My father also played golf for the Glendenning's team in the Drum Federation Golf Tournaments. In fact in his first match for the Drum Federation held in Chepstow he won first prize in the Blagden Trophy, which was great news as they were, at that time, Glendenning's big competitors. They never had ladies in the Drum Federation Golf Matches at that time. That was until my mother, never one to be left behind, decided to start a ladies team.

In 1995 my father was due to play a golf match at Whitby Golf Club on the east coast of Yorkshire. He received a telephone call from a relative of Petty Officer Cook who was aboard HMS *Neptune*. Again he was subjected to a series of questions as to how the ship met her end and again relayed the story of the sinking of the *Neptune*. He informed the enquirer, Bob Field, that he was playing golf in Whitby and Bob was delighted when my father agreed to meet up with him there. Stories like these occurred so often in my father's life and continued till his dying days. The thirst for knowledge from relatives of *Neptune* casualties of how their loved ones had met their death never ceased. 'Missing presumed dead' was a statement so difficult to accept for so many families when the sinking of *Neptune* was hidden in secrecy for so many years.

It was pleasing to see at the funerals of both my mother and my father a large number of representatives from the golfing fraternity and many wishes of sympathy declaring what a loss they were to the club.

My father was also a member of the Pudsey Bowling Club where he played snooker and dominoes for the club teams. He was still a competitive character even though the pace of engagement may have slowed from his days in boxing, football and water polo. He continued to attend the Bowling Club on Smalewell Road up to the last weeks of his life. My parents were also well known in the Fox and Grapes public house near their home again joining the pub's darts and dominoes teams and becoming very good friends with the landlords, Sam and Gladys Leach.

The festive season at my parents' home was well remembered by all who knew them over the years. It was always open house on Christmas Day and New Year's Eve. No invitations were ever sent but the house was always full of people and there was food and drink a plenty catering for any number of guests. My father was particularly known for having long pockets.

He retired from Glendenning's Containers Limited in 1985 with a party at the usual company watering hole, the Albion public house, Armley Road in Leeds. Barry's youngest son Ian was taken under my father's wing when he taught him all he knew about the business. Barry Glendenning's sons Simon and Ian continue to run the business to this day.

A most memorable event in my parents' latter years was the celebration of their golden wedding. As the date approached in November 1993 it coincided with the twenty-first birthday of their first grandchild, Nicola, who dearly wanted to share the celebration with her grandparents. The result was a joint golden wedding and twenty-first celebration with over 100 guests, including family and friends from far and wide. It was a celebration we all continue to treasure.

CHAPTER 12

Living Links

THE YEARS WERE GOOD to my father and January 1986 saw him celebrating his sixty-fifth birthday with his family, colleagues from Glendenning's Containers in Leeds, golf partners from Fulneck Golf Club in Pudsey and the friends he had made during the past twenty-five years living and working in West Yorkshire. The memories of his war experiences and especially his experience of surviving the sinking of HMS *Neptune* were buried deep in his heart. My father rarely spoke about his experiences in the Second World War not even in his latter years, preferring to live for today. He often advised me not to dwell on the past or think too much about the future but to live for the moment and that was what he did. He had worked hard all his life and was now looking forward to his retirement years with my mother.

Around this time, unbeknown to my father, there were two men who lived many miles across the sea from England, who were considering the possibility of writing a book, and he was soon to be asked by them to recount his story and re-open again the memory box from over forty years previously.

In America, Captain James E. Wise, Jr., was considering writing a book he was to call *Sole Survivors of the Sea*. He had come across a sole survivor story and was intrigued to find out if there were other sole survivors of similar incidents at sea. Finally he began to dig further into the subject, and with the help of various historical archive sources, sole survivor incidents began to surface. As James Wise explains:

> As I found more incidents of sole survivors I tried to gain a better perspective on why certain people survived catastrophes against all odds. Many were lucky. They were in the right place at the right time. Others seemed to possess such a tenacious will to live that they were able to endure unbelievable hardships and survive while others perished. Still others have never been able to find a satisfactory explanation for their good fortune.

My father never answered his own question, 'Why me?'

In New Zealand another author by the name of Jack Harker who lived in Auckland, was collecting information about the cruiser HMS *Neptune*. Jack Harker decided to write about *Neptune* as it was to have been New Zealand's fourth cruiser of World War II. The biography of the ship and its fateful end would then complete his work on New Zealand's World War II cruisers.

So it was, that by the end of the 1980s my father had received two letters, one from the USA and one from New Zealand both asking him if he would assist them with their manuscripts regarding his sole survival of the sinking of HMS *Neptune* as he was the only eyewitness as to how so many men had died that fateful night. Very little had been done around the world, and especially in the United Kingdom, to publicly commemorate the tragic loss of *Neptune* with 764 lives in December 1941.

On 24 September 1981 a feature appeared in the *Yorkshire Evening Post* in honour of the fortieth anniversary of the Second World War, which included an appreciation of *Neptune* and the sole survivor Norman Walton. The article had a far-reaching effect. The story of the loss of *Neptune* had been offered to the newspaper by a descendant of one of the ship's crew who felt that the time to commemorate the ship was long overdue. The feature generated extensive interest and correspondence that soon provided a channel of communication for some of the descendants of those who perished, and brought an unanticipated result in giving an outlet for the emotions of not only the relatives but also my father, that had been suppressed for more than forty years.

The publicity escalated and other newspapers began to contact my father with more articles being written with the *Neptune* story as the focal point. This is what my father always wanted to avoid, he felt it was a glorification of himself as a survivor rather than what he wanted which was to commemorate the shipmates he had been so proud to be amongst: the seamen of courage who bravely fought albeit in vain to save themselves and others. After more than forty years he was again inundated with letters and was greatly moved by the communications he received from all over the world. My father never wanted publicity for just staying alive. He felt an element of shame about the fact that he could not ease the suffering and the death of his shipmates. The guilt bothered him and he hated the idea that others would write about the tragedy in a glorified way. He often said to me that there was nothing glamorous about watching your mates dying around you.

On 18 November 1981, he received a letter from Jack Harker in Auckland, New Zealand:

> I have received a letter from Bob Whittle in New Zealand, saying that you were the survivor from *Neptune*.
>
> Well Norm, I feel very humble in asking you to assist me with my manuscript about your ship HMS *Neptune*. You have been the centre of a lot of controversy here and in your country and I expect you are fed up with people worrying you for your story of that fateful event.

It was true that the letters he received overwhelmed my father but after many months of heart-searching he finally made the decision that the time had come to put the story straight after the many years of speculation, and began to write again about what he had experienced in December 1941. He already had his notes and the diary he wrote in the prisoner of war camp in Italy. They were in his Naval ditty box that sat in the loft; untouched and unseen for forty years. The memories, once released, came flooding back and he engaged in the emotional journey back to 1941. He also decided to reply to the request of James E. Wise and by 1991 *Sole Survivors of the Sea* by James E. Wise and *Almost HMNZS Neptune* by Jack Harker had been published.

The publishing and promotion of these books coincided with an event in 1991 that was to have a profound effect on my father and bring comfort and a final peace to him and some of the descendants of the 150 New Zealanders who had perished with the ship.

The events in New Zealand came about by the persistence and tenacity of John and Barbara Newton who live in Nelson, South Island, New Zealand. An old shipmate of my father's, John Newton arrived on a UK visit in 1986 to join a Navy reunion for the 'Algerines', in Blackpool, where he made extensive enquiries about my father, or Geordie as he called him, but to no avail. His shipmate Geordie was a Leading Seaman on HMS *Rowena* when John knew him.

John Newton explained how he knew my father:

> We were both on the HMS *Rowena*, a fleet minesweeper operating in the Mediterranean, then after the German surrender, *Rowena* moved out to Trincomalee Naval Base in Ceylon (now Sri Lanka), and after they dropped

the atomic bombs on Nagasaki and Hiroshima in 1945, the *Rowena* proceeded to Singapore where I, the only Kiwi on board *Rowena*, was put ashore and I never had contact with him after that.

I tried to find him in 1986, when I visited the UK, but could find no trace of him. During 1988 I wrote several letters to Jack Williams in Blackpool, who is Secretary of the Algerines Association who I met in 1986 and he advertised for information on Norman in the *Navy News* newspaper, Royal Navy Circulars, British Legion etc. but nothing came up.

Eventually Jack Williams wrote to me to say that Don Stevenson, a New Zealander, had Norman's address. Don had seen a note about Norman in the *Navy News* and written to Jack with Norman's details. I decided to write to him, wondering how he had Norman's address. He replied that he had, in the Returned Services Branch scrapbook a photograph of Norman and Irene taken from an English newspaper, dated 1981 and sent to him by Wally Ware, a member of the New Plymouth Branch of New Zealand's healthy Returned Services Association. Apparently a variety of folk all over New Zealand knew about Norman Walton and here was I trying like hell to trace him.

Our interest in Nelson was that we have, for a number of years, had a parade and service to remember the 150 New Zealanders lost on *Neptune* and in particular Trevor Comish, Lawrence Nalder and William Gibbs all sons of Nelson. Nelson was not alone in remembering *Neptune* as services were held all across North and South Island of New Zealand organised by the Ex-Naval Men's Associations.

Don Stevenson wrote to John Newton explaining their plans for the RNZN fiftieth anniversary to be held in 1991, along with the memorial celebrations for HMS *Neptune*:

> We have a Project Officer for the RNZN 50th Anniversary and being a combination of the RNZN and *Neptune* sinking anniversaries it would be most interesting if you could trace Norman Walton. As I mentioned I'm a bit baffled as to how he served with you on *Rowena* for the years stated as we were under the impression that he was a POW of the Italians until after the war. If he escaped or something we would be pleased to hear as I will use it in the Newsletter.

In reply to the letter John Newton told Stevenson that Geordie was in fact on the *Rowena* and he could vividly recall sitting on the mess deck at Malta when he was told about HMS *Neptune*. Stevenson replied on 14 August 1990:

> Seems I was right on one thing at least – this chap Walton is one who keeps to himself. Not sure when and where I heard that but repeated a couple of times at least and your remarks confirm it. I was also under the impression (apparently incorrect) that if a serviceman from any of the forces were

repatriated for any reason he had to sign under oath he would not take an active part in the war again. One is always learning!

A very substantial contribution was made to Allied forces by the Commonwealth countries, which proved invaluable but sadly, led to a considerable loss of life. The smallness of New Zealand's population meant that the losses sustained by her forces during World War II were relatively high, compared with those of more highly populated countries such as the UK. Nowhere perhaps was this more evident than in the loss of *Neptune* with the lives of 150 New Zealanders. As the banter regarding Norman Walton spread across New Zealand through the postal and email systems of the Ex-Naval Men's Associations a Neptune Committee was being formed by John Newton, Peter Malone and Allan Horgan in Nelson to discuss plans for *Neptune*'s fiftieth anniversary. The Committee had the inspired idea of inviting my father and mother over for the occasion as their guests of honour. Since he had already displayed his reluctance to answer mail that he found traumatic, John Newton made a personal telephone call to his old friend. At 1 p.m. UK time on Friday 17 August 1990, my mother picked up the telephone and the chain of events began that led to a tour of New Zealand by my parents.

John personally felt that he had found a long lost brother. It would be forty-six years since they last saw one another and he felt all the effort had been worthwhile. So with the enthusiastic support of the city's Mayor at the time, Peter Malone, and the backing of Ex-Naval Men's Associations and other organisations throughout the country, the stage was set for a memorable visit. The plans for the visit escalated as the Committee received more requests for my father to visit their Returned Services Associations branches and speak to descendants of the men who had lost their lives in *Neptune*. The itinerary was extended to incorporate as many of the organisations and individuals that wanted to meet my father, as was possible.

Plans were also being drawn up for another annual event that would prove to be a highlight of my father's trip to New Zealand. In 1951 the late Mr P. J. McComish donated the Neptune Cup to Nelson Yacht Club, in memory of his son Trevor and all his shipmates that went down with HMS *Neptune*. Since the first race in 1952, the Nelson Yacht Club had hosted the event annually with up to twenty keelers for, at times, fifty Returned Services Association members to skipper or crew. The race to compete for the Neptune Cup planned for December 1991 would be held in conjunction with a civic reception to commemorate the fiftieth anniversary of the sinking of *Neptune* and my father would be invited to sail.

In July 1991, Peter Malone visited England and when he arrived in Pudsey, West Yorkshire to see my parents they made him very welcome, introducing him to the family at parties and barbeques and their friends in the Golf Club and Bowling Club. Peter was a retired veterinary surgeon and a keen horseman so my father brought him to my house in Clifton, Brighouse to meet his grandchildren. My daughter Nicola had horses of her own that she kept at the local farm and Peter could not resist a visit to the stables to take a ride on her pony Tara. It was an exceedingly funny sight to see, as Peter was getting on in years and had a false leg both of which did not hinder his progress in galloping across the fields near our home. Sadly Peter Malone passed away in 2004 but our family still holds the memory of him riding the pony close to our hearts.

My father had already begun the process of recalling his experiences in December 1941, after many months of thought and discussion with his family. Even though he still felt some fear and trepidation at facing the relatives of the sailors who had died he decided to accept the kind invitation from New Zealand. Peter Malone was pleased and handed him the air tickets that were kindly provided by the sponsorship of the event by British and New Zealand airlines. Peter then assured them that there would be hosts waiting to welcome them in every town and city across New Zealand.

When Peter Malone returned to Nelson an itinerary was drawn up in consultation with the Ex-Naval Men's Association of NZ branches for my parents' stay in the country. This brought tremendous encouragement, support and co-operation for the organisers who were delighted with the response and kind offers to host the couple during their stay. The busy itinerary to visit up to thirty towns and organisations across the length and breadth of New Zealand was finally agreed. Peter's reassurances were an understatement of the welcome and friendship that my parents received in New Zealand.

My parents held the friendship of Peter and his wife Trish close to their hearts along with those of the many other hosts and families that they were so fortunate to meet during their trip. They also formed a close lifelong friendship with John and Barbara Newton who had been the instigators of the memorable trip and worked tirelessly to find my father and subsequently help him through his difficult visit to the islands.

The guests of honour arrived at Auckland Airport on 6 December 1991 at 5.45 a.m. to be met by John and Barbara Newton. My father recognised John instantly and the memories of his service aboard HMS *Rowena* were the earliest to flood back. Their first duty was to attend a press conference where they also had the pleasure of meeting the author Jack Harker, to whom my father had spoken many times on the telephone, when relaying his stories of that fateful night in December 1941. My father began talking, answering the many questions that the people of New Zealand had regarding the largest loss of New Zealand life in any Naval disaster; tired and emotional he found it difficult to contain himself. The car journey to Thames to attend the Commemoration Service to be held there on Saturday 7 December provided a brief respite before meeting the host of Returned Service Association members and relatives. A newspaper article published in the *Thames Star* by Andrew Schmidt sums up my father's introduction to a unique visit:

Ship's Sole Survivor comes to comfort

Norman 'Geordie' Walton has been fighting most of his life. Now he's fighting back the emotion. The 71 year old Yorkshire man is the sole survivor from the HMS Neptune, a ship sunk by in the Mediterranean on December 19th, 1941, with the loss of 764 lives. The ship's contingent of 150 New Zealanders perished.

There were a few teary eyes and breaking voices around the Thames R.S.A. on Saturday, Norman's mate John Newton of Stoke, Nelson, leans over and confides, 'He was crying this morning.' 'It is going to get emotional in some places,' says Norman Walton. 'When it's one of the relations of the lads on the raft you expect that. I'm going to take it day by day. I don't know who I'll meet each day.

I just want to comfort everybody, that's what I've come to do – relive the memories with the relatives.' The Waltons have been receiving letters from some of the 150 New Zealanders' children, brothers, sisters and widows since the war finished.

'It's been 50 years of wondering for some of them. I want to ease the path if I possibly can. I'm indebted to do this,' says Norman Walton.

Across the table John Newton opens one of the many letters he has received since Mr Walton's visit was announced. A small black and white photograph falls out. The letter is from Kathy Houghton of New Plymouth. The picture, of her brother, killed when the *Neptune* went down.

It's all getting a bit much for Norman Walton. 'We'll open the letters at each stop,' says John Newton, putting the letter away.

One letter lingers longer in his hands than others. It's of Able Seaman D. P. Munro of Christchurch, a shipmate on the *Neptune*.

'This is the one I'd really have liked to have met. But they all seem to ring a bell. His mother first contacted my wife in 1943. She wrote for twenty years, then the letters stopped. She must have died,' says Norman Walton staring down at the photograph. 'Used to send Christmas cake,' he adds as an afterthought. With the letters regularly arriving, the sinking of the *Neptune* has never been far away. He prefers not to talk about it. 'The hospitality has been out of this world. It's only the second day and I've already met so many beautiful people,' says Norman Walton steering the conversation back to the present.

John and Barbara Newton provided their practical and emotional support to my parents throughout their tour and their lifelong friendship was held in great esteem. On 8 December my parents were driven to the Returned Service Club Rooms at Whangamata and were impressed by the well-appointed Club Rooms with a large dance floor and bar and a superb Naval plaque. They enjoyed an outdoor buffet right next to a sandy beach in the beautiful sunshine. On their return to Thames my father had the chance to talk with the daughter of a *Neptune* casualty, called Val.

It was a few weeks later that Val called in to New Zealand Radio as they interviewed my father in Christchurch. Her sentiments in that call revealed an element of the emotion that was commonly felt amongst the many relatives of *Neptune* casualties that my father met over the remaining weeks of his tour:

Excuse my emotion but I just wanted to thank Norman for explaining about the disaster. We always wondered why it was you that survived. Now you have cleared my mind of so many thoughts wondering about how my father died and I am so grateful . . . It is a big thing to know how a loved one dies – why we want to know I don't know but we do . . . Dad was thirty-two and I was ten when he died. Now I know he is at rest, I can rest. Not enough information was put out about the circumstances of how they died. There was very little publicity at the time.

I met Norman in person in Thames and he kissed my cheek. I said to my husband, 'Don't kiss that side and I'm never going to wash it again.'

Everyone laughed at Val's last comment and my father then replied, 'Thank you Val – you and everyone in New Zealand has also helped me to face what I have been carrying around with me all these years and I have now been able to let out the emotion with you.' The tremble in their voices could be heard across the airwaves, such an uncanny flow of emotion after so many years.

The initial welcome by the Kiwis was to be the standard of the welcome that my parents received right across the islands of New Zealand. My father had the honour of meeting many relatives including Vic Robertson, the brother of Able Seaman Malcolm Robertson, born in Feilding and enlisting in Auckland, Mrs Ashford from Mount Albert, the sister of A. B. Cosgrove; and Mrs Crosby the sister of Petty Officer J. E. More both *Neptune* casualties. There was also a collection of letters at each stop that my father made throughout the tour sent by relatives and friends who wanted to hear from him and he attempted to reply to them all. An evening at the Imperial Hotel with relatives and friends ended with a happy singalong, and one of the many presentations from the Returned Services Association to my father that was repeated across North and South Island. The plaques and presentation gifts made by all the Associations that my parents visited during their tour were displayed with great pride in their home in Pudsey, adorning the walls of their semi-detached home until their deaths. A video of the commemoration in Thames was sent to the then commander of HMS *Neptune*, the Naval base in Faslane, Scotland, by a descendant of a *Neptune* casualty. This prompt resulted in my father being invited in 1992 to the ship's namesake HMS *Neptune*, the Nuclear Submarine Base in Faslane on the Clyde by the then Captain of the Base, Captain Kerr. My father also made contact with a previous Captain of HMS *Neptune*, Captain R. D. Butt, CBE, RN who wrote to him later that year:

Captain Kerr kindly sent me a copy of your letter about your heart-warming visit to New Zealand. I am not surprised at the welcome you got, as they are a warm people with a great pride in the memory of HMS *Neptune*.

She was my first ship and I joined her in Chatham in early 1941 on the day she arrived home. I had many close friends in her and it was with some reluctance that I left her for training in HMS *Jervis* at Alexandria in October, 1941. We were in company covering the passage to Malta of HMS *Breconshire* a few days before you were sunk and that was the last time I saw her. I was supposed to have rejoined her at Alexandria before she sailed for Malta, but owning to the sickness of our gunner (T) in *Jervis* I could not be spared to do so.

The memorial service at Faslane in December last was a very moving occasion and we all felt happier that Captain Rory O'Conor and his gallant ship's company had at long last been properly honoured. I was to serve in three more cruisers, *Birmingham* in Korea, *Gambia* in the East Indies and finally in Command of HMS *Blake* worldwide; but it is *Neptune* that will always have a special place in my heart. I was so pleased to have heard from you, who had the worst time of it than anyone else.

I hope the enclosed picture may remind you of some good times in the ship.

With every good wish. Ronnie Butt.

Another example of the series of coincidences that led to this chapter of living links and to the many special relationships being formed so many years after the sinking of *Neptune* in 1941.

The next port of call for my parents in North Island, New Zealand on 9 December 1991 was Tauranga where another welcoming crowd awaited them at the Ensign Club Rooms, including the Presidents of the Ex-Naval Men's Association, Tom Verran and Dave Stephenson and his wife Jean. They were treated to a flight in a small aircraft piloted by Tom Verran to view the sights of North Island then on 11 December they visited Rotorua, hosted by Rotorua and Taupo Associations and had a wonderful time at the Agradome watching a demonstration of sheep-shearing followed by an outdoor session of sheepdog trials. Their destination of the hot springs and whirlpools, the Maori village and display of traditional crafts and the unusual and highly ornamental St Faith's Church in the Rotorua area was something they would never forget. They were overwhelmed by the kindness of their hosts from the Rotorua Ex-Naval Men's Association, President Brian Palmer, in showing them this beautiful area of the country and the many afternoon teas and barbecues with the members at branches across the country that followed.

It prepared my parents for the events to come as they flew to Wellington via Lake Taupo to their hotel room at Lower Hutt. They were guests of honour at an assembly and reception at the imposing Naval base of HMS *Olphert* on 14 December and an evocative picture of HMS *Neptune* next to a roll of honour caught their eye as my father realised more and more how the sinking of *Neptune* had affected so many people in New Zealand. He spoke to many of the company assembled and signed copies of Jack Harker's book *Almost HMNZS Neptune*, which had provided some insight to the events of 18/19 December 1941.

The day of 15 December 1991 was devoted to another commem-oration event for *Neptune* organised by the Taita R.S.A. at Lower

Hutt. The day began with a ceremonial march past of guardsmen accompanied by a band and followed by relatives with smart young cadets, officers and marines bringing up the rear. The service was led by Rodney M. Murphy (Chaplain); my father was honoured to lay a ceremonial wreath. The official speeches by local dignitaries that followed in the crowded hall at the formal reception were, like the many that followed throughout New Zealand, pertinent and commendably short. They, as others, commented on the fact that the loss of life with *Neptune* was greater than in any other single engagement since Gallipoli and that this fiftieth anniversary represented a 'good part of most people's lives'. Captain Westoff, representing the Chief of Naval Staff, expressed the view that as well as remembering the past, we needed to look to the future, hoping for a better and more peaceful world. A sentiment shared by all in the room.

The 'distinguished guests, the sole survivor of *Neptune* Norman Walton and his charming wife Irene' were officially welcomed. My father responded by thanking all concerned for their wonderful hospitality. He then had the great pleasure of presenting cups to the best turned-out male and female cadets and in return, received a badge of membership for their Association. The commemoration service followed, ending with the traditional prayer of remembrance. A delightful social occasion enabled my father to meet with more relatives. He was particularly moved when he met with the relatives of James Quinn and his close friend on board *Neptune*, Ronald Quinn who abandoned ship with my father and spent the long days on the raft with him before his unfortunate death on the third day. My father was unable to continue speaking when the memories of his friend returned.

On 16 December my parents departed North Island for a six-day stay in Nelson with John and Barbara Newton who had worked tirelessly to support them during their tour in North Island. Nelson is a beautiful city bordered by long stretches of sandy beaches and surrounded by mountains, snow-capped in the winter. It nestles in the top western corner of South Island and boasts having the highest sunshine scores in South Island. It was certainly a lovely sunny day when they arrived and quickly gained reports on their itinerary for South Island.

By 19 December, the actual anniversary of *Neptune*'s tragic loss, they were in Christchurch where a memorable function was held at

HMS *Pegasus*. As they entered the function room the roll of honour including photographs of the New Zealand seamen who perished and a wreath in the shape of an anchor caught their eye. A similar wreath lay on my father's coffin on 20 April 2005 with a note signed by me and his grandchildren as a poignant reminder of the visit to New Zealand that had such an impact on my father in his later life.

A memorial dinner was held in Christchurch R.S.A. where my father paid tribute to all those who served in *Neptune* including Captain Rory O'Conor whom he described as 'one of the most caring and humane of Captains who interviewed personally everyone who joined the ship'. He then added his admiration for the Kiwis in particular saying, 'Anyone who can't get along with the Kiwis must have something the matter with them. They are some of the nicest people I have ever met.' He asked all present to 'raise their glasses to the memory of all those who went with *Neptune*', paving the way for Chief of Naval Staff Rear Admiral Sir Ian Hunter. The Rear Admiral outlined the profound effect *Neptune*'s loss had on the Navy; he thanked my father and was pleased to give New Zealand people a better understanding of their history. He ended his address by saying, 'It is easy to gloss over past events especially when they can be hurtful but being able to face up to them with courage is a sign of maturity. In helping to do this we owe a vote of thanks to all who have organised and participated in this special occasion.' It was added that my parents had, 'provided an added impact to the occasion and brought it all home most dramatically' and brought the formal proceedings to an end by offering a heartfelt vote of thanks to their guests of honour.

My father was interviewed for television and radio, again being asked to recall the events on the night of 18 December 1941 and speaking to many who called into the radio programme to ask questions of him, some giving thanks for his presence at New Zealand's bicentennial commemorations for *Neptune*. He described how this felt in an interview with a journalist from the *Nelson Evening Mail* on 21 December:

> I found it difficult at first because it kept bringing back all the terrible memories. It has been very emotional. I've broken down a couple of times. In Wellington after meeting relatives of my Kiwi mate Quinny I was too choked with emotion to speak. But the visit has been therapeutic, in a sense, both for myself, and the families of the Kiwis. I hope I have set their minds

at rest. It's really got to me at times, talking to all these people, but for them and me it's put the final piece in the jigsaw after all these years.

A civic dinner was held in my father's honour back in Nelson on the evening of 21 December attended by more than 100 people. A most memorable Remembrance Service held in Anzac Park, Nelson, followed the next day. When my parents arrived in Anzac Park with John and Barbara Newton and Peter Malone the beauty of the park in the middle of the city, impressed them. The imposing Naval memorial was flanked by four young sailors who stood motionless throughout the ceremony. The commemorative service was conducted by Rev. Peter Swears of Manuela, a former Navy chaplain, and attended by Rear Admiral Sir Ian Hunter who again praised the New Zealand Navy for its steadfast continuity and described this special day as 'a significant part of all we are trying to do which is symbolised by the Cross and all it stands for.' Peter Malone in his address referred to the tragic loss of HMS *Neptune* and the 150 New Zealanders who went down with her and added that the presence of the sole survivor Norman was most significant to all who mourned their loved ones. My father laid the first wreath followed by all dignitaries who stood side by side with members of the Nelson community, in silence, as an expert bugler played the Last Post. The words, 'We will remember them' drew the service to a close.

One of the highlights of their visit to Nelson was when my father was invited to take part in the Neptune Cup Yacht Race in the afternoon. They were special guests at the annual Neptune Cup regatta held by the Nelson Yacht Club. My father showed he had lost none of his seafaring skill by helming the yacht *Politeia*, owned by Mike Heath, to victory. He was presented with the Neptune Cup and his name remains on the cup with *Politeia* as cup winners for 1991, a fitting tribute to his fellow crew member, Trevor McComish.

Jean Tapper of Christchurch presented the trophy awarded in memory of her brother Trevor McComish, a Nelson Yacht Club member and one of 764 *Neptune* crewmen who died. Mr McComish's father first presented the Neptune Cup in 1951.

Three members were killed when *Neptune* went down. Two sisters of one of the victims, Bill Gibbs, were present at the event as well as his former fiancée who had travelled from Blenheim. Relatives of Laurie Nalder, the third club member who perished also attended and met my father at the Yacht Club.

Twenty-eight keelers lined up in testing conditions for the race. The Neptune Cup boats are crewed by guests from the Nelson R.S.A. and made a crew record of seventy-five keelers in all on the day. My father was delighted to win and remembered with great affection the people he met on what was a magnificent day. In fact on his return to England he spoke so highly about the event to his family that it inspired my daughter Nicola and me to visit Nelson when we went to Australia and New Zealand in 1996. We were so pleased to be able to meet some of the many friends my parents had made in 1991 and were kindly invited by the R.S.A. members to crew the keeler *Politeia* in the same annual Neptune Cup regatta that my father had taken part in five years previously. *Politeia* may have come last in the race of 1996 but we did hope to return to New Zealand to try again. Whilst in Nelson my parents were invited over to Blenheim and stayed at Terri Ruffles' home. Terri is an ex-Wren and was the first woman in New Zealand to be President of the Ex-Naval Men's Association, and was awarded the Queen's Service Medal (QSM). On arrival, Terri poured my father a rum; she had been saving the small amount left in the bottle especially for him as you could not buy it in NZ at that time. It is another example of the great kindness shown to my father by the New Zealand people. It was Terri who later read out my father's thank you letter to New Zealand to all those assembled at the unveiling of the Neptune Memorial in Nelson.

December 1991 had been exhausting for my parents both mentally and physically. Consequently they were very pleased to spend a peaceful Christmas in Nelson with John and Barbara. They managed to fit two other visits at the end of December to Montueka with their hosts Jim and Audrey McGregor, and Blenheim to see members and relatives of *Neptune* casualties before returning to Nelson for New Year's Eve.

It was in Picton where a poignant meeting took place when they were able to meet Joan Taylor, the niece of Mrs Munro. My mother had communicated with Mrs Munro since 1943 for twenty years before the letters had stopped. My parents were taken to the house from where she had written so many letters to the sole survivor. Duncan Munro, a casualty of *Neptune* was the only adopted son of Jack and Nell Munro. A meeting with Mrs Lily Naismeth, a 96-year-old Wren also from Picton was very moving as she had sadly lost her fiancé to the disaster fifty years previously. My parents' spirits were lifted when they were invited to Maraenui Golf Course for a few welcome holes of their favourite hobby.

They were on the move again on 2 January when Peter Malone flew them in his own aeroplane to Westport R.S.A., then on 5 January they visited the R.S.A.s at Greymouth and Hokitika on the west coast of South Island. Another quick three-night visit across the island in Christchurch where they were guests of Jack Stewart, a member of the Woodstock Group; Commander Collins kindly provided an evening barbecue where a great time was had by all.

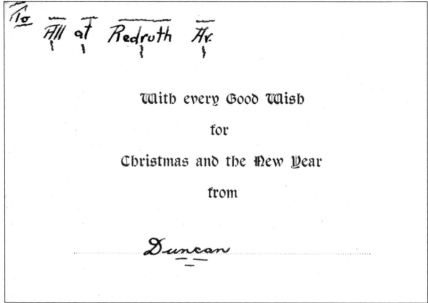

An HMS Neptune *printed Christmas card sent by Able Seaman Duncan Munro, RNZN, to his family. He was reported missing at sea in December 1941. The card shows the ship's crest on the front. Duncan's mother communicated with my family for twenty years.*
By kind permission of Duncan's cousin, Joan Taylor

On 10 January they travelled to Timaru to stay with their hosts June and Ray Carter who had organised another group gathering to meet the couple. A long car journey down to Dunedin followed on 11 January by a reception at the Senior Ratings Mess HMNZS *Toroa*. A three-day stay with Commander Perry, where the Royal Naval Reserve entertained them concluded their stay in the area.

Royden Thomson, the son of one of *Neptune*'s casualties, Paymaster Lieutenant Bruce Thomson, living in Cromwell, South Island had heard about my father's visit to New Zealand and attempted to get to Dunedin in time to meet him. He and his wife Sandie unfortunately never caught up with my father but in July 2005 at the Memorial Celebration for *Neptune* and *Kandahar* held at the National Arboretum in Alrewas in England, I was fortunate enough to meet them both. They were too late again to meet my father who had passed away only months before but our families formed a special relationship that began in 2005 and still continues today. Thirty young men from the Dunedin Area of New Zealand were serving on HMS *Neptune* on 18 December 1941 and lost their lives, including Paymaster Lieutenant Bruce Thomson, RNZN, and Midshipman Brian E. McPherson, RNZN, aged seventeen years. So many friendships have been formed between the families of *Neptune* casualties and our family over the years providing lifelong memories. I am sure that the sailors serving in *Neptune* on that fateful night in 1941 and clinging together on the Carley raft could never have imagined what an effect their passing has had on the development of strong friendships that have formed and enriched the lives of the generations that followed.

My parents' tireless travels continued throughout January and February 1992. To Invercargill where they were entertained by June and Allan Bowie and met Ex-Naval Men's Association Southland branch President John Smith and his wife Joyce, before flying from the south back to Nelson. My father was able to celebrate his seventy-second birthday on 15 January with John and Barbara Newton again back in Nelson. When arriving at the Newtons' house they had a lovely surprise visit from my mother's sister Betty and her husband Barry who were on a world tour at the time and had been staying in waiting with John and Barbara.

Visits were becoming fast and furious again when they visited Palmerston North, went back to Hutt Valley and Napier R.S.A., Gisborne, and ending with six nights in Auckland with memorable functions and meetings with members and relatives. At Te Kuiti R.S.A. they were treated to a barbecue organised by Lorna and Dick Spraggs and – much to my parents' pleasure – a round of golf at St Andrew's Golf Club. A final guest who was keen to meet my father before he returned to England just managed to catch up with him during his last week. He was Tim Riley, who was my father's asdic instructor who had not seen him for fifty years, another coincidence that helped make the trip so special for my father. Trevor and Joan Stacey hosted the couple during their final days in New Zealand topped off by a visit to Devonport Naval Base directed by Commodore Tony Lewis.

Before leaving South Island there was another emotional meeting for my father. Nelson mother of seaman Bill Gibbs who worked in the engine room of HMS *Neptune* when his life was taken in December 1941 had heard from her daughter that the sole survivor was back in town. For Nattalea O'Toole the meeting with my father on 11 February 1992 revived memories of her beloved son Bill. The 97-year-old said her son was in his mid-twenties when he died. His birth had been in tragic circumstances. Her first husband died while fighting overseas in World War I and Bill was born a few months later. He joined the British Navy at the outbreak of World War II and was proud to be in the New Zealand branch of the Royal Navy until his tragic death. They held hands and talked about Bill. Even though my father had not been with *Neptune* for long and did not know many of the ship's company well he was a good listener and it transpired he was to be a special counsellor to the many relatives who contacted him over the years.

It was a fitting end to their eight-week stay in New Zealand where they had visited the wealth of Returned Service Associations that New Zealand had to offer and spoken to hundreds of relatives and friends who had wanted to know finally after fifty years the details of the death of their loved ones from the only seaman left who could tell them. The exhausted but happy couple left on their return flight to England from Auckland with very special memories and a host of new friendships.

The visit embodied the strength of feeling New Zealanders have for the relatives of their 150 countrymen who perished with HMS *Neptune*. It had been the journey of a lifetime for my father who spoke privately to me after the visit when I asked him how he coped:

It was a bit like opening a safe, one click at a time, as I travelled the country and back in time in my memory. When I met the relatives of my shipmates and heard their stories of loss and their feelings and desires for final closure and peace I felt it became a shared responsibility to find that peace. To see and be amongst those people who were remembering and grieving for their sons, husbands, nephews and friends after all that time reminded me of the bodies I saw and the seamen I knew. The guilt at the time was overpowering, knowing there was nothing I could do about it. That guilt stopped me being able to reply to the hundreds of letters that fell at my door in 1943. I did not know how to tell them what I saw. This visit helped me to unlock the safe, tell the story and the guilt I always felt started to go as if I was able to let some light into my mind and feel some sort of relief.

My father's official 'thank you' to New Zealand read as follows:

To all R.N.A.s (Royal Naval Associations) and R.S.A.s, I say thank you from the bottom of my heart for the way my wife and I were treated everywhere we visited, both in the North and South Islands. The places of exceptional scenery that our hosts have shown us in this beautiful country of New Zealand; the way in which we have been welcomed at every function that we have attended on this 50th anniversary of the Royal New Zealand Navy, and also commemorating the tragic loss of HMS *Neptune*, when 150 New Zealanders perished, in honour, on duty, for their country.

To the relatives of my lost shipmates whom I have met and talked with, who sent me letters of appreciation for speaking to each one of them and relieving them of the wondering how and why the ship sank so suddenly. I go home a much more relieved person, after fifty years someone else is sharing the experience with me. All I can say is – thank you all.

I am much indebted to British Airways for sponsoring my wife and I, enabling us to visit this lovely country. Also to Air New Zealand and Nelson Air Link for all internal domestic flights.

I would also like to extend my grateful thanks to my old shipmate John Newton who, like a British bulldog, never lets go; and to his lovely wife, Barbara, for looking after our every need. And my deep appreciation to the Mayor of Nelson, Peter Malone, whose liaison with British Airways made our visit to New Zealand possible. He visited us in England when on a business trip and assured my wife and I that we would be well looked after during our stay in New Zealand. He wasn't spinning a yarn – New Zealanders are very special.

I would also add my sincere thanks to members of the 'Neptune 1991' Committee, for all their hard work in organising the itinerary. The New Zealand phrases I have learned and digested are, 'No problem', 'Good on you' and 'Don't worry about it'. People here have always time for you. In the street politeness is the key word.

Regarding the many highlights of my visit, in my view, still being seafaring in mind, was being invited to participate in the Nelson Neptune Cup race.

Mr Mike Heath, the owner of the keeler *Politeia* invited me to take over the helm. I said that it had been some thirty years since I cox'nd any boat. However, by the time we had waited for our starting time I thought I have the wind in my sails, and the rudder under control. I've never concentrated so much since I won my last golf medal. It was a great day with more such days to follow. Everywhere the R.N.A. had organised a visit for us was a highlight in some way or another.

The meeting with the niece and nephew of my special Kiwi mate on *Neptune*, R. F. Quinn ('Quinny'), brought a few tears and was traumatic for us all, but a relieving time for me as well as for the niece and nephew. Also the meeting with the soldier who had been in the same POW hospital as me, but later was sent to different POW camps – more memories.

The meeting with the mother of Bill Gibbs in Nelson, 'very touching'. Then meeting the 96-year old Wren in Picton; also meeting a cousin to the son of Mrs Munro who had written to us from 1943 to 1963. Not only did her niece tell us what happened to her but we were able to visit the house in which she had written so many letters. Then came the meeting with Tim Riley, my old Asdic instructor (after *Neptune*) whom I met in Browns Bay – more memories.

I've had a lot of memories to take home, and a lot to thank New Zealand for, and most of all, to be invited to the commemoration of the sinking of HMS *Neptune*. Thank you New Zealand, thank you all.

PSSX26921 John Norman Walton

John Newton wrote the following paragraph about my father's visit:

> Norm's visit was a closing chapter for all wives, siblings, sweethearts etc. as they were able to talk to Norm about the sinking of HMS *Neptune* and he set a lot of minds at rest being able to tell them what chance their loved ones would have had as the ship went down. Response all over NZ was unbelievable.
>
> Irene and Norm were great ambassadors for their country, extremely popular and well liked and respected by all who came in contact with them. At the beginning of their trip around NZ, there were a lot of tears shed over the remembrance of shipmates and loved ones but as the journey throughout NZ progressed, the healing became obvious so that when Norm left NZ shores, he appeared a much more relaxed man having been able to talk about the tragic sinking of *Neptune* and loss of so many shipmates. His journey meant so much to so many New Zealanders.

It was to be another ten years before my father was again approached to recall the story of *Neptune*'s fateful end. Commander John McGregor, OBE, RN and son of *Neptune* casualty Paymaster Commander Jack McGregor initially traced my father through his brother Richard. He explained what occurred:

My brother Richard first saw the cutting about Norman from a Leeds' newspaper dated 1981 in the Simonstown Naval Museum in South Africa. I went to Richard's son's wedding in South Africa in October 2000. On the last day I visited the Simonstown Naval Museum, saw the article and someone had written on it Norman's address as 90 Smalewell Road, Pudsey, Leeds. On my return in November 2000 I found his telephone number from Directory Enquiries and rang him up. We spoke for about three-quarters of an hour and I found the whole conversation fascinating. In January 2001 I drove up to Leeds and met him. I was intrigued with all he had to say and we became firm friends.

I felt an empathy with Norman from the very first. I found him a particularly warm person with an open friendly personality. He was intelligent and articulate with a low gravel voice and a strong Geordie accent. I listened with closest attention to his memories of the *Neptune* tragedy and his traumatic time in the water, on the raft, his rescue and time as a POW. When I researched the *Neptune* story with the Naval Historical branch I found that his account remained consistent throughout the sixty years since the sinking and that he hadn't embellished it with the passing of time. I have always been a keen sportsman and was fascinated to hear of Norman's boxing career and his swimming, football and water polo skills.

I put Nixie Taverner in touch with Norman and she went up to visit him in February 2002.

Nixie Taverner, the adopted daughter of *Neptune*'s Captain Rory O'Conor had been assembling material for her book about the life of her father called *A Torch Among Tapers* and was naturally curious about the sole survivor but was led to believe he had 'crossed the bar'. It was only when she met some special *Neptune* contacts, John McGregor, Ken Auger and Ken Oakley who had spoken to my father that she was assured he was alive and kicking and living in Leeds.

When the telephone in my father's house rang out on an otherwise ordinary day the call stirred again his memories. The caller was Nixie Taverner. I initially spoke to Nixie and told her that as my mother needed a great deal of care from me and my father due to problems related to advanced osteoporosis and osteo-arthritis at the time, it would not be possible to bring my father down to London to meet her. When I spoke to my father about the telephone call he was amazed that the Captain's daughter had contacted him and invited her to his home. I rang Nixie with the invitation and expressed how happy my father would be to meet her and help in any way he could with material for a book she wanted to write about her father's ship *Neptune* and those who sailed with her. My father was very moved when he heard that Nixie had recently taken up the gauntlet and decided to contact him as he was the last person that had spoken to Captain Rory O'Conor before he passed away in his arms on the fourth day in the raft in December 1941.

In February 2002 Nixie visited my father at his home with her son John. They brought with them a camcorder, so that a recording of the unique meeting could be made. I was able to arrange for my mother to attend a respite day centre and travelled from my home in Huddersfield to support him through what I knew would be a very emotional meeting for them both. My father commented that he never thought he would live to meet the Captain's daughter.

He described his initial interview with the Captain when he joined *Neptune* some sixty years previously, who he said noted his boxing prowess and made him captain of the water polo team explaining to Nixie that he had played a great deal of sport representing the ship. My father was very complimentary about his Captain, which pleased Nixie and he mentioned several times how *Neptune* was a 'very happy ship.'

Nixie began to ask my father many questions about that fateful night to settle the doubts she had on the death of her father and was comforted to know that his 'Skipper' had died in his arms only two days before he was rescued by the Italians. He spoke in a voice thick with emotion. After an affectionate hug between them Nixie told my father that the meeting had been one of the most special occasions of her life and that he would be the first person to receive a copy of *Neptune's Legacy*, her forthcoming book.

The health of my father's beloved wife Irene was deteriorating and by 2002 she was only a shadow of her former self. He hardly recognised this five-stone, curled-up ball propped up in the hospital bed, with pain showing in every line of her face. He found difficulty in accepting why such a lovely lady had to suffer so badly when all her life she had cared for everyone else. My mother in her final months was unable to speak and had to be fed by tube until she could bear no more and left us alone on 28 November 2002. My father and I were heartbroken and lost without her as she had been the backbone of our life. My father's health and mental agility began to deteriorate but he was determined to continue living in their home and continued with life in the same fighting fashion he had always displayed.

Nixie Taverner and John McGregor decided to form the Neptune Association in December 2002, and both agreed that the President should be my father. He was pleased that sixty-one years after this much-neglected ship was sunk she was at last being commemorated by the inception of the Neptune Association and he was delighted to accept the invitation. I was happy to support him and thought at the time that this would help him in his grieving for my mother.

Initial publicity through Nixie Taverner's book *Neptune's Legacy* and the Association brought together ninety members including some from South Africa and New Zealand. A website was also set up by the Neptune Association which provided the opportunity of a special ongoing channel of communication to honour the ship that had become so close to the hearts of the relatives of those who perished with her. The popularlity of the website escalated rapidly and by the year 2007 there were 280,000 hits on the *Neptune* website and members of the Neptune Association had risen to 250.

The inaugural meeting of the Neptune Association was held at the Union Jack Club, in London on Friday 20 December 2002 to commemorate the sixty-first anniversary of the ship's tragic destruction. My father and I travelled to London by train and had a quiet journey where he stared out of the window most of the way contemplating the reception he would receive and looking worried. He would be again facing the same questions, How could so many men die and why were they not saved? Where were the lifeboats? Why were you on the upper deck? And so the questions would go on but this time there was a difference. Because of his momentous pilgrimage to New Zealand he now felt he could face the questions without the overpowering guilt he had felt for so many years and he hoped he could answer them all as calmly and clearly as he could. When we arrived arrangements had been made for him to be interviewed privately by ITN Producer Rob White and a cameraman, with a few press reporters, away from the main meeting room. My father was surprised by this but did his usual trick of ordering a tot of rum to give him thinking time. The outcome was a comprehensive feature in *The Times* and a filmed interview that formed part of a compilation video recording of the meeting. This became available to Members for a fee, which raised valuable funds for the Neptune Association's plans.

A warm welcome was given when my father joined Committee Members at the 'top table'. John McGregor, the Chairman, through his research provided a thought-provoking presentation on the circumstances leading to the destruction of Force K that was helped by eyewitness accounts from Harry Bradbear and Harry Jones aboard the cruisers that followed my father on *Neptune* that night. It all shed further light on the cloak of silence and mystery that had enveloped the ill-fated *Neptune* for so many years. The meeting was concluded by Rev. Ron Paterson and it was wholly appropriate that a message sent by Pat Win, the Secretary of the Nelson branch of New Zealand's Ex-Naval Men's Association was read, 'We are proud to be part of the newly formed Neptune Association and wish you well on the occasion of the inaugural meeting. May our links continue to grow and strengthen.'

It was later, to my father's delight that the idea to build a much-belated memorial for those who lost their lives in *Neptune* and *Kandahar* was put forward. In July 2004, the Neptune Association gathered at the National Arboretum in Alrewas and the thirty-four members present decided it would be a grand idea to build a permanent monument for *Neptune* and *Kandahar*. The committee approved this and in October the dedicated few set about getting the stone pyramid built and raising the necessary funds. Dedication day was 9 July 2005 and attended by 405 relatives and friends from across the world. Sadly my father passed away before he was able to see the end result but through John McGregor's visits at his home he was kept involved in the progress of the monument to the end.

CHAPTER 13

Closing the Circle

AFTER MY PARENTS RETURNED from New Zealand, the publicity that the trip had spawned travelled far and wide, and relatives of HMS *Neptune* casualties in the United Kingdom, after the many years of silence were finding opportunities to hear and meet the sole survivor through the newly formed Neptune Association. Over the past sixty years my father had accepted the mantle of counsellor, through no choice of his own, and continued to wear this mantle to his final days. More and more relatives of casualties were making contact and now had a network through which they could share their stories. The work on the monument and commemoration day at Alrewas was going well and my father took a great interest in the progress of the Association.

In July 2004 my father was contacted by John Peel's *Home Truths* programme which went out on Radio 4 every Saturday morning at the time, and was a programme which had a very wide audience nationally. My father was asked if he could attend an interview in the London studio but I had to inform the BBC that as his health was deteriorating he would not be able to make the journey. In response they decided to send a 'sound man' to 90 Smalewell Road in Pudsey and my father was expected to take part in a three-way interview with John Peel and Nixie Taverner who they had interviewed in London. When I arrived at my father's house to support this wonder of technology I found him with a telephone receiver in one hand and microphone in the other attempting to compensate for his lack of hearing and poor concentration levels. It was quite hilarious watching the confusion on his face as he answered the questions, but with excellent editing the programme was broadcast on Saturday 17 July. Nixie's interview fitted in well and the whole broadcast produced fourteen minutes of quality radio. Many told me later how much they enjoyed hearing my father speak and what a unique connection he had to all those interested in the fate of HMS *Neptune*.

The programme followed one with Gillian Cross on 15 May. She is the daughter of Lieutenant Frank Woodward killed in *Neptune*.

John Peel had seen a report in the *Nottingham Evening Post* of Gill hearing her father's voice for the first time after sixty-two years. The recording of the Christmas message of 1941 from Captain Rory O'Conor for New Zealand radio had never been broadcast due to the sinking. Many years later Radio New Zealand had found the tape in their archives. On the tape, Lieutenant Woodward (Gill's father) described what *Neptune* had been doing and this was followed by messages from the New Zealanders on board to their families back home. Gill was born seven days after *Neptune* sank and had never before heard her father speak.

John Peel was fascinated by the stories, and thanks to his interviews another eight families of casualties made contact with the Neptune Association. John Peel, a well-known, respected and popular radio presenter whose career spanned the 1960s to 2004 died not long after the programmes were broadcast. He was on holiday with his family in Peru when he suffered a fatal heart attack and sadly died on 26 October 2004. He was greatly missed by the British public.

Since the death of his beloved wife my father found coping with life without her very difficult as she had organised him and taken care of his every need for nearly sixty years. He tried to move on as he had always done in the past, living in the same house and to all those outside looking after himself and the house very well. His lifeline was his nightly visit to the Pudsey Bowling Club just a five-minute walk across the street. He would lean on the bar downing his two pints of beer and two 'bubblies' (tots of rum) with friends around him, and once a week he was joined by his brother-in-law Ronnie Dodds for a game of snooker. I had moved with my family to north Lincolnshire in August 2002 but visited my father regularly as did his grandchildren Nicola and Michael. The light of his life was the new addition to our family, his great-grandson Thomas Michael Keating born on 17 May 2001. They spent many happy hours together over the few years he had left. He taught Thomas to play dominoes, never letting his great-grandson win of course until he had mastered the skill, just as my father had done with his grandson Michael over the years. On my twice-weekly visits Thomas would be with me and would while away the hours with his Grandpa, playing the mouth organ and 'chewing the fat'.

One of my favourite memories of the two together was on a cold winter's day when we were making our weekly trip to Pudsey Town

Centre. My father insisted on saving his small state pension in the building society from where he would draw out enough money to cover his household bills. We would take his pension on a short walk across town to his bank where the calculated funds were deposited. I had suggested numerous alternative ways to pay his bills that would make life easier for him and his failing legs but he was set in his ways and preferred his own method, and who could blame him. I was having great difficulty in the bad weather negotiating the streets with an 84-year old on one arm and three-year old on the other and so decided to take the risk and deposit the two in a local café. After choosing their libation and sticky buns I left them to it and carried out the financial transactions across town. On returning to the café I watched them through the window, their heads together engaged in conversation and engrossed in each other's company. It is a memory I hold very dear.

In November 2003, my husband and I took a trip to Australia over the Christmas period to visit our son Michael, who had been working and travelling over there. We met up with Michael and his girlfriend Laura in Cairns and travelled together down the east coast of Australia visiting friends in Sydney and Melbourne. I had organised a carer to visit my father daily but in the New Year he suffered from a chest infection and was admitted to hospital where they took a number of X-rays. He always hated hospitals, never visited the doctor or the dentist and still had his own teeth. After a couple of days in Leeds Infirmary he had had enough and walked out of the hospital, hailed a taxi and returned home.

When I returned from Australia I convinced him to go back to the consultant at the hospital, after he had received a number of letters requesting him to do so. At the consultation I learned that my father was suffering from advanced lung cancer, which had shown up by chance on the X-rays. He was still plodding through life quite happily, visiting his bowling club each evening and having lots of visits from his family, and I decided it would not be beneficial to him to tell him the bad news as it was the view of the consultant that the cancer was terminal and nothing could be done to help. It seemed his time was up.

John McGregor and Nixie Taverner had kept in constant contact with my father since their first meeting and were supportive friends up to his dying moments. John had visited him at the end of February

2005, and brought with him the models of the memorial for *Neptune* and *Kandahar*. My father listened intently to any news of the Association's progress and they talked excitedly about the forthcoming Memorial Service to be held at Alrewas in July 2005 which my father hoped desperately to attend.

My husband had arranged a special trip to Venice to celebrate our silver wedding anniversary in March 2005 and again I was concerned to leave my father with his visiting carers. He did not cope well with change and when the carers found him in a confused state they again sent for an ambulance to take him to Leeds Infirmary. When I returned this time it was evident that he was no longer capable of returning to his home. We could only stand by and watch as my gentle giant of a man was reduced to a skeletal frame within weeks. At 5ft 11inches tall he had always seemed the big strong hero to the women in his family and to watch him fade away so quickly in his hospital bed was heart-wrenching. As the cancer spread to his brain and the morphine was increased my father appeared to hallucinate as he made his arms move, imitating the front crawl and attempting to punch the air with his fists. As the family watched him we had to agree that he was not going to be able to swim or fight his way to survival this time. By the last few days his arms lay silently on the clean white sheets, occasionally his hands would flap like a bird with a broken wing. On the morning of 20 April 2005 my father, Norman Walton, passed quietly away to join his beloved wife and son, as he believed he would. I held his hand and stared at his white and painfully thin arm where the tattoo of his two love-birds seemed to shine brightly carrying the banners that represented the two women he loved dearly, his mother and his wife.

The young male nurse who attended him began clinically clearing his locker when he found photographs of the memorial that John McGregor had left with him and which he must have taken into hospital with him. The nurse asked what the photograph of the memorial was about and I began to explain about *Neptune* and how important the monument was to my father. The nurse was fascinated with the story of *Neptune* and simply replied that he must have been 'a remarkable man'.

This response was echoed by many people who attended the service for my father at Rawdon Crematorium in Leeds. John McGregor kindly spoke an oratory for him at the service to a crowd that spilled outside the doors. All who came were invited to the Pudsey Bowling Club to celebrate my father's life and it was here that his friends remarked to John how little they knew about my father's experiences during World War II and his life in the Navy before he moved to Yorkshire. John McGregor was told a few stories about my father that he had not heard. One story told by my father's friends from the bowling club made him smile. They recalled that one night when Norman left the club around his usual time of 11.30, he had struggled down the steps with his walking stick, as he did every night, to cross the car park and make his way to 90 Smalewell Road. Only on this night a youth with a wooden stick was lying in wait in the car park and came out of the dark and confronted him. He poked him in the stomach asking for his wallet. Still a quick thinker in his old age my father pleaded informing the youth that the wallet was in his back pocket but he couldn't let go of his stick to get it. As the youth started to bend over to retrieve the wallet father's survival instinct kicked in and he 'struck on the nut', smashing the nose of the youth with his forehead. From the corner of his eye he saw another youth coming in from the right and swung round with his stick, catching the youth with a blow to the head. The weapon was dropped and the youths ran off, whereupon my father calmly walked across the road and into his house. My mother panicked when she saw his head bleeding and immediately rang the police. When questioned by the police about his injuries my father simply stated that it was probable that the nose of his attacker had ended up in a worse state.

John McGregor and Nixie Taverner wrote tributes to my father whose obituary was published in the *Daily Telegraph*, *The Times*, *Yorkshire Evening Post* and *Newcastle Evening Chronicle*. Responses to the obituary arrived from friends, neighbours and boxing associates from the north-east of England, friends and work colleagues from Yorkshire as well as those with connections with HMS *Neptune*, providing a wealth of anecdotes and stories that are featured in this memoir by the kind permission of those concerned. John McGregor and Nixie Taverner remained good friends of the family as did many of the relatives of *Neptune* casualties.

It was at the end of 2006 that I received a notice from John McGregor, the Chairman of the Neptune Association, which described some exciting plans for 2007:

In April 2007, members of the Neptune Association, mostly relatives of those who died, will be going for 9 days to Malta and Tripoli. In Malta from where the ships set out, we will be unveiling a memorial plaque in the Maritime Museum and presenting a parchment scroll with the names of the 837 men who died in the two ships (*Neptune* and *Kandahar*).

In Tripoli we will visit the graves of some of the *Neptune* casualties and make a pilgrimage on board *Barberousse*, a Libyan ship, to the site 16 miles north-east of Tripoli, where *Neptune* and *Kandahar* both struck mines and *Neptune* sank.

It was an exciting possibility that there could be an opportunity for my father's wishes to be returned to his shipmates to be fulfilled. A trip that I never thought would be possible seemed to be on the cards. My father had always said that when he left this life it was his wish to be returned to the sea to rest with his mates in the 'Med'. I immediately contacted John and asked if it would be possible for me to join with other members and relatives of the men who had perished with Force K to travel to Malta and Tripoli and take with me the remains of my father to scatter on his final resting place.

John responded to me immediately with his thoughts on the matter, 'When I heard that you wanted to bring Norman's ashes to scatter over the sea above where I believe *Neptune* lies, I knew it was just right.' I set about planning for the exciting and unique trip to Malta and Tripoli.

The jar that held my father's ashes had been with me for a while as I contemplated what would be the right thing to do. When I visited the grave of my brother in the cemetery in Blaydon-on-Tyne to scatter my mother's ashes I was quite clear that this was the place she wanted to rest, with the son she loved so dearly and lost. There was no dilemma when my mother died. It was simple for me to recall her wishes as we had a special closeness that we shared. It was that unique bond between a mother and her daughter, the kind that is never replaced by any other. The yawning gap left by Mother's death now widened with the passing of my final guru and I wanted to do the right thing by him.

I deliberated long and hard until eventually deciding to scatter most of his ashes on the site of my brother's grave with my mother's ashes; it felt that the family lost so long ago had been reunited again. The scattering of the ashes had been carried out only days before the news arrived from the Neptune Association of the pilgrimage to

Malta and Tripoli. Once again I took to the A1 road and made the long drive to Blaydon Cemetery. It was an impulse reaction that I set about by the graveside with a garden trowel in one hand the container in the other and proceeded to scrape away the topsoil. Some may feel it was rather ghoulish or even worthy of reporting to the authorities that decide on the rules and regulations governing cemeteries. I did not stop to think about whatever the rules are governing consecrated ground; I did not know or even care. As I collected the soil, it was not the grains of earth that mattered but the symbol of his life that I would carry lovingly with me back to his mates who he had left in Libya.

On the anniversary of my father's death on 20 April 2007 the jar containing his remains was carefully packed into the case when I collected my belongings together and boarded the train to London. The next day I met up with the other pilgrims at Heathrow Airport and what a happy band they were, many in their seventies and eighties, some in wheelchairs, all determined to retrace the steps of their loved ones on that fateful day in December 1941. Soon settled into our airline seats we set off on the long-prepared and awaited visit to Malta and Tripoli. For some, to scenes of nostalgia, others to recognise their memories from letters and diaries describing the locations where husbands, fathers, grandfathers, brothers, uncles and sons had lived and fought during World War II. Eagerness was tempered by apprehension and some trepidation as to how individuals might themselves react to scenes that implied and evoked so much of those times of more than sixty years ago. On arriving at the assigned hotel we began to share our stories and the realisation of the uniqueness of the event in which we were to engage started to dawn.

The first opportunity for the group to commemorate the loss was on Sunday 22 April, when the Neptune Association joined with the George Cross Island Association to attend a service in St Paul's Cathedral in Malta. This was followed in the afternoon by a sea tour of the waters around the Valletta area, including the very impressive Grand Harbour from whence Force K had sailed on 18 December 1941. The tour was keenly nostalgic for the few war veterans in the party, including Frank Brown who had been an eyewitness to the events on 18 December 1941, in the destroyer HMS *Havock*.

On the Monday we experienced the 'history' of Malta: the Lascaris War Rooms where we walked the underground stone corridors, peering down from the balconies inside the caverns onto the board-room tables where Admirals, Vice Admirals and Captains, heads over the sea charts, plotted their manoeuvres over sixty years ago. Later we saw the stone steps that led to the harbour down which Captain Rory O'Conor certainly returned to his ship with urgency to get the sortie for Force K underway. This was where the long battle against the Axis siege of Malta was conducted. The period 1941–43 saw the immense courage and untold suffering of the Maltese people, and the struggles and losses suffered by the Royal Navy, the Army and the Royal Air Force in their defence. The battle was conducted to an agonising but victorious end. A modified version of an Admiralty Statement taken from *East of Malta: West of Suez* published 1941/2, sums up the importance of the time:

> The work of the Royal Navy in the Eastern Mediterranean from 1940 to 1943 and its supremacy in these waters has been vigorously asserted at Taranto and Matapan and in many other actions large and small, from Tobruk to protecting convoys to Malta, attacking enemy convoys to North Africa, bombarding enemy land forces on both Syrian and Libyan coasts and by its constant sea-going vigilance which greatly discouraged Italian fleet action and limited both Italian and German submarine and small craft operations, maintaining, throughout our most desperate period in '41 and '42, before sufficient protective aircraft could be spared to cover any of its many and varied activities and when grievous losses of men and ships were frequently occurring, the high standard of duty and discipline associated with the Senior Service and consequently the precious advantage of high morale.

This is a Naval story but to understand its full significance it is necessary to look beyond the narrow seas in which it was enacted, for the part played by the Navy in the Mediterranean has an importance in world strategy, which would be difficult to exaggerate. If, during those eighteen months, the Navy had failed to control the Eastern Basin against greatly superior enemy forces, Malta, Suez and Alexandria might all have fallen, the campaigns in Abyssinia, Syria and North Africa would not have been possible. Our whole Middle Eastern position would have been endangered and the Axis powers might have reached the Indian Ocean from the west and joined victoriously with their Japanese allies. Such was the Royal Navy's achievement in the Mediterranean in those vital years.

What had been a disparate group of travellers was now becoming a closely-knit unit determined to continue with the next and most important stage of the trip, leaving Malta on the short flight into Libya on Tuesday 24 April. The weather was unusual for the Mediterranean at that time of year with cold winds; rain and storms were brewing. The group made comments on how the poor weather differed from their experiences of holidays around the Mediterranean coast and there was a realisation of how bad weather conditions would have affected the men in Force K during their sortie in the depths of winter with stormy seas and black skies. The bus ride to the hotel was a pleasant surprise for most, with flourishing fields of fruit trees and flowers, Italian architecture and a great deal of Venetian and Roman influence across the land. The hotel made a token gesture to Western tastes attempting to attract tourism to the region and provided a very pleasant stay.

A visit to the glorious Roman city of Leptis Magna approximately eighty kilometres east of Tripoli was not dampened by the heavy rain that persisted all day. Avoiding the albino frogs that hopped between the cracks in the water-logged Roman roads, the group tramped through great temples, baths and harbour buildings, amazed by the vastness of what must have been a truly great harbour city in Roman times. As we drove back to Tripoli along the Libyan coast my mind drifted back to my father and memories of when he was picked up, having been sighted in the raft near Misurata and taken to the Tripoli hospital. The port of Misurata was not far from the Roman city of Leptis Magna and as I looked out of the window of the coach as we travelled the eighty kilometres back to Tripoli I thought about his body suffering the long journey up the coast of a foreign land and what he must have been thinking as he regained consciousness on that Christmas Eve in 1941, finally arriving alive on the Libyan coast.

On the return to Tripoli a visit and service had been arranged by the Neptune Association at the Commonwealth War Graves Cemetery, which was attended by the British Ambassador, Sir Vincent Fean. The cemetery was impressive and the service, conducted by Father Robbie Prakasam, a Libyan Anglican priest, was emotional. A more poignant period followed as the group found six named and four unnamed graves of *Neptune*'s men. Feelings for those men washed ashore so long ago ran high as relatives looked over the six named graves for casualties from HMS *Neptune* in the 1941 plot which was surrounded by twenty graves marked 'Soldier known unto God'. Remembrances (poppy crosses) were placed on each by individual members of the Association. Frank Brown from HMS *Havock* described the scene:

> I felt deeply honoured to make this gesture for 22-year old 2nd Class Stoker Brookes. My thoughts for his parents as this time that their son had the touch of a kindred spirit on their behalf and that this might offer them, and their family, solace and some comfort. I was nearly undone emotionally and glad no one spoke to me for some minutes afterwards. I walked through the headstones later reflecting on the number of sailors, soldiers and airmen – my head full of memories and sombre thoughts.

An evening reception in the British Embassy was hosted by Sir Vincent and Lady Fean and attended by one hundred guests including the ambassadors of South Africa, Australia (representing New Zealand), Malta, Germany and Italy. The Neptune Association representatives were able to share their stories with those attending and also had the opportunity to talk to British residents of Tripoli, gaining an insight into their life in Libya in the twenty-first century.

An unveiling ceremony at the Malta Maritime Museum in the presence of the President of Malta, Dr Edward Fenech-Adami was held on Saturday 28 April when the group returned to Malta and was reported by the *Sunday Times* on 29 April. The report highlighted the effort that should be made to remember those who sacrificed their lives so that we may enjoy the freedom we have today and described how members of the Neptune Association presented a scroll of honour naming the casualties of Force K to the Maritime Museum while President Edward Fenech-Adami unveiled a memorial to those who lost their lives in the sinking of HMS *Neptune* and HMS *Kandahar.*

Thanks were given by the Association's Chairman, John McGregor:

> The Neptune Association is honoured that His Exellency Dr Edward Fenech-Adami, the President of the Republic of Malta, has shared with us in this ceremony and would like to take this opportunity to thank him for his support and participation by unveiling the new Memorial; to the British High Commissioner and Heritage Malta for their encouragement and guidance as well as generously hosting the reception; to the Maritime Museum for allowing us to share in their dream; to Canon Tom Mendel and Father Joe Caruana for taking the service of dedication; to the R.N.O.A., the R.N.A., the R.B.L., the G.C.I.A. and John Mizzi for their welcome, help and enthusiasm throughout; to the Sea Cadets and the Standard Bearers;

and finally to our members for their continued encouragement and support
and for the great effort it has taken many to be here today.

The members commented on their return to Malta that the event
was what they had all been waiting for; the event they would never
forget had taken place off the coast of Tripoli two days before. The
group had hoped that weather conditions would improve enough to
sail out to where HMS *Neptune* most probably lies. The weather had
in fact improved with rain and strong winds subsiding by the second
day in Tripoli. The ship they were to take out to sea had also been
improved upon. The original idea was for the Association to hire a
tourist ship named *Barberousse*, that lay in Tripoli harbour, but on
closer inspection the group leaders John McGregor and Nick Wright
made the decision to seek elsewhere the transport for their journey
out to sea, much to the relief of the rest of the group. A Libyan
suction dredger of 1,500 tons also lay in harbour, a more suitable sea-
worthy vessel than the *Barberousse*. The group leaders set about
negotiating a deal with the captain of the Libyan suction dredger, to
take the group out to the site where *Neptune* probably sank. The
captain and his crew were bemused by the idea but did agree to take
this large group of British pilgrims aboard and ship them nearly
twenty miles out to sea to perform a special ceremony.

The process of authorisation for the trip by harbour authorities was
a long one and the group waited patiently for hours in the harbour
building as Libyan officials and the ship's crew made preparations for
the trip. Masses of red roses and white lilies, picked from the Libyan
fields that morning, surrounded the passengers. Over 200 flower
arrangements were to be cast into the sea, with written messages from
the loved ones of those who perished, some who were there and
some who were not. Libyan officials scurried around outside the
harbour, checking papers and safety conditions on board. The ship's
captain had sent for lifebelts, food and drink for his guests. Soon all
on the harbour and aboard were nodding approvingly and the group
boarded the dredger while locals watched with curiosity then waved
enthusiastically to this unusual group of British travellers.

The Libyan dredger named *Jarif* eventually began to negotiate
Tripoli harbour and make its way out to sea with the precious cargo.
The charismatic captain with his wide friendly smile made his bridge
open to all. As I stood on the bridge looking out to sea I turned back

to the harbour entrance and looked over the city of Tripoli as it now stood in the twenty-first century and wondered how it would have looked when my father had been brought there on Christmas Eve 1941 by the Italians. The Central Hospital was visible, as were many of the old buildings still standing on the main drag up from the harbour and I wondered if that old hospital, built by the Italians, was where my father had been taken and his life saved over the Christmas period in December 1941. I decided then that I would investigate the possibility the next day. Today was about commemorating those he had left behind, all those men who had died around him.

As the group journeyed out to sea there was a growing need to prepare, to organise to keep busy. As a few of us peered over the bridge we saw a hive of activity below. The roses and lilies had been spread across a large table and an organised group was busily constructing wreaths, stringing together tributes and attaching messages. As we watched Simon Hayhurst (the grandson of *Neptune* casualty Stoker Frederick Pascall) commented how very 'British' and 'Women's Institute' the scene looked and we laughed. In fact there was a growing feeling of 'British bulldog' abroad, the party was determined to see their plans through and beat any obstacle that might get in the way of their plans to pay tribute to the 837 men who rested in the waters and whose sacrifice, they felt, had been ignored for so long. The ship 'hove to' at the accepted chart calculation. The location at 33.07N 13.25E in Libyan waters, near the site of the mining of HMS *Neptune* and HMS *Kandahar* on 19 December 1941, had been plotted by the technical divers who were on board. The Libyan crew watched in wonder as did the Libyan television crew who had boarded in Tripoli to record the event, as the party organised themselves along the starboard side of the ship to begin the Service of Remembrance.

The Service of Remembrance was conducted at sea on 25 April 2007 near the site of the mining of HMS *Neptune* and HMS *Kandahar* on 19 December 1941, and was led by Commander Nicolas Wright, RN, son of Lt. Humphrey Wright, Trustee to the Neptune Association. This next is a short summary of the service.

Psalm 107, verses 23 and 24 provided the opening Sentence:

> They that go down to the sea in ships, and occupy their business in great waters. These men see the works of the Lord, and his wonders in the deep.

After the Welcome, Judith Littlewood, daughter of L. S. Frank Gardiner read the prayer from the Neptune Memorial Service at St Christopher's, New Zealand, remembering the sinking of *Neptune* and *Kandahar* with the loss of so many lives.

The first reading by Valerie Pennifer, daughter of Stoker Edmund Lidbury of *Kandahar* was from John 15, v 13, 'Greater love hath no man than this, that a man lay down his life for his friends' and was followed by The Lord's Prayer. Diana Clayton, daughter of Sgt. William Crocker, RM, gave the second reading, an anonymous seaman's poem:

> There are no flowers on a sailor's grave
> No lilies on an ocean wave
> The only tribute is the seagull's sweep
> And the teardrop on a loved one's cheek.

This was followed by the Naval hymn, 'Eternal Father, Strong to Save' written by the Rev. William Whiting in 1860 after a terrible storm in the Mediterranean Sea. The Exhortation was read by Royden Thomson, son of Pay Lt. Bruce Thomson, RNZN:

> They shall grow not old, as we that are left grow old,
> Age shall not weary them, nor shall the years condemn.
> At the going down of the sun, and in the morning
> We shall remember them

with the response 'We shall remember them'.

Then the Silence.

The Kohima Epitaph was read by Geoff Staley, son of Stoker Leonard Staley, 'When you go home, tell them of us and say, For your tomorrow, we gave our today.' The response was 'We will not break faith with you.' Jean Horsham, daughter of Cpl. James Auchinlech, RM read the next prayer to dedicate and commit the Wreaths of Remembrance which were then cast into the sea, together with the White Ensign, and individual flowers and messages. Norman Walton's ashes were scattered.

After the Act of Commitment came the Blessing:

> God grant to the living grace, to the departed rest,
> To all people unity, peace and concord.
> May the blessing of God Almighty, Father, Son and Holy Spirit be with us all and remain with us always.
> Amen.

All contributors had played their part and the lowering of a White Ensign presented by the current HMS *Neptune* at Faslane in Scotland was conducted. A second Ensign, representing the New Zealanders on board *Neptune*, was lowered by Royden Thomson, a New Zealander whose father, Bruce Thomson, went down with *Neptune*. A piece of rock brought by Royden from South Island, New Zealand, weighed down the Ensign, a poignant reminder of how far his fellow countrymen were away from home at their deaths. When the procession of relatives cast 250 floral tributes into the sea they spoke out loud the names that were known of the men who lay beneath then silence followed.

This was my cue as I walked slowly and apprehensively to the guard rail. Unscrewing the top from the jar that held my father's remains, his experiences of hanging onto the guard rail on the night of 18/19 December 1941 came rushing into my head and I began to lose my composure and involuntarily and shakily began to speak to my father: 'I am returning you to the mates you left behind as you wanted Dad, may you now rest in peace.' I was overcome by the feeling that a circle had finally been closed now his soul was returned to the deep.

Silence fell over the ship – without engines – only the flapping of *Jarif*'s flag in the wind and the slap of the sea against her sides. There seemed to be a drawing together in comfort, hugging close to friends, a clasping of hands, a hand on an arm or a shoulder, round a waist; sharing this very precious and never-to-be-forgotten time was unique and very special. From that moment, a loose association of people became members of the same family, sharing comfort and relief as though this was what they had been waiting for through all those years – an ending.

There was much talk and companionship throughout the rest of the trip and the return journey. Later John McGregor described the moment my father was returned to the sea, 'All sixty-three of us (descendants of the casualties of Force K) were profoundly moved on that special day when Norman joined his mates. It was the climax of our amazing remembrance journey.'

There were a few hours spare the next morning before our flight back to Malta and I managed to gain the help of our Libyan guide to leave the hotel and visit the Central Hospital in Tripoli. The guide kindly escorted me explaining that this hospital would more than likely be the hospital where my father was taken in 1941. The Central Hospital based near the harbour was built in 1923 and controlled then by the Italian forces in Tripoli during the Second World War. On arriving at the hospital after a swift and hairy drive through the streets of Tripoli, we left the taxi and slowly toured the building. I was looking for any signs of the scanty description my father had given about his rescue all those years ago. I remembered him saying that all he could recall about his time in Tripoli was the sight of arches overhead as he was taken to the hospital and the kindness and care of a male nurse who attended him there. On our walk around the main hospital there were no arches to be found. I was introduced to the manager of the hospital who explained that any records from 1941 would have either been burned or transferred to storage elsewhere and would be difficult to locate. As a last resort I asked the hospital manager if there was another hospital or building nearby that would have been used at that time. The hospital manager explained that the building he described as the 'old nursery' could have been used; it was now not in use but being refurbished and he proceeded to give directions to the site. Following his directions I turned a corner to the entrance of the 'old nursery' to be faced by rows of arches lining the building. Tears welled and overflowed as I felt the presence of my father next to me, finally closing the door.

Before the group returned to England, I made another visit to the Malta Maritime Museum privately and quietly to enjoy to the full what was such a special and interesting place, and to reflect by the memorial plaque that sits in the fitting private cloister. I was keen to experience the trip across the harbour in the small gondolas to the area my father described as 'the gut'. John McGregor and I took the short trip across the water as we made our way back to the hotel. I knew this would have been a trip made many times by my father and recalled he was not the type for words or ceremony but actions; he grabbed life by both hands and lived it to the full never wasting a moment of the precious gift. A smile crossed my face as I imagined him enjoying every aspect of what this area full of bars and girls would have to offer during what little respite the sailors would have had here from the toils of war.

Appendices

Role of Honour of those lost with HMS Neptune *sunk on 19 December 1941*

Royal Navy

Abell, Frederick J. Leading Supply Assistant
Adsetts, William I. Ordinary Seaman (South Africa)
Allen, George E. Plumber
Allen, Joseph F. Stoker
Allridge, Arthur Ordinary Seaman
Arbuthnot, Peter C. R. Lieutenant
Argulus, Edward A. Leading Telegraphist
Armour, Daniel Ordinary Seaman
Ashton, Charles Master at Arms
Aspinall, Jack Leading Sick Berth Attendant
Auger, Thomas F. Ordnance Artificer
Badcock, Charles D. E. Midshipman
Bailey, Edward Stoker
Baker, Ernest Able Seaman
Baker, William Cook (S)
Baker, Walter Leading Seaman
Baker, Walter J. Stoker
Baldwin, Cornelius Stoker
Ball, William F. Petty Officer Stoker
Ballinger, Frederick Petty Officer Stoker
Barlow, William H. Stoker
Barnes, Albert J. Chief Stoker
Barnett, William Leading Stoker
Bartlett, Owen J. Able Seaman
Barton, Malcolm R. Ordinary Telegraphist
Bastable, Philip H. C. Midshipman
Batt, William J. Chief Shipwright
Baxter, Ronald Steward
Bell, Reginald Stoker
Belsom, Richard A. Ordinary Seaman
Bennett, Alfred Stoker
Bennett, Edward D. Leading Seaman
Bennett, Geoffrey Joiner
Berry, Philip A. Commander
Bevan, David R. L. Sub-Lieutenant
Billington, William Stoker
Birmingham, William Ordinary Seaman
Bisby, Bernard Ordinary Seaman
Black, Thomas F. Leading Stoker
Blake, Frederick C. Able Seaman
Blight, James H. Engine Room Artificer
Boddington, Fred Able Seaman
Booth, Alan V. Ordinary Seaman
Bosley, George C. S. Ordinary Seaman
Bowron, Leslie C. Ordinary Seaman
Brabyn, Kenneth A. Engine Room Artificer
Bradburn, Ernest Able Seaman
Bradwell, Arnold H. Engine Room Artificer
Branson, Wilfred F. Chief Petty Officer
Brant, John N. Able Seaman
Braunton, Thomas J. Leading Stoker
Bright, Reginald W. Leading Seaman
Bristow, Franklin W. Able Seaman
Brooks, James S. Able Seaman
Brough, Arthur Boy Seaman
Brough, Caleb D. S. Chief Petty Officer Telegraphist
Buckingham, William Leading Stoker
Bull, James W. Able Seaman
Bull, R. Thomas G. Sick Berth Attendant
Burdett, George Ordinary Seaman
Burley, Morris Petty Officer Stoker
Burns, Ellick T. E. Stoker (South Africa)
Burton, Albert H. Able Seaman
Buxton, Richard Engine Room Artificer
Came, Edgar R. Stoker
Campbell, Keith Able Seaman (Australia)
Canterbury, Fred Able Seaman
Carroll, Frank Stoker
Carter, George Leading Stoker
Carter, Thomas Able Seaman
Carthy, James G. Petty Officer (Eire)
Carty, John J. Petty Officer Telegraphist
Chamberlain, Albert H. Stoker
Chamberlain, Frederick J. Leading Seaman
Charles, David W. Petty Officer Steward
Charman, James P. Leading Steward
Clark, John C. Sick Berth Attendant
Clayden, Victor J. Chief Stoker
Cleary, Patrick J. Coder
Clemm, William E. Stoker
Cock, Edwin A. Boy Telegraphist
Cole, Raymond M. Boy Seaman
Coleman, Ernest C. Chief Petty Officer
Connor, John Stoker
Cornish, Reginald E. Chief Petty Officer Cook (S)
Costello, James S. Petty Officer
Coulton, Richard T. Lieutenant
Cousins, Ernest G. Electrical Artificer
Creek, John A. T. Chief Petty Officer Sick Berth Attdt
Cregoe, Albert E. T. Petty Officer Stoker
Crisp, Kenneth S. F. Telegraphist
Crook, Ernest Leading Seaman
Crossley, Harold Stoker
Cunningham, David C. Lieutenant
Cunningham, Thomas Petty Officer Stoker (South Africa)
Curtis,Cedric C. Canteen Assistant
Darcy, Richard Ordinary Seaman
Darton, William G. S. Petty Officer
Daulton, Raymond G. Stoker (South Africa)
Davies, Alan S. Stoker
Davies, Thomas W. Ordinary Seaman
Day, Robert F. Boy Seaman
Denney, Raymond Ordnance Artificer
Desoer, Allan Ordinary Telegraphist
Dixon, James A. Telegraphist
Dixon, James B. Stoker
Dodd, William J. Boy Seaman
Donaldson, James N. Able Seaman
Donaldson, Thomas Able Seaman
Donoghue, Stanley C. Able Seaman
Donovan, John Able Seaman
Dornom, Herbert E. Shipwright
Dowle, Percy G. Stoker
Drake, Kenneth Boy Telegraphist
Duffy, John A. Wireman
Duncan, Harold Able Seaman
Durham, Victor G. R. Boy Seaman (South Africa)
Edmans, Edgar T. Commissioned Gunner
Edwards, Frank B. Stoker
Edward, Thomas G. Ordinary Seaman
Elder, Alexander Able Seaman
Elliott, Ernest H. Ordinary Seaman
Ellis, George H. Yeoman of Signals
Elson, Dudley V. Leading Seaman
Ensell, Maurice A. S. Midshipman
Esterhuyse, Adriaan J. Stoker (South Africa)
Evans, Edward T. Leading Seaman
Evans, John Leading Signalman
Evans, John C. Electrical Artificer
Evans, Moses W. Warrant Mechanician
Evans, William H. Petty Officer
Falzon, Angel G. F. Steward (Malta)
Farish, Robert J. Leading Seaman
Feltwell, Thomas G. Petty Officer Stoker
Fenn, Charles Ordinary Telegraphist
Fewins, Arthur K. Engine Room Artificer
Field, Ronald F. G. Ordinary Seaman
Field William A. A. Petty Officer Cook (S)
Fielding, George S. Leading Telegraphist
Flaherty, Harold L. Leading Seaman
Flett, Arthur Seaman
Flowers, Ernest R. Chief Engine Room Artificer
Forbes, David B. Midshipman
Ford, Edward W. G. Supply Chief Petty Officer
Forrest, Alexander J. Leading Steward
Forster, Thomas Leading Stoker
Francis, William Petty Officer Stoker
Fraser, Cameron Surgeon Lieutenant
Freeland, George E. A. Lieutenant (E)
Gailes, Wilfred Wireman
Gardiner, Frank R. Leading Seaman
Garner, Percival Ordinary Seaman
Garry, Desmond J. Ordinary Seaman (Eire)
Gaudern, William H. Engine Room Artificer
Gill, Frank G. Stoker (South Africa)
Gilchrist, Peter H. Able Seaman
Gillingham, Alfred M. Leading Stoker
Glancy, John Able Seaman
Glanville, E. John Chief Engine Room Artificer
Glover, Charles G. Able Seaman
Goff, Sidney E. Ordinary Seaman
Good, Cecil G. Ordinary Seaman
Gore, James A. Petty Officer Stoker (South Africa)
Gorey, Wallace M. Able Seaman
Grant, Alistair Macdonald Boy Seaman
Grant, Michael E. Leading Cook (S)
Gray, Edwin Wireman
Green, Frank B. Petty Officer Stoker (South Africa)
Green, Kenneth Supply Assistant
Greensmith, Harry Stoker
Grierson, William Ordinary Seaman
Griffith, Henry E. Petty Officer Writer
Griffiths, Robert A. Ordinary Telegraphist
Griffiths, Trevor E. Petty Officer Stoker
Griffiths, William Leading Stoker
Griffiths, William E. Able Seaman
Gritton, Thomas Ordinary Seaman
Gundry, W. Gerald Petty Officer Stoker
Guthrie, John W. Joiner
Hague, Douglas Signalman
Haines, Walter Boy Seaman
Halford, Jonathan (Jack) H. Ordinary Telegraphist
Hall, Clifford A. Stoker (South Africa)
Hall, John W. Stoker (South Africa)
Hall, Edwin L. Leading Stoker
Hall, Leonard G. Ordinary Seaman
Hall, William A. Chief Stoker
Hamilton, Albert Able Seaman
Hancock, Christopher U. Chief Mechanician
Handford, Bertram C. Leading Cook (S)
Hanley, Bernard H. Boy Seaman
Hannaford, William H. Stoker
Harbon, Reginald E. Chief Yeoman of Signals
Harland, Frederick Able Seaman
Harper, Frank Stoker
Harris, Ernest W. S. Leading Stoker
Harris, Lionel H. Ordinary Seaman
Harris, The Rev'd Thomas Chaplain
Harrison, David A. C. Stoker
Harrison, Fred Stoker
Harrison, John A. Stoker
Hassell, John Stoker
Hatcher, Sidney G. W. Stoker
Hathaway, Cyril D. Petty Officer Telegraphist
Hawkins, John H. Petty Officer
Hay, Duncan E. G. Chief Petty Officer
Hedges, George H. Stoker
Heighes, John (Jack) W. Ordinary Seaman
Henry, Bernard Stoker
Henry, Michael W. Steward (St Helena)
Hicks, Stanley Stoker
Hickson, Joe Stoker
Hill, Alan B. Lieutenant
Hill, James Stoker
Hill, Richard Yeoman of Signals
Hinson, George A. Stoker
Hoad, John H. Able Seaman (New Zealand)
Hoar, Harold Warrant Shipwright
Holden, Edgar G. Boy Seaman
Holiday, Keith A. Ordinary Telegraphist
Holloway, Douglas R. Midshipman
Holt, Arthur Engineer Commander
Holyome, George J. Wireman
Honeywood, Hubert T. Ordinary Seaman
Hooper, Leonard Sailmaker's Mate
Hopkinson, Joseph Leading Stoker
Hopwood, George Ordinary Seaman
Horton, Douglas E. Stoker
Hosking, Reginald Boy Seaman
Houston, David A. Midshipman
Hudson, John Engine Room Artificer
Hughes, Edward Ordnance Artificer
Hughes, John Able Seaman
Hunter, Cyril G. Wireman
Hussey, Edward J. Able Seaman
Hutchings, Hubert R. Leading Cook (S)
Hutchinson, Horace Stoker
Hyem, Ian McConnachie Coder
Irwin, Leslie C. Chief Petty Officer Cook (O)
Jackson, Frederick A. V. Lieutenant (E)
James, Arthur B. Blacksmith
James, Peter Petty Officer
Jay, A. David Midshipman
Johns, Arthur S. Chief Petty Officer Cook (S)
Johns, William C. A. Leading Stoker
Johnson, Edward W. Petty Officer
Johnson, Harry Ordinary Seaman
Johnson, Herbert Engine Room Artificer (South Africa)
Jones, Alwyne Chief Electrical Artificer
Jones, Harry Wireman
Jones, John Able Seaman
Jones, Peter K. Canteen Assistant
Jones, Reginald D. Ordnance Artificer
Keefe, Abel Able Seaman (Canada)
Kemp, Alexander A. Able Seaman (Australia)
Kennedy, Robert Ordinary Seaman
Kenworthy, George E. Petty Officer Stoker
Kerr, Charles S. G. Stoker
King, Charles L. Leading Seaman
Kingston, Charles C. Stoker
Kinross, John B. Petty Officer Stoker
Kitts, Richard K. Stoker
Knight, John Able Seaman (South Africa)
Knowles, James M. Lieutenant (E)
Laban, Cyril K. Commissioned Gunner
Lake, Courtenay W. Leading Seaman
Lambert, Louis C. Able Seaman
Lancaster, Frederick G. J. Able Seaman
Lanchbury, Charles W. Petty Officer Cook (O)
Lang, Albert W. Petty Officer
Larkworthy, Thomas C. MID Surgeon Commander
Lavis, Ernest G. Petty Officer
Lawson, Donald L. Engine Room Artificer (South Africa)
Legg, Robert J. Able Seaman
Lewney, Kenneth Ordinary Telegraphist
Light, John R. Leading Stoker
Lloyd, James Able Seaman
Lobb, Thomas H. Leading Stoker
Lock, John Chief Electrical Artificer
Lockie, James Able Seaman
Logue, William R. J. Able Seaman
Long, Norman F. Stoker
Longston, Aubrey J. Stoker
Loughland, Jack Cook (O)
Lowe, John F. Electrical Artificer
Lowings, George W. R. Regulating Petty Officer
Lowthian, John E. Ordinary Seaman
Lunn, James G. Cook (O)
Lynes, William B. N. DSM Petty Officer Telegraphist
Lyons, Arthur Stoker
Mabb, George E. Stoker
Markwick, Anthony A. Midshipman
Mantle, James A. E. Petty Officer Cook (S)
Marsden, Thomas Ordnance Artificer
Marshall, Michael B. H. Paymaster Lieutenant
Martin, Cyril R. W. Engine Room Artificer
Martin, Francis L. Leading Seaman
Mason, William H. Ordinary Seaman
Mawson, Michael G. H. Paymaster Midshipman
Mayes, William Stoker
McBride, John P. Able Seaman
McCarthy, Michael J. Stoker (Eire)
McGlead, Patrick J. Boy Seaman
McGowan, Garnet D. W. Able Seaman
McGregor, John (Jack) H. Paymaster Commander
McLean, John L. Ordinary Seaman
McNally, Daniel Leading Seaman (Eire)
McSweeney, Timothy Leading Stoker (Eire)
McTigue, Charles J. Ordinary Seaman (Eire)
Mead, Ronald H. Ordinary Signalman
Medland, W. Howard Stoker
Medlicott -Vereker, Patrick B. Midshipman
Medlow, Wilfred H. D. Able Seaman
Mee, Leslie E. Stoker
Metcalf, Douglas Schoolmaster
Miller, William Able Seaman
Montanaro, Emmanuele Steward (Malta)
Moody, Donald E. R. Able Seaman
Morey, Ernest J. Stoker
Morris, Arthur H. Mechanician
Morris, David L. W. Boy Seaman
Mortimore, Cyril A. Petty Officer
Morton, Edwin G. T. Stoker
Mossop, John Stoker
Munro, Stanley Stoker
Murphy, John Blacksmith
Mustoo, Norman C. Able Seaman
Needham, George W. Stoker
Nelson, Walter H. Petty Officer
Newell, William A. Able Seaman
Newton, Emmanuel Leading Stoker
Nicholls, Henry H. Stoker
Nicholls, Joseph C. Leading Steward
Norrish, William S. Able Seaman
North, The Right Hon. Baron Lieutenant
O'Brien, Arthur Able Seaman
O'Brien, Frank Stoker
O'Conor, Rory C. Captain (in command)
Oldham, William A. Able Seaman
Oliver, Thomas Leading Seaman
O'Mara, Donald H. Able Seaman
Oosterberg, Leslie Stoker (South Africa)
Orman, Leslie F. Able Seaman
Osborne, William H. Instructor Lieutenant
O'Shea, James Ordnance Artificer
Ovenstone, Peter Wireman
Oxley, Ronald Able Seaman
Oxley, William Ordinary Seaman
Painter, Ronald Engine Room Artificer
Palmer, Ivo Able Seaman
Parrott, Philip H. Sick Berth Attendant
Paske, Robert A. Petty Officer Stoker
Paskell, Frederick W. Stoker
Paver, William G. M. Boy Seaman
Payne, Charles G. Boy Seaman
Payne, Herbert J. Stoker
Pearson, Sydney F. Boy Seaman
Peel, Alan Able Seaman
Pereira, Cecil A. Stoker (South Africa)
Perkin, David C. Leading Stoker
Perkins, David O. Petty Officer Stoker
Perrin, Ernest R. Stoker
Phillips, David Chief Petty Officer Stoker
Phillips, Frederick W. Able Seaman
Phipps, Alfred Leading Stoker
Phipps, William G. Able Seaman
Pidden, John F. Stoker
Pilling, Douglas Ordinary Seaman
Plackett, Gilbert G. Able Seaman
Platt, Frank F. Petty Officer
Pollard, Albert Able Seaman
Powell, Raymond M. Ordinary Seaman
Price, Albert W. F. Able Seaman
Price, George A. Petty Officer
Price, Hanley B. Chief Engine Room Artificer
Priestley, John T. Able Seaman
Prince, Frederick C. Commissioned Gunner
Pritchard, William F. Leading Seaman
Pugh, Cyril W. Able Seaman
Quine, Henry T. Leading Stoker
Quinn, Joseph B. Ordnance Artificer
Ralph, Edwin Stoker
Rawcliffe, Ted Leading Seaman
Read, Victor S. Boy Seaman
Reed, Arthur Leading Seaman
Reed, Denis Petty Officer (South Africa)
Rees, Humphrey D. Supply Assistant
Regan, Donal Mechanician (Eire)
Richardson, Edwin Stoker
Riding, Eric B. Surgeon Lieutenant
Ridsdale, Ernest Petty Officer Stoker
Roberts, Bertram A. Stoker
Roberts, Edwin S. Petty Officer
Robertson, Robert M. B. Ordnance Artificer
Robinson, Edward C. Paymaster Midshipman
Rodhouse, Norman W. Able Seaman
Rogers, Alfred (Billy) W. Stoker
Russell, Edward J. Petty Officer Stoker (South Africa)
Rutherford, James D. Petty Officer Supply (South Africa)
Sainty, Ernest W. E. Warrant Engineer

We will remember them

Roll of Honour of those lost with HMS Neptune *sunk on* 19 *December* 1941

Royal Navy

Sanders, Eric W. Stoker
Savage, Burnham N. Steward
Scamp, John A. D. Steward
Scholes, Patrick J. Boy Seaman
Scott, George Able Seaman
Scott, John W. Supply Assistant
Scrine, Robert Leading Stoker
Sears, Leonard W. Able Seaman
Sears, Ronald G. Able Seaman
Shaw, Douglas Able Seaman (Rhodesia)
Shay, Douglas Leading Stoker
Sheppard, William F. E. Petty Officer Steward
Shilston, Edward A. C. Petty Officer Stoker
Short, Alfred J. Able Seaman
Simm, Joseph Ordinary Seaman
Sisk, Phillip D. Able Seaman (Eire)
Skellam, James A. Stoker
Skentelbury, John L. Shipwright
Skinner, Thomas H. Leading Seaman
Sly, Leonard G. H. Canteen Manager
Small, John W. Ordinary Coder
Smith, John Ordinary Seaman
Smith, Leonard A. A. Stoker
Smith, Stanley Able Seaman
Smith, William H. Leading Telegraphist (New Zealand)
South, Alfred E. Petty Officer Stoker
Speake, Norman S. Telegraphist
Spink, Sydney Stoker
Spivey, William A. Ordinary Seaman
Spriggs, Frederick J. Ordinary Seaman
Stainsby, Thomas F. Stoker
Staley, Leonard Stoker
Stannard, Colin F. Leading Seaman
Statham, Sydney Wireman
Stewart, Joseph Ordinary Telegraphist
Stowers, George F. J. Able Seaman
Street, Stanley W. H. Boy Seaman
Symes, Richard J. Stoker
Symons, William C. F. Boy Seaman
Taylor, Frank Ordinary Seaman
Taylor, Harold Able Seaman
Taylor, James A. Ordinary Seaman
Taylor, Joseph Able Seaman
Taylor, Stanley A. Boy Seaman
Tetley, Ian B. Lieutenant (E)
Thacker, Charles E. Able Seaman
Thomas, Francis H. Stoker
Thomas, Edgar W. G. Petty Officer
Thomas, Francis H. Stoker
Thomas, Frederick Petty Officer
Thomas, Hubert Cook (O)
Thompson, Edward A. Leading Seaman
Thorne, Walter J. Mechanician
Thornhill, Frederick H. Petty Officer Stoker
Tiley, Alfred J. Stoker
Tinkler, Francis M. Ordinary Seaman
Tinsley, William R. C. Canteen Assistant
Tipping, Joseph S. Able Seaman
Titcombe, Reginald Able Seaman
Tomkinson, John Stoker
Tostevin, Donald E. Leading Stoker
Townsend, Henry C. Stoker
Tracey, John Stoker
Travers, Cecil J. Ordinary Seaman
Trench, David S. C. Ordinary Seaman
Truby, William H. Able Seaman
Tucker, Rupert F. Petty Officer Stoker
Tudge, Edwin R. Able Seaman
Tull, Leslie C. Petty Officer
Turley, Reginald (Tommy) C. Leading Seaman
Turner, Ernest R. Leading Writer
Turner, Harry A. Ordinary Seaman
Underwood, Arthur S. Able Seaman
Van Rensburg, Johannes F. Petty Officer (South Africa)
Vivian, Henry W. Able Seaman
Waldron, Sydney F. E. Able Seaman
Walker, Harry G. Ordinary Seaman
Walters, Francis T. Able Seaman
Walters, Harold Able Seaman
Walters, Howard A. Ordinary Telegraphist
Walton, Robert F. Stoker
Ward, Henry Engine Room Artificer
Warley, James M. Able Seaman
Wateridge, Frank Ordinary Signalman
Waterworth, Clifford Able Seaman
Waterworth, Harry Ordinary Seaman
Watson, Harold Ordinary Seaman
Webber, George D. R. Petty Officer
Weiss, Frederick Petty Officer
Welling, Herbert N. Petty Officer Cook (S)
Wesson, Donald S. Able Seaman
West, John E. Boy Seaman
White, Henry Boy Seaman
White, Richard R. Stoker

White, William H. Stoker
Whyte, Hugh M. Leading Steward
Wilby, Arthur N. Ordinary Telegraphist
Wilks, Vivian T. W. J. Warrant Electrician
Williams, Clarence A. Ordinary Seaman
Williams, Hayden P. Able Seaman
Williams, Samuel C. Petty Officer Stoker
Williams, Thomas Petty Officer Stoker
Williams, William Able Seaman
Willing, Jack Boy Seaman
Willis, Mark Petty Officer Cook. (S)
Wilton, John T. Leading Stoker
Windsor, Frederick R. Able Seaman
Winsor, Bertram P. Ordinary Seaman
Wilson, Donald J. Lieutenant
Wood, Thomas R. Steward
Woodford, Leslie Shipwright
Woodriffe, Leonard G. Chief Engine Room Artificer
Woodward, Alfred Able Seaman
Woodward, Frank A. Lieutenant
Worth, Harold W. Leading Seaman
Wright, Ernest Stoker
Wright, F. Humphrey Lieutenant
Wright, Sydney Petty Officer Supply
Wright, William Engine Room Artificer
Wylie, Samuel Boy Seaman

Royal Marines

Auchinlock, James W. Corporal
Barlow, William S. Marine
Blackwell, George Marine
Boxall, Leslie A. Marine
Burrows, Verdun C. M. W. Marine
Chambers, George H. Marine
Cloughly, Norman D. S. Marine
Coppock, Colin F. Marine
Corner, Arthur E. G. Musician
Cray, Terrance C. Marine
Crocker, William H. Sergeant
Croke, William T. Corporal
Dale, Dennis I. T. Marine
Day, James E. Marine
Dick, David Musician
Dickens, George Marine
Dowle, Sidney J. Marine
Dubber, Ronald A. Marine
Dufton, John Marine
Evoy, James Marine
Facer, G. Bernard Marine
Glover, Reginald J. Marine
Goddard, Hayward T. C. Musician
Greaves, Dennis Musician
Green, Frank Marine
Harris, Brynmor I. Marine
Harrison, Robert L. Marine
Hartnoll, H. Digory DSC Lieutenant RM
Hawkins, Thomas C. Marine
Hayward, Charles E. E. Corporal
Hendy, Norman Marine
Hill, Thomas W. Marine
Hollick, Percy E. Marine
Hooper, William Marine
Hooper, William H. R. Sergeant
Hopkins, George A. Marine
Hynard, Walter G. Marine
Joyce, Donald F. Bandmaster
Lavis, George Sergeant
Lewis, Robert J. Marine
Lovett, Frederick C. Marine
McGuffog, Andrew Marine
Medcalfe, Ernest W. Marine
Millar, Noel L. W. Captain RM
Murch, William E. Sergeant
Nuttall, James Marine
O'Brien, Patrick G. Sergeant (Eire)
Partridge, George W. Marine
Patterson, John Marine
Phipps, Reginald C. Corporal
Plain, Charles H. H. Musician
Poole, Cyril E. Musician
Preece, Douglas (Val) R. V. Corporal
Raby, Albert F. Marine
Raindle, William J. Marine
Randall, Douglas A. Musician
Reffold, Leonard Marine
Roberts, John O. Musician
Robins, Henry A. Marine
Rogers, William J. Boy Bugler
Sergison, Andrew H. W. Marine
Shackleton, William T. Marine
Simpson, John W. Marine
Smith, Albert R. Boy Bugler
Sommerford, Jack Marine

Southgate, William A. Musician
Spence, Walter A. Musician
Tebworth, Albert G. Marine
Vosper, Sydney A. Marine
Walford, Selby H. L. Corporal
Whitworth, James Marine
Wilcock, Joseph Marine
Willis, Oswald G. L. Marine
Wright, Stanley H. G. Marine
Young, Ronald J. Marine

(Gardner, Hubert R. Marine)

South African Naval Forces

Adams, Thomas A. Able Seaman
Bullimore, Denis J. Lieutenant RM
Calder, Frank T. Able Seaman
Campbell, Roy M. Able Seaman
Dixon, Serfas Able Seaman
Few, Jim Able Seaman
Haines, Eric G. Able Seaman
Hook, Aubrey C. Able Seaman
Howard, Harold D. Signalman
Hubbard, Wallace S. Able Seaman
Kemack, Brian N. Signalman
Merryweather, John Able Seaman
Meyrick, Walter Signalman
Morris, Rodney Ordinary Signalman
Rankin, Cecil R. Signalman
Thorp, Edward C. Signalman
Thorp, Francis D. Able Seaman
Wild, Ernest A. Able Seaman

Royal New Zealand Navy

Alder, Edwin P. Able Seaman
Anderson, Henry B. Able Seaman
Anderson, William J. Able Seaman
Andrew, Norman R. Able Seaman
Andrews, Albert G. R. Shipwright
Armfield, Harry J. Leading Signalman
Ashton, Lindsay R. Leading Seaman
Atkinson, Basil M. Able Seaman
Atkinson, Roy V. Leading Seaman
Ball, Jack P. Able Seaman
Barford, Bryan J. Able Seaman
Barker, Frederick R. Able Seaman
Barron, Alexander G. Able Seaman
Barstow, John A. Supply Assistant
Baskett, R. George Able Seaman
Biggs, Hudson W. Able Seaman
Birss, James A. Able Seaman
Blackley, James B. E. Able Seaman
Boaz, Ernest G. Able Seaman
Brackenridge, Ian H. Able Seaman
Brookes, Norman G. Signalman
Brown, Alan H. Supply Assistant
Brown, James Engine Room Artificer
Brown, William W. Able Seaman
Brownie, Revell E. Leading Seaman
Buckley, Ross B. Able Seaman
Burt, Ian Cook (S)
Button, Kenneth A. Signalman
Calvert, James W. Able Seaman
Campbell, Albert V. Able Seaman
Campbell, William A. Petty Officer
Capon, Arthur N. Leading Seaman
Carr, Patrick A. Stoker
Carrigan, John Able Seaman
Carter, Alan H. J. Able Seaman
Christie, Herbert H. Electrical Artificer
Clark, Ronald H. C. Able Seaman
Collins, Thomas Able Seaman
Cook, Norman Able Seaman
Cooper, Howard Supply Assistant
Coote, James M. Able Seaman
Corbin, Donald H. H. Able Seaman
Cormack, Colin A. Able Seaman
Cosgrove, Charles A. Able Seaman
Cronquest, Robert M. Able Seaman
Dawson, Graeme D. Leading Stoker
Dennison, George S. Able Seaman
Denton, Leo R. Able Seaman
Diehl, Arthur E. Able Seaman
Dimmock, John B. Able Seaman
Dobbs, Raymond P. Leading Telegraphist
Doussett, Edward D. Leading Seaman
Dyer, Robert F. Engine Room Artificer
Elstob, Norman J. Able Seaman
Evans, George D. Joiner
Evans, Victor R. D. Telegraphist

Forgie, Kauru S. Supply Assistant
Friedman, Maurice W. Supply Assistant
Garlick, Bruce C. Able Seaman
Garmson, Alan T. Cook (S)
Garrett, Kenneth E. Leading Seaman
Gibbs, William H. Engine Room Artificer
Gilian, Reginald C. Able Seaman
Gregory, Douglas A. Stoker
Hansen, George Able Seaman
Hardie, Geoffrey B. Cook (S)
Harris, Herbert E. Able Seaman
Harvey, Douglas M. Petty Officer
Heaney, Arthur J. Engine Room Artificer
Hook, Roy D. Able Seaman
Howlison, James R. Able Seaman
Hubbard, Stanley J. Engine Room Artificer
Hubble, Linus E. Signalman
Hull, George B. Able Seaman
Jenkins, A. Wally J. Signalman
Johns, John W. Able Seaman
Johnstone, William Joiner
Jones, Mervyn G. Engine Room Artificer
Kennedy, Ian A. Signalman
Kingdon, Stanley L. Able Seaman
Knewstubb, John W. Engine Room Artificer
Land, Arthur C. Able Seaman
Leckie, James C. DSM Leading Telegraphist
Leyland, Frank Writer
Lord, Lloyd N. Able Seaman
Lovett, Arthur F. Cook (S)
Macaulay, Desmond G. Engine Room Artificer
MacDonald, Robert A. Able Seaman
Macintosh, Ivan W. Stoker
Marett, Hamel W. Able Seaman
Marsden, Harry Able Seaman
McCabe, Gilbert Able Seaman
McCallum, Frederick G. Engine Room Artificer
McComish, Trevor J. Engine Room Artificer
McGee, Noel F. Engine Room Artificer
McIver, Alexander H. H. Stoker
McKinnon, P. Bruce Supply Assistant
McLeod, Alan J. Engine Room Artificer
McPherson, Brian E. Midshipman
Moore, John E. Engine Room Artificer
Morley, Roland Telegraphist
Mosley, Thomas J. P. Able Seaman
Munro, Duncan P. Able Seaman
Murray, Gordon Able Seaman
Nalder, Laurance N. Engine Room Artificer
O'Connell Leslie J. Engine Room Artificer
O'Neil William J. Assistant Cook
Patterson, Samuel J. S. Petty Officer
Payne, Stanley R. A. Painter
Peat, Reginald Leading Signalman
Percival, Raymond S. Leading Seaman
Perry, Ronald J. Able Seaman
Perry, William G. Able Seaman
Petherick, James D. Able Seaman
Quinn, James B. Able Seaman
Quinn, Ronald F. Able Seaman
Raper, Allan S. Leading Seaman
Reid, John R. Stoker
Riley, Bernard D. Leading Seaman
Robertson, Malcolm D. Able Seaman
Rodgerson, George Joiner
Ross, John V. Able Seaman
Rowe, Frederick Assistant Cook
Ruddick, Edward W. Leading Seaman
Scott, Jack G. Able Seaman
Simpson, Alfred G. Able Seaman
Simpson, James A. Engine Room Artificer
Smith, George E. Electrical Artificer
Steedman, John J. D. Painter
Stewart, John E. Leading Telegraphist
Sturgeon, Albert V. Engine Room Artificer
Tamplin, Edward H. Able Seaman
Thomson, Bruce A. Paymaster Lieutenant
Toomey, Austin K. M. Writer
True, Jack G. Able Seaman
Vazey, Edward H. Able Seaman
Vercoe, Henry B. Plumber
Walker, Alexander J. Able Seaman
Walkinshaw, Lewis R. Signalman
Walpole, Henry Supply Assistant
Wangford, William B. Shipwright
Wardle, John C. Leading Seaman
Watson, David M. Leading Telegraphist
West, Selwyn F. Able Seaman
White, Morgan A. Able Seaman
White, William B. Stoker
Wilson, Samuel G. Able Seaman
Wood, Cecil J. S. Able Seaman
Wright, Cyril G. Leading Seaman
Wright, Ernest E. Signalman

We will remember them

Role of Honour of those lost with HMS Kandahar *sunk 19 December 1941*

Royal Navy

Atherton, George H. Able Seaman
Austin, James Able Seaman
Azzopardi, Joseph Leading Cook (O) (Malta)
Bell, Alfred G. Able Seaman
Bellenger, Albert S. Leading Stoker
Bertuello, Joseph Petty Officer Steward
Burton, Arthur B. Leading Seaman
Carson, William J. Writer
Clee, Joseph Engine Room Artificer
Collins, Leslie A. Ordinary Telegraphist
Connolly, William Able Seaman
Cooke, Albert E. Able Seaman
Cook, Henry J. Leading Seaman
Cooper, Harold Sick Berth Attendant
Dance, Neville F. Able Seaman
Davies, Gilbert Able Seaman
Davies, William T. Petty Officer Stoker
Day, Roy V. Stoker
Dowling, Francis H. Stoker
Dunn, Alan T. Leading Seaman
Ellis, Francis Able Seaman
Ellis, Samuel E. Able Seaman
Evans, William Able Seaman
Fanning, Michael Petty Officer Stoker
Forty, J. Maurice MID Able Seaman
Gibson, William T. Ordinary Seaman
Gibson-Watt, Martin R. DSC Lieutenant
Gratton, John G. Able Seaman
Hambly, Cyril Albert Medal Leading Seaman
Hancock, Albert P. Leading Stoker
Heal, Sydney E. Leading Stoker
Holmes, Ronald Stoker
Jackson, James G. Ordnance Artificer
Jenkins, William G. Able Seaman
Johnson, John W. Stoker
Jolly, Frank Ordinary Seaman
Jones, Robert S. Stoker

Jude, Herbert Able Seaman
Lacey, Leslie Able Seaman
Lewis, Bertram H. Able Seaman
Lidbury, Edmund J. Stoker
Lloyd, Cyril J. Petty Officer Stoker
Martin, James Able Seaman
McDowell, George Albert Medal Leading Signalman
McFadyen, James Stoker
Miller, Colin C. Able Seaman
Millington, Harry Able Seaman
Moore, Samuel R. Able Seaman
Mulliss, Stanley J. Able Seaman
Needham, Thomas E. Able Seaman
Orgill, Arnold Able Seaman
Pascoe, Leslie MID Petty Officer Stoker
Price, Ronald C. Able Seaman
Quarrington, John H. Able Seaman
Reilly, James A. F. Leading Seaman
Render, George W. Ordinary Signalman
Rice, John C. D. Able Seaman
Richardson, William Stoker
Robbins, Alfred T. Able Seaman
Sanderson, Fred S. Stoker
Schembri, Andrew Leading Steward
Shortland, Ernest C. J. Able Seaman
Smith, John T. Able Seaman
Speirs, John Able Seaman
Sprackling, Sidney Able Seaman
Starr, Thomas Petty Officer
Tatham, Lyster J. Midshipman
Tindall, Charles P. Stoker
Towns, Robert D. Able Seaman
Webb, James Able Seaman
Wigham, Ronald B. Able Seaman
Wilson, Arthur F. Leading Seaman
Wilson, Rupert S. Engine Room Artificer

We will remember them

"There are no flowers on a sailor's grave
No lilies on an ocean wave
The only tribute is the seagull's sweep
And the teardrop on a loved one's cheek"
Anon

Members of Neptune Association who made the pilgrimage to Malta and Tripoli in April 2007

	Name	Relationship to Neptune Casualty
1	Pauline Anwyl-Jones	none – member of Neptune Association
2	Harold Brooks	son – Marine Ronald Dubber
3	Frances Brooks	daughter-in-law – Marine Dubber
4	Frank Brown	eye-witness to sinking of Neptune
5	Diana Clayton	daughter – Sergeant William Crocker, Royal Marines
6	Robin Clayton	son-in-law – Sergeant William Crocker
7	Richard Coulton	son – Lieutenant Richard Coulton
8	Patricia Coulton	daughter-in-law – Lieutenant Richard Coulton
9	Mary Cunningham	sister-in-law -Lieutenant David Cunningham
10	Debbie Cunningham	niece – Lieutenant David Cunningham
11	Fiona Britten	niece – Lieutenant David Cunningham
12	Liz Dean	niece – Leading Seaman Cyril Hambley (K)
13	Christine Pittman-Corner	sister-in-law – Musician Arthur Corner
14	Graham Davies	nephew – Leading Stoker William Griffiths
15	Keith Evans	none – Vice-Chairman Hood Association
16	Nancy Edwards	sister – Able Seaman Alfred Woodward
17	Janet Edwards	niece – Able Seaman Alfred Woodward
18	Adrian St Clair Fewins	nephew – ERA Arthur Fewins
19	Rorie Grieve	none – friend of Captain O'Conor's family
20	Elaine Gray	sister – Lieutenant Alan Hill
21	Sarah Beall	niece – Lieutenant Alan Hill
22	John Green	none – member of Neptune Association
23	Rose Green	none – member of Neptune Association
24	Maureen Hayhurst	daughter – Stoker Frederick Pascall
25	Simon Hayhurst	grandson – Stoker Frederick Pascall
26	Vi Cornish	widow – Corporal James Auchinlech, Royal Marines
27	Jean Horsham	daughter – Corporal James Auchinlech
28	Bill Horsham	son-in-law Corporal James Auchinlech
29	Norma Hudson	daughter – Petty Officer Norman Walton – survivor
30	Mike James	nephew – Blacksmith Arthur James
31	Janet James	wife of Mike James
32	C.R. (Butch) James	nephew – Signalman Cecil Rankin (SA)
33	Angela Lindley	niece – Paymaster Commander Jack McGregor
34	Peter Lindley	husband of Angela Lindley
35	Judith Littlewood	daughter – Leading Seaman Frank Gardiner
36	Harold Mason	brother – Ord. Seaman William Mason
37	Susan Rawlings	niece – Ord. Seaman William Mason
38	Stephen Rawlings	husband of Susan Rawlings
39	Neil Rawlings	great nephew – Ord. Seaman William Mason
40	John McGregor	son – Paymaster Commander Jack McGregor
41	Richard McGregor	son – Paymaster Commander Jack McGregor
42	Lesley McGregor	daughter-in-law – Paymaster Commander McGregor
43	Shirley Murphy (NZ)	niece – Able Seaman John Ross (NZ)
44	Tony Osborne	son – Lieutenant William Osborne

45	Valerie Pennifer	daughter – Stoker Edmund Lidbury (K)
46	Peter Pennifer	son-in-law Stoker Edmund Lidbury
47	Geoff Staley	son – Stoker Leonard Staley
48	Royden Thomson NZ)	son – Paymaster Lieutenant Bruce Thomson (NZ)
49	Sandie Thomson (NZ)	daughter-in-law Paymaster Lieutenant Thomson (NZ)
50	Gillian Wadden	daughter – Surgeon Commander Thomas Larkworthy
51	Tessa Sale	daughter – Surgeon Commander Thomas Larkworthy
52	Susan Healy-Fenton	daughter – Surgeon Commander Thomas Larkworthy
53	Nick Wright	son – Lieutenant Humphrey Wright
54	Gerry Wright	daughter-in-law Lieutenant Humphrey Wright
55	Stan Welsh	nephew – Able Seaman John Glancy
56	Fiona Welsh	niece – Able Seaman John Glancy
57	Elizabeth Pye	niece – Able Seaman John Glancy
58	Dave Kennaugh	none – friend of Stan Welsh
59	Bob Goodman	none – member of Neptune Association
60	Sue Thompson	none – representative of Remembrance Travel

Index